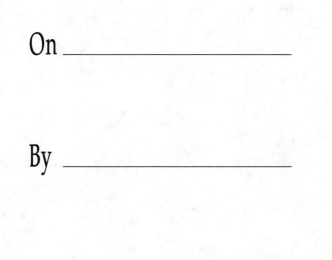

Presented to

_____

On _____

By _____

FROM

Faith To Faith

A DAILY GUIDE TO VICTORY

FROM

Faith To Faith

A DAILY GUIDE TO VICTORY

BY

Kenneth And Gloria Copeland

"For I am not ashamed of the gospel of Christ: for it is the power of God unto salvation to every one that believeth; to the Jew first, and also to the Greek. For therein is the righteousness of God revealed from faith to faith: as it is written, The just shall live by faith." **(Romans 1:16,17)**

KCP

Kenneth Copeland Publications
Fort Worth, Texas

From Faith to Faith
A Daily Guide to Victory

ISBN 0-88114-833-4   #21-0005

© 1990 Kenneth Copeland Ministries, Inc.

All Rights Reserved. Reproduction in Whole or Part Without Written Permission is Prohibited. Printed in United States of America.

Unless otherwise indicated, all Scripture quotations are from the KING JAMES VERSION.

Cover painting by Helen Cuthbertson, "Summer Pastels," from the Hummingbird Gallery, Fort Worth, Texas

Published by Kenneth Copeland Publications
Fort Worth, Texas 76192

Dear Friend,

It's been almost 25 years now since we first determined to live by faith. Since then our lives have been more glorious and thrilling than we ever imagined they could be. We've seen more victories than we can count. Spiritual victories. Physical victories. Financial victories.

But it's important for you to know, those victories didn't come our way overnight.

Our bank account didn't double the first time we jumped up and said, "My God meets my needs according to His riches in glory by Christ Jesus!" Sickness didn't flee forever the first time we confessed, "By His stripes, I am healed."

We won those victories because once we took hold of the Word of God, we refused to let it go. Even when that Word didn't appear to be working, we kept on meditating it and speaking it out. We kept on feeding our faith with it…day after day after day.

Eventually, just like Mark 11:23 said it would, that faith began to move the mountains in our lives.

That's why we're so excited about the book you're holding in your hands right now. It's designed to help you feed your faith, not just occasionally, but every single day. It's designed to encourage you daily, to keep you going until you develop the kind of mountain-moving faith that will make you more than a conqueror in every area of life.

Years ago, the Lord told Gloria, "In consistency lies the power."

It's our prayer that this book will help you become so consistent in the Word that its power will explode in you. We know from experience, that power will keep you moving from faith to faith and from victory to victory for the rest of your life!

Kenneth & Gloria Copeland

A Prayer of Protection from Psalm 91

Father, I praise You that I dwell in the secret place of the Most High and that I shall remain stable and fixed under the shadow of the Almighty [Whose power no foe can withstand]. I will say of You, Lord, "The Lord is my refuge and my fortress, my God; on Him I lean and rely, and in Him I confidently trust!"

For then You will deliver me from the snare of the fowler and from the deadly pestilence. Then You will cover me with Your pinions (feathers), and under Your wings shall I trust and find refuge. Your truth and Your faithfulness are a shield and a buckler.

I shall not be afraid of the terror of the night, nor of the arrow (the evil plots and slanders of the wicked) that flies by day, nor of the pestilence that stalks in darkness, nor of the destruction and sudden death that surprise and lay waste at noonday.

A thousand may fall at my side, and ten thousand at my right hand, but it shall not come near me. Only a spectator shall I be [inaccessible in the secret place of the Most High] as I witness the reward of the wicked.

Because I have made You, Lord, my refuge, and the Most High my dwelling place, there shall no evil befall me, nor any plague or calamity come near my tent. For You will give Your angels especial charge over me, to accompany and defend and preserve me in all my ways of obedience and service. Your angels shall bear me up on their hands, lest I dash my foot against a stone.

I shall tread upon the lion and adder; the young lion and the serpent shall I trample underfoot. Because I have set my love upon You, therefore will You deliver me. You will set me on high, because I know and understand Your name.

I have a personal knowledge of Your mercy, love, and kindness. I trust and rely on You, knowing You will never forsake me, no, never. I shall call upon You, and You will answer me. You will be with me in trouble. You will deliver me and honor me. With long life will You satisfy me and show me Your salvation!

(Taken from *The Amplified Bible*)

A Happy New Year

"For whosoever shall call upon the name of the Lord shall be saved."
(Romans 10:13)

Today people everywhere are gathering together to celebrate the first bright moments of the New Year.

Yet, for thousands of others, this day will be the toughest 24 hours of their lives. For those people, New Year's will serve only as a dim reminder of loneliness and loss. It will simply mark the beginning of another year of failure.

What about you? What's this year really going to be like for you?

You may appear to be happy enough. You may be passing out seasonal smiles and holiday greetings just like everybody else. But inside, you may hurt. You may be disappointed. You may even feel like you can't go on.

If so, I want you to know something. All of that can change in an instant. You can start your life over today and make this New Year's Day the most joyful day of your life!

How many times have you said to yourself, "If I could just start over, I'd do it all differently"? That doesn't have to be simply an idle wish. Jesus Christ has actually made it possible. That's His Christmas present to you. He paid the price for all your sins. He paid the penalty for all your mistakes.

That's the reason He came to earth. That's the reason He was born—so you could start over!

You may look at your life and say, "But I've made some terrible mistakes. I've done some despicable things." That doesn't matter. Jesus paid the price for them all!

How can you make a new start? Romans 10:9 says that "if thou shalt confess with thy mouth the Lord Jesus, and shalt believe in thine heart that God hath raised him from the dead, thou shalt be saved." It's as easy as saying, "Jesus, I'm turning my life over to You. From this day forward I'm Yours."

What better time to turn your life around than on this first day of the New Year. Right now, wherever you are, just give your life to Jesus. Then jump up and down and holler, "Praise God, I'm starting all over!" And find out what it really means to have a Happy New Year!

SCRIPTURE READING: Romans 10:1-13

Look Up!

"Consider [Jesus] that endured such contradiction of sinners
against himself, lest ye be wearied and faint in your minds."

(Hebrews 12:3)

*ook up...because in times like these,
your very life may depend on it.*

Some time ago, the Lord showed
me that a spirit of weariness is trying
to work its way into our lives these
days through all the pressure and bad
news that surrounds us. It's working
to get our eyes off the Word of God by
bombarding us with negative forces.
It's trying to get us to look down at
defeat instead of up at Jesus.

If you let that happen, your spirit
man will begin to lose his dominion.
And the Word tells us what the results
of that is. It says you will "be wearied
and faint in your minds."

Jesus put it this way in Mark 4. He
said that when the cares of this world
enter into your heart and mind, they'll
choke the Word and cause it to become unfruitful. And since your faith
is the product of the Word, that means
your faith will wither. Once that happens, you're headed for disaster.

What can you do to stop this chain
reaction of weariness?

Look up! Get your eyes back on
Jesus. I remember on the field of ath-
letic competition that when an opponent allowed himself to drop his head,
he was no longer dangerous. He could
be very easily defeated. So keep your
head up. Keep considering Jesus, the
Author and Finisher of your faith.
Consider Him instead of the cares of
this world. Consider what God says in
His Word. Be moved by the thoughts
of God. Let His thoughts become
your thoughts.

Look up! Get your eyes off the circumstances around you and onto your
heavenly Source. Don't be afraid you're
going to lose everything. God is your
Source, not the world. He can take
care of you regardless of what happens around you.

If you've gotten weary lately, begin
to lift your eyes. Raise your head up
instead of looking down. God is up.
Jesus is up. The devil is down—under
your feet. Look up!

SCRIPTURE READING: Isaiah 40:21-31

Be a Blessing

"Let those who favor my righteous cause and have pleasure in my uprightness shout for joy and be glad, and say continually, Let the Lord be magnified, Who takes pleasure in the prosperity of His servant."

(Psalm 35:27, AMP)

If traditional religion has taught you that God wants you poor and oppressed, I have good news for you today. The Bible says, "God takes pleasure" in your prosperity. God *wants* you to prosper!

Not just in the financial realm but in every area of your life...spirit, soul, and body.

No matter where you are or who you are, God wants to see you delivered from every adverse situation.

Why? Because He loves you and He has a job for you to do. He wants you to help meet the needs of mankind and He's smart enough to know that you can't give away what you don't have. You can't give to spread the gospel or buy food for the hungry when you're broke. You can't go out laying hands on the sick when you're lying in a hospital bed. You can't minister joy to others when you're being held captive by depression. No! You have to be blessed to be a blessing.

If you really want to tap into the riches of God today, make up your mind to be a blessing to others, and before you know it, you'll be receiving more from God than you ever dreamed of.

That's what happened to me. I decided years ago, first and foremost, to be a giver. I developed a life-style of giving. Today, I literally "live to give." And I don't mind telling you, God dumps blessings on me by the truckload!

He'll do the same for you if you'll become His servant—if you'll lay down your time and your money and your love for those who need it. Become a giver—and God will take pleasure in prospering you!

SCRIPTURE READING: Genesis 12:1-4, Genesis 13:1-4

Let the World Know

"Neither pray I for these alone, but for them also which
shall believe on me through their word. ...that they may be one,
even as we are one: I in them, and thou in me, that they may be
made perfect in one; and that the world may know that
thou hast sent me." **(John 17:20,22,23)**

Over the years the Church has come up with all kinds of elaborate ways to evangelize the world. We get together and map out plans and strategies and raise money for it. But through it all, we rarely mention the plan that Jesus gave us.

Most believers don't even realize that He gave us the key to winning the world, but He did. He prayed about it right before He went to the cross. He asked the Father to bring us into a place of such oneness with each other and with Him that the *world would know* that He had been sent from God.

If you and I and all the rest of the Body of Christ would get together and start loving each other, we'd evangelize the world so fast it would make your head swim. It's true. But until recently, we've been too busy scrapping with one another and getting our feelings hurt to give it much thought.

But, praise God, it's beginning to dawn on some folks now that we need to stop that stuff. We need to start treating Jesus' command that we *love one another* as a *command* instead of an *alternative*. We need to drop our silly arguments and be unified by the Spirit of God.

Do you want to take a step toward evangelizing the world today? Then start praying for oneness. Make up your mind that you're going to start loving your fellow believers instead of criticizing, complaining, and talking ugly about them.

Start confessing that the Church of God is going to rise up together in faith and love like one glorious body driven by the power of Jesus Himself. We are, you know. Jesus prayed that it would happen, and the Holy Spirit is already bringing it to pass.

Satan would like to stop it, but he can't. It's far more powerful than he is—and it's going to blast a hole in his operation that's big enough to drive a train through. It's going to let the whole world know that Jesus truly is Lord!

SCRIPTURE READING: John 17:9-26

You are Righteous

"...not having mine own righteousness, which is of the law, but that which is through the faith of Christ, the righteousness which is of God by faith."

(Philippians 3:9)

I don't care how badly you may have messed things up yesterday or how many mistakes you made, I want you to begin this day knowing you are *righteous!* Not because of anything you've done but because you've received, by faith in Jesus, the very righteousness of God.

Just look at the kinds of benefits the Word of God says that righteousness will bring:

"The righteous shall flourish like the palm tree" (Ps. 92:12).

"When it goeth well with the righteous, the city rejoiceth" (Prov. 11:10).

"The seed of the righteous shall be delivered" (Prov. 11:21).

"For the eyes of the Lord are over the righteous, and his ears are open unto their prayers" (1 Pet. 3:12).

"For thou, Lord, wilt bless the righteous; with favour wilt thou compass him as with a shield" (Ps. 5:12).

"The righteous cry, and the Lord heareth, and delivereth them out of all their troubles" (Ps. 34:17).

"I have been young, and now am old; yet have I not seen the righteous forsaken, nor his seed begging bread" (Ps. 37:25).

"The righteous shall inherit the land, and dwell therein forever" (Ps. 37:29).

"The Lord loveth the righteous" (Ps. 146:8).

Don't let the devil rob you of even one of these blessings by telling you you're unworthy of them. Run him off. Shout out loud, "I am the righteousness of God!" Then step out in faith and enjoy the privileges God has prepared for you!

SCRIPTURE READING: Romans 3:21-28

Created to Praise

"Let every thing that hath breath praise the Lord.
Praise ye the Lord." **(Psalm 150:6)**

We're created to praise God. Some people don't know that. When the praise service starts, they sit back and say, "I'm not comfortable with all that singing and shouting. I guess praise is just not my thing."

Yes it is! According to the Bible, if you breathe, you were meant to praise.

And don't try to slip by with saying, "Well, I have praise in my heart." That's not enough. The Word says you need to have it in your mouth as well! (Ps. 34:1). Psalm 132:9 says, "Let thy saints shout for joy." You can't shout and be quiet at the same time.

When you first begin to truly praise, it may seem awkward to you, but if you'll keep it up, it will become a way of life. Why? Because praise causes the glory of God to manifest in your life. It causes you to walk in the light of His countenance (Ps. 89:15). It will start a revival inside of you!

"But, Gloria, if I start to praise like that, people will think I'm some kind of fanatic."

Well, good! Did you know that every revival in history has been started by people the world considered absolute fanatics? God does things differently than the world. So when you set aside your inhibitions and start letting His Spirit operate through you, you're going to look strange to those who are strangers to His ways...but you're going to look wonderful to the Lord!

And, by the way, don't just think of praising Him in the congregation. Praise Him in your own private prayer time and throughout your day. Learn to maintain an attitude of praise and thanksgiving. When praise becomes natural to you in your own private life, it won't be difficult to praise Him in the midst of the congregation.

Are you longing for a revival of God's presence in your life? Are you tired of just hearing about the glorious manifestations of His power in the past? Then open your mouth and your heart and do what God has created you to do. Praise!

SCRIPTURE READING: Psalm 150

God Has Something to Say

"The sheep listen to [the Shepherd's] voice and heed it, and he calls his own sheep by name and brings (leads) them out." **(John 10:3, AMP)**

Don't ever be so afraid of making a mistake, you miss out on the joy of acting on the voice of the Lord. Instead, trust the leadership of the Holy Spirit and let Him show you how. He'll begin by speaking to you about the little things in your life, and as you grow accustomed to hearing and obeying, He'll speak to you about weightier things.

That's how it happened with Gloria and me. When we first accepted Jesus as Lord, we didn't have any idea how to hear God. Our spirits weren't yet trained to distinguish His leading. But since the Bible promised we could do it, we began to approach our prayer time and Bible study time *expecting* to hear God's direction and He began to give it.

I'll never forget the first time it happened to Gloria. She'd been reading the Bible and she just stopped for a few minutes to see if God would say something to her. Right down on the inside of her, she heard the Lord say, "The light is on in your car."

It didn't occur to her that God would speak to her about something so trivial, so she just brushed that thought aside and went on listening. Pretty soon, He said the same thing again. He kept on repeating it until finally, she got up and walked out to the car. Sure enough, the light was on.

Why would God bother with something as insignificant as a car light? Because He cares! He knew Gloria was home alone that night with two small children, and if that battery had run down, she'd have been stuck there. God was watching out for her, and He told her just exactly what she needed to know right then.

Yet, at the same time, He knew she was a beginner where listening to His voice was concerned, so He gave her an instruction she could follow without much risk. I mean, what if she had gone out there and the light *hadn't* been on? What if she'd missed it? She would have felt foolish but that wouldn't have hurt anything.

If you'll trust Him, the Holy Spirit will do the same thing for you that He did for Gloria and me. He'll bring you along one step at a time in a way that will help you, not hurt you.

The biggest mistake you can make is to be afraid to follow that inward witness which is the number one way God leads all His children (Rom. 8:14). So don't be afraid. Take time to listen today. Expect to hear in your spirit. God has something to say to you.

SCRIPTURE READING: 1 Corinthians 2:6-16

Step Across the Faith Line

"And being not weak in faith, [Abraham] considered not
his own body now dead, when he was about an hundred years old,
neither yet the deadness of Sarah's womb: He staggered not at the
promise of God through unbelief; but was strong in faith,
giving glory to God." **(Romans 4:19,20)**

In the years I've spent living by faith, there's something I've learned to do that helps me receive from God in the toughest of situations. It's something I call stepping over the faith line.

A *faith line* is what you need when you want God to do the "impossible" in your life. It's what you need when you want to be firm in your faith and yet you keep wavering back and forth between your circumstances and God's promises – believing first one, then the other.

It's what can make you like faithful Abraham. You know, Abraham had natural facts to deal with just like we do. He knew there was no natural way for God's promise to him to come true.

Yet the Word says Abraham considered not his own body. In other words, Abraham ignored the natural evidence around him and believed only God's promise.

Somewhere he stepped across the line of faith.

He made an irreversible decision to go with the Word of God. He made a final commitment. He chose to step past the point of no return. And if you and I are ever going to see God do the impossible in our lives, we're going to have to do the same thing!

How do you draw that faith line?

Begin with the Word. Search the promises of God and purposely believe what He has said, and is saying, about your need. Meditate on those promises until faith rises in your heart.

Then draw the line of faith. Draw it in your mind and heart. Draw it across the floor in your prayer room. Say, "In the presence of God, in the presence of all the angels in this room, and in the devil's face, I am stepping across the line of faith. From this moment on, I consider this matter done. From this day forward, I give God the praise and the glory in the name of Jesus."

From that moment on, speak only as if your miracle has already happened. Turn your back on the problems, on the doubts, and turn your face toward Jesus.

God *will* do the impossible in your life. Dare to step across the faith line!

SCRIPTURE READING: Romans 4:13-21

No Time for Clay Pots

"But in a great house there are not only vessels of gold and of silver, but also of wood and of earth; and some to honour, and some to dishonour."

(2 Timothy 2:20)

Are you destined for greatness in the kingdom of God?

Ask most believers that question and they'll humbly assure you they're not. "You know we can't all be golden vessels," they'll say. "Like the Bible says, some of us are just called to be little clay pots."

Praise God, the Bible doesn't say any such thing!

Certainly there are going to be some golden vessels in the kingdom and there are going to be some clay pots, but we are the ones—not God—who determine which kind we will be. Second Timothy 2:21 tells us that "whoever cleanses himself [from what is ignoble and unclean]—who separates himself from contact with contaminating and corrupting influences—will [then himself] be a vessel set apart and useful for honorable and noble purposes, consecrated and profitable to the Master, fit and ready for any good work" (AMP).

Golden vessel or clay pot, the choice is up to you!

Why then do so many believers choose to do menial work in the kingdom of God? Why are they content to remain clay pots?

Because they lack one thing every golden vessel must have. They lack dedication. They haven't made a quality decision to separate themselves from contaminating influences. They haven't been willing to turn away from the ways of the world and go on with God past the point of no return.

My friend, God is doing some exciting things on this earth right now. He's working signs and wonders, paving the way for Jesus' return. This is a thrilling time, but it's definitely no time for clay pots! So if you haven't yet made the kind of commitment that will turn you into a golden vessel, admit it. Then take the time to get before God and study His Word and get your will in line with His. Let the Holy Spirit deal with you until you're willing to leave the ways of the world behind and walk in higher ways—the ways of God.

Do it now. The hour is late. The glory of God is spilling over the earth in one final thrilling wave. It's not trickling out of clay pots. It's being poured through golden vessels—and that's exactly what God is calling *you* to be.

SCRIPTURE READING: 2 Timothy 2:15-26

Turn Your Kids Around

"And all thy children shall be taught of the Lord; and great shall
be the peace of thy children." (Isaiah 54:13)

Too many Christian parents today are wasting time *worrying* about their children.

Years ago, Gloria and I saw the devil trying to get a foothold in our children's lives, so one weekend we got our concordance and four or five translations of the Bible. We began to search out scriptures and write out agreement prayers concerning them.

We tore into the devil with the Word of God and started saying, "Thank God, our children are not going to hell. Thank God, they are taught of the Lord and great is their peace!" Instead of walking the floor and worrying about the problem, we walked the floor and praised God for the solution.

Things didn't change instantly. We still had to go through some tough times, but the Word began to turn things around. Today, my children are serving God with all their hearts.

If your kids are headed for trouble, don't waste time worrying. Start believing! Get the Word working in their lives. Bind the devil with it and tell him he can't have them. Then follow the instructions in Matthew 9:38: "Pray the Lord of the harvest to send out laborers" into the field who can reach your children. God knows who they'll listen to, and He knows how to bring those people into your children's lives at just the right time.

Grab hold of God's Word and refuse to let go where your children are concerned—and sooner or later, that Word will grab hold of them.

SCRIPTURE READING: Psalm 127

Don't Look at the Storm

"But when he saw the wind boisterous, he was afraid;
and beginning to sink, he cried, saying, Lord, save me. And immediately
Jesus stretched forth his hand, and caught him, and said unto him, O thou
of little faith, wherefore didst thou doubt?" **(Matthew 14:30,31)**

If there's any way the devil can get your eyes away from the Word, he'll do it. He'll cause trouble. He'll make the circumstances around you pitch and roll like a rowboat in a hurricane. He'll do anything he can to get you to concentrate on the realm of the physical senses and the situation around you instead of on the promise of God—because he knows that if he doesn't, you'll take that promise and beat his brains out with it.

That's what he did to Peter. When Peter first jumped out of the boat that day in response to Jesus' word, what happened? He walked right along across that water without a problem. His whole being was fastened on that word Jesus had spoken to him, "Come!"

But when he took his eyes off that word, he started looking at the storm. He started looking at the impossible thing he was doing. After all, he was a fisherman. All his training and experience told him when the waves were that high, you were going under. He started to focus on what he knew in the natural instead of what Jesus said; and when he did that, his faith slipped out of gear and he started to sink.

Don't let that happen to you. Once you get a revelation from the Word of God, hang onto it. Don't focus on anything else.

The devil will do everything he can to get you to turn loose of it. He'll stir up things around you. He'll try to get you into fear. He'll push every button he can from the past to get you back into your old way of thinking.

But don't let go. Keep your eyes on the Word of God until it's more real inside you than anything else. If you do, you'll be able to walk your way across the water just fine.

SCRIPTURE READING: Matthew 14:22-33

Our Only Hope is Jesus

"Therefore did my heart rejoice,
and my tongue was glad; moreover also my flesh shall rest in hope:
Because thou wilt not leave my soul in hell, neither wilt thou
suffer thine Holy One to see corruption." **(Acts 2:26,27)**

Twenty-one years ago, God said something to me that will mark my ministry forever. It was this: *The only hope that any man has anywhere in the world is faith in Jesus Christ.*

In light of what's happening around us today, the truth of the statement is more painfully obvious than ever before. We are a generation with diseases no man can heal, with problems no man can solve. What fleeting successes we have are quickly overshadowed by new and greater crises.

All too often, that's as true for believers as it is for unbelievers. It shouldn't be. But it is. Believers are being killed by the same diseases that are devastating the rest of the world. They're being plagued by the same problems. And many are walking around without hope—just like the rest of the world.

Why? Because the only hope that any man has is faith in Jesus Christ. And the majority of Christians don't know how to live by faith.

Instead of being filled with the Word and with faith, they've been stuffed full of religious tradition and superstition. And they're suffering. When the devil hits them with sickness and disease, with poverty or depression or divorce, they often stand by helplessly as it destroys them. They simply don't know what else to do. The Bible says, "My people are destroyed for lack of knowledge..." (Hos. 4:6).

But you know. Your hope is in Jesus. Trust Him. And tell the world—their hope is in Him too.

SCRIPTURE READING: Mark 4:35-41

In Good Times and Bad

"Because he hath set his love upon me, therefore will I deliver him:
I will set him on high, because he hath known my name. He shall call upon
me, and I will answer him: I will be with him in trouble; I will
deliver him, and honour him." **(Psalm 91:14,15)**

God is called by many names. He is the Lord our Healer, our Provider, our Banner, and our Righteousness. He also promises to be our Deliverer. In this troubled world that may very well be what we need Him to be most often.

But there are many believers who never experience God's mighty delivering power because, instead of walking closely with Him day by day, they wait until danger strikes to call upon Him. That just doesn't work. If you want God to rescue you in the bad times, you have to fellowship with Him in the good times. Why? Because God responds to faith. Our faith, not our need, is what causes Him to act on our behalf. And we'll never be able to develop that kind of faith, that kind of trust and confidence in Him, if we don't spend enough time with Him to get to know Him.

First John 3:20-22 tells us that we have confidence toward God when we do the things that are pleasing in His sight. If we only serve God half-heartedly, then we will not have confidence in Him to deliver us from trouble. When danger surrounds us, instead of being filled with faith, we'll find ourselves paralyzed with fear.

Love and serve God with your whole heart. Walk closely with Him in the good times. Then, when you need Him to be your Deliverer, you'll know without a doubt you can trust Him to care for you!

SCRIPTURE READING: Psalm 108:1-6

Under Your Feet

"The Lord said unto my Lord, Sit thou on my right hand, Until I make thy foes thy footstool." **(Acts 2:34,35)**

Even though Satan lost all his authority on this earth the day Jesus rose from the dead, for the past 2,000 years he's been running around as a spiritual outlaw—continuing to kill, steal from, and destroy all who will let him. But, you know, he's not going to be able to do that much longer. There's coming a day when he's going to be put out of business completely. There's coming a day when the evil he's done here on earth will be put totally underfoot by the power of God.

Most believers know that's true. They've shouted and rejoiced over it—but they haven't really understood how it's going to happen. They haven't realized that *they* are the foot that's going to trample down the works of the devil!

Jesus is the Head of the Church. You and I are the feet. We are the ones who are going to take His authority and power and stomp on sin and sickness and every other demonic thing in this earth. We are the ones God is going to use, as Acts 2:35 says, to make Jesus' enemies His footstool.

That's what Jesus was telling us when He said, "Go ye into all the world, and preach the gospel to every creature... lay hands on the sick and...cast out devils" (Mark 16:15-18). He was saying, "Go ye and be My foot." He was saying, "All power and authority has been given unto Me, both in heaven and in earth. Therefore, you take it and use it to put the devil under."

But instead of obeying Him, we've waited around wondering when God was going to do something about this mess here on earth. We've sat around wondering why it's taking so long for Jesus to come back.

We're the reason it's taking so long! Jesus is waiting on you and me. He's waiting on us to step out in His power, put the devil in his place, and win the world. He's waiting on us to drop our silly doctrinal differences and get busy doing what God said we would do.

The Bible says that one can put a thousand to flight and two can put ten thousand to flight. Every time we get together, we increase our strength astronomically. If we'd just get together and figure out who we are, if we'd realize that *we're* the feet of Jesus, we could kick Satan out of earth's affairs with ease.

Do you want to hasten Jesus' return? Then quit sitting around staring at the clouds! Start stomping around in the Spirit. Start putting the works of the serpent under your feet and we can wrap this thing up and go home to glory real soon!

SCRIPTURE READING: Genesis 3:1-14

Don't Worry!

"Therefore do not worry and be anxious." **(Matthew 6:31, AMP)**

God is vehemently against worry. Jesus preached against it. Paul preached against it. The whole Bible preaches against worry because it was designed by Satan to produce stress, strain, and death.

Yet many of us still act as if it's an option, as if we're free to worry if we want to. But we're not! Worrying is a sin. It's one of those things the Word of God directly commands us not to do.

What are you supposed to do then with all the concerns you have about your problems? In 1 Peter 5:7, God says you should "cast them *all* upon Him." All. Not 75 percent of them. Not all of them but the ones about your kids. All of them!

Your confession every morning should be, "I do not have a care in this world because I've cast every one of them onto my Lord."

Let me illustrate how that works. Let's say you were standing about 20 feet away from me and I tossed my car keys to you. If someone else were to come to me and say, "Brother Copeland, I need the keys to your car. I need to use it." I would say, "I can't help you. I cast my keys over on him. I don't have them anymore."

That's what you need to do with your worries. You need to cast them over on the Lord and not take them back. If Satan brings a worried thought to your mind, saying, "What if this terrible thing happens?" then you can tell him to talk to God about it. It's in His hands, not yours!

Once you do that, changes will start to take place in your life. Problems you've been fretting about for years will start being solved. You'll no longer be tying God's hands with your worrying. His power can begin to operate because you've acted in faith and cast your cares on Him!

Remember, though, God will not take your cares away from you. You have to *give* them to Him. Then you have to replace those worries with the Word. You are the one who has to keep your thoughts under control. But you can do it. The Greater One dwells within you. He is able to put you over. Commit to it. You'll never have to worry again.

SCRIPTURE READING: Psalm 55

Jesus Can Set Them Free

"And as ye go, preach, saying, The kingdom of heaven is at hand. Heal the sick, cleanse the lepers, raise the dead, cast out devils: freely ye have received, freely give." **(Matthew 10:7,8)**

There are those who've said that some of the diseases that are on the rampage right now, diseases such as AIDS, are God's way of punishing immoral people today. There is absolutely no scriptural basis for that!

God does not bring disease on the human race. In fact, if there's anybody in heaven and earth who hates it, it's Jesus. The devil is the one who's trying to tell us otherwise. He's promoting a lie, trying to get us to believe God is the one who's inflicting these diseases on people because he knows that if the victims believe that, it will drive them further from God than ever. And that's his aim.

It's time you and I as believers put a stop to that lie. Some time ago, the Lord spoke to my heart and told me so. He said, "Reach out to those who are suffering. Let them know I didn't do this to them. Let them know I'm their Deliverer!"

That word was not just for me, it was for the whole Body of Christ. We need to tell people who've been afflicted with AIDS or any such disease that Jesus is Lord over it. We need to tell them that God loves them dearly, and He has the desire and the power to heal them.

God is not responsible for the suffering we're seeing around us. That's just a nasty lie the devil is passing around. And if you and I do our job right, very soon another word is going to start spreading through the streets. The news is going to get out that Jesus Christ is not their captor, He's the One who can set them free!

SCRIPTURE READING: Matthew 9:18-26

Let God Do It His Way

"Elisha sent a messenger to him, saying, Go and wash in
Jordan seven times, and your flesh shall be restored, and you shall be clean.
But Naaman was angry." **(2 Kings 5:10,11, AMP)**

So often we miss out on what God wants to do for us because He doesn't do it the way we think He should. We work up an idea in our minds about how He's going to heal us, for instance. We think He's going to send some famous preacher to lay hands on us or that He's going to knock us off our feet with a blast of His power. When He doesn't, we let our faith drop and foul up what He had actually planned to do.

That's what Naaman did. He went to Elisha expecting to be healed in a particular way. When it didn't happen that way, the Bible says, he went away in a rage.

What Elisha told him to do was simple. Dip seven times in the Jordan. Naaman could do that. But it didn't fit his idea of how his healing should take place. He thought Elisha would heal him by waving his hands around and calling on the name of the Lord.

Naaman stormed away and he would have missed out on his healing if one of his servants hadn't talked him into giving Elisha's instructions a try.

I used to be like that. I wanted spectacular experiences from God so badly I was missing out on the experiences God had planned for me. Once I realized that, I quit looking for feelings and spectacular manifestations and just started expecting God to keep His Word.

I remember I went to a meeting one night with my ankle messed up terribly. The pain was so severe it went from my foot all the way up to my shoulder blades. But I went into that meeting expecting God to heal me.

During the praise service, I ignored the pain in my foot and just sang and worshiped with everyone else. When the preaching started, I got my Bible and got involved in the Word. Sure enough, sometime during that service I was healed. I don't know when it was. I didn't feel anything. I didn't see any sparklers go off. I didn't even realize I'd been healed until after the service. I got about halfway to the door and thought, "Glory to God, my foot's well."

Don't let your own ideas of how God's going to work rob you of your healing or your deliverance or your prosperity. Just trust Him and let Him do things His way. He *will* work mightily in you.

SCRIPTURE READING: 2 Kings 5:1-14

Get Yourself Together

"Can two walk together, except they be agreed?" **(Amos 3:3)**

When it comes to faith, a lot of believers feel like they have one foot nailed to the ground. No matter how hard they try, they just can't seem to make any progress.

If you'll watch them, you can see why. They literally haven't "gotten themselves together." One minute they'll be telling you, "Oh yes, amen, I believe the Word," and the next minute they'll be spouting unbelief like it's going out of style. "I know God says He'll prosper us, but I'll tell you what, my business is doing so badly, it's about to give me ulcers. I can't sleep at night for worrying."

Dig a little deeper and you may find out that they've pulled their actions out of line with the Word as well. "Well, you understand, brother, I can't possibly *tithe* with my income like it is. I'd go under!"

Faith just won't work for a person like that.

You see, you're a triune being. You are a spirit. You have a soul, which consists of your mind, will, and emotions. And you live in a body. Each of those areas has a specific role to play in your faith walk. You have to get them all three in agreement before you can go anywhere at all!

Start by feeding your spirit on the Word of God. Just like the body produces physical strength when you nourish it with food, the spirit produces spiritual strength when you nourish it with the Word. That spiritual strength is called faith. Develop that faith, and instead of your spirit being dominated by the other two areas, it will be the one in charge.

Next, bring your soul in line. Set your mind on "things above." Meditate on the Word until your thoughts begin to agree with it. Keep your attention on it until even your emotions yield.

Finally, bring your body in line. Once you truly get your spirit and soul established on the Word, that won't be hard. The body is a follower, not a leader. It will do whatever you train it to do. Begin teaching your body to act on the truth you've planted in your mind and spirit, and it will follow right along.

Don't try to walk in faith with your foot nailed to the ground. Get yourself together! Bring your spirit, soul, and body in harmony—and the Word will take you as far as you want to go.

SCRIPTURE READING: 1 Thessalonians 5:14-24

From Messes to Miracles

"A fool's mouth is his destruction, and his lips are the snare of his soul."

(Proverbs 18:7)

We have what we say. As believers, we know that's a vital biblical truth. We can see it in Mark 11:23, Matthew 21:21, James 3:2, and many other verses. Yet we often let it slip.

We allow ourselves to begin talking like the world instead of talking the Word. And eventually we get what we've been asking for—a big mess.

If that's happened to you, remember, whatever you have in your life is a product of what you've been saying. In order to change what you have, you must change what's coming out of your mouth. To head your life in a different direction—from death to life, sickness to health, failure to success—you must take charge of your words.

That's a lot easier said than done. But that's the key: It must be said in order to be done!

How do you start?

First, realize that it can't be done just in the natural. This is a spiritual law, so it must be handled with spiritual power.

James 3:7,8 says the tongue can't be tamed with the same power with which man tames animals. It takes God's wisdom from above. God's Word is His wisdom (Prov. 2:6). He also said His words are spirit and life. That means it takes God's words to tame our tongues.

Second, repent before God for ever allowing your tongue to be used by anyone except the Holy Spirit. Then give Jesus your tongue. Be determined to speak His words of love, faith, joy, peace, and grace. Words of faith stop the fiery darts of hell.

The third thing is to do what Jesus said to do in Mark 4:24. Take heed, or listen, to what you hear. Listen to yourself! Think, *Do I want what I just said to come to pass?* If the answer is no, then stop and correct yourself right then. Replace those negative words with praise (Eph. 5:4).

If you've gotten sloppy about what you say, change your course today by changing your words. Ask God to help you set a watch over your mouth (Ps. 141:3). Put the power that's in your tongue to work for you instead of against you. Stop using it to make messes, and start using it to make miracles. There is a miracle in your mouth!

SCRIPTURE READING: James 3:1-13

Believe the Love

"And we have known and believed the love that God hath to us."

(1 John 4:16)

One day I was walking along a highway through a park praying and I asked a simple question, "Lord, what do You want me to tell Your people?" Without a moment's hesitation, these words came ringing through my spirit and my mind:

Tell them how much I love them.

They were so filled with love and compassion that it defies words to express it. For days afterward all I could think of was 1 John 4:16. "And we have known and believed the love that God hath to us."

We've read about God's love. We've heard about it. But I don't think many of us have really believed it. If we did, it would totally change everything about us and everything around us.

It's that love that caused Jesus to lay down His life for us and to experience for Himself all the pains and weaknesses we experience. It's that love that says to us, even when we feel so unworthy, "Come to Me and get what you need. Don't be shy about it. I've been there. Come boldly to the throne of grace that you may obtain mercy and find grace to help in time of need."

Think about it. God is in love with you—so in love, He's given you everything He has! He's given you all the healing, all the wisdom, all the wealth, all the strength you could ever need.

"But what about my terrible past?"

That's what His mercy is for! It's taken care of your past. It's covered every sin and failure you ever had. All you have to do now is believe and receive His love.

What a shame it is that people suffer at the hands of sickness and disease and every other cursed thing just because they can't believe the love God has for them. Don't let that happen to you. Learn to believe the love.

Believe the love God has for you. It's already been released in the blood of Jesus.

Believe the love. It's already been released in Jesus' name.

Believe the love. It's already been released in His Word.

Meditate that scripture over and over. Say it to yourself again and again all day, "I believe the love Jesus has for me." Once it gets down in your heart, you'll never be the same again.

SCRIPTURE READING: Psalm 139:1-18

Heaven's Economy

"Giving thanks unto the Father...Who hath delivered us from the power of darkness, and hath translated us into the kingdom of his dear Son."

(Colossians 1:12,13)

If, in spite of all the Bible's promises about prosperity...in spite of all the prayers you've prayed...you are still struggling financially, consider this question: *Where do you think God is going to get the resources to meet your needs?*

Many believers limit God without even realizing it by training their eyes on the limited resources of this world rather than the unlimited riches of God's kingdom. Their faith fails when they think of the troubled economy on the earth, of the shortages and scarcity that surrounds them. They wonder, "How is God going to bless me in the middle of all this?"

If that's what you've been thinking, here's some news that will turn those thoughts around!

The Bible says God has "delivered us from the power of darkness, and hath *translated us into the kingdom of his dear Son.*" To be translated means to be taken out of one place and put into another. In other words, your citizenship is not primarily of this earth. You are not primarily American or Canadian or Australian—you are first and foremost a citizen of the kingdom of God.

That means this planet doesn't have any right to dictate to you whether your needs are met or not. The Bible says God will meet your needs according to His riches in glory! (Phil. 4:19). You can live by heaven's economy, not earth's economy—and in heaven there is always more than enough.

Wake up to the abundance of heaven that's been made yours through Jesus. Wake up to the fact that you've been translated out of a world of poverty into a kingdom of abundance. Rejoice. Heaven's unlimited resources have been made available to you!

SCRIPTURE READING: Psalm 105:37-45

Live Like Jesus

"But [Christ Jesus] made himself of no reputation, and took upon
him the form of a servant, and was made in the likeness of men."

(Philippians 2:7)

The truth of this verse hasn't really dawned on most people. They mistakenly think that Jesus was able to work wonders, to perform miracles, and to live above sin because He had divine powers that we don't have. Thus, they have never really aspired to live like He lived.

"Oh my," they say with great humility, "I could never live like Jesus did. After all, He had an advantage. He was God!"

They don't realize that when Jesus came to earth, He voluntarily gave up that advantage, living His life here not as God but as a man. He had no innate supernatural powers. He had no ability to perform miracles until after He was anointed by the Holy Spirit as recorded in Luke 3:22. He worked wonders, not by His own power but by the power of the Father, saying, "The Father that dwelleth in me, he doeth the works" (John 14:10).

And when He prayed, He prayed not as a divine One who had authority as God, but as a man who walked obediently *with* God. And, as Hebrews 5:7 says, "His prayers were heard not because of His deity, but because of His reverence toward God" (AMP).

Jesus, the divine Son of God, set aside the privileges and powers of deity for a time and lived as a man on earth. Once you grasp that, it will absolutely thrill your soul! Why? Because it means that you, as a reborn child of God, filled with the same Holy Spirit as Jesus was, have the same opportunity to live as He lived on earth. In fact, that is exactly what He intends. For in John 17:18 He said to the Father, "Just as You sent Me into the world, I also have sent them into the world."

Jesus has sent *you* into the world to live as He lived. Through the new birth, He's enabled you to exchange the sinful nature of Adam for the sinless nature of God.

He's given you the ability and the command to live above sin, to live in fellowship with the Father, to preach the gospel, to heal the sick, to raise the dead, to cast out demons, and to make disciples.

Once you realize that, you'll throw off the shackles of doubt that have held you back. You'll begin to live as Jesus meant for you to live—not as a sin-ridden son of fallen man, but as a reborn child of the Most High God. Then those around you will actually begin to see Jesus—in you.

SCRIPTURE READING: 1 John 3:1-8

Grow Up!

"Like newborn babies you should crave — thirst for, earnestly desire —
the pure (unadulterated) spiritual milk, that by it you may be nurtured
and grow unto [completed] salvation." **(1 Peter 2:2, AMP)**

Have you ever been in a room full of babies? Infants crying. Crawlers hollering for certain toys. Toddlers pushing and whining to get their way. It can be quite a handful, can't it?

When a bunch of spiritual babies get together, it's just about the same way! Of course, there's nothing wrong with being a spiritual baby. All of us start out that way. When we're first born into the kingdom of God, we're much like physical newborns. We're not very strong or well-developed. We blunder around trying to learn how to operate in our new environment. That's how we all have to begin. But God never meant for us to stay that way.

That's why in 1 Peter 2:2 He says we should "desire the sincere milk of the word, that ye may grow...." He intends for us to grow up! He intends for us to feed on His Word, moving from the milk of the Word to the meat of the Word until we grow up into mature sons and daughters.

Begin now finding your nourishment in His Word and enjoy the reward of growing up in Him!

SCRIPTURE READING: Ephesians 4:12-16

Do Your Own Praying

"Is any one among you afflicted —
ill-treated, suffering evil? He should pray." **(James 5:13, AMP)**

The Greek word translated *afflicted* doesn't mean the result of sickness and disease. It means "troubled."

If you're in trouble, you need to pray. That's what the Word says. Notice it didn't say your pastor needs to pray for you or your friends need to pray for you. It says *you* need to pray.

Too often we try to find a quick fix to our problems by asking everyone else to pray for us. There's nothing wrong, of course, with having others pray for you, but you'll never get your life to a place of permanent victory until you begin to pray yourself.

The biggest church in the world is in Seoul, Korea. It's pastored by Dr. Paul Cho, and the last I heard, it had more than 700,000 members. How did that church grow to be so large? According to Dr. Cho, the key is prayer. Not just his prayers but the prayers of his people. Praying is a way of life in that church. They have a place called Prayer Mountain where thousands of people come every day to pray.

I once heard Dr. Cho's mother-in-law on television talking about the emphasis they put on prayer. She said that when their church members are in trouble, when they have marriage problems or problems in their personal life, before anything else is done, those church members are told to go and fast and pray for 24 hours.

We need to do more of that here in our churches in the United States. We need to quit training our people to run around asking others to pray for them and train them instead to do their own praying.

You see, if I pray for God to solve one problem for you, you may enjoy success for a while, but then another problem will come along because you'll still be making the same old mistakes that got you in trouble the first time. But if you buckle down and do that praying for yourself, if you discipline yourself to start searching out the things of the Spirit, you'll get permanent answers. You'll learn how to make adjustments in your life that will keep those problems from cropping up again.

If you have made Jesus your Lord, you have access to the throne of Almighty God. He has every solution to every problem you'll ever have, and He's just waiting for you to come to Him, so He can give you the answer. It may take some private time alone with Him for you to hear it, but He will never disappoint you.

Don't depend on others to do your praying for you. Go personally to the throne of God today.

SCRIPTURE READING: Psalm 5

You Hold the Keys

"I have pursued mine enemies, and overtaken them...
they are fallen under my feet." **(Psalm 18:37,38)**

If you've been standing around wringing your hands and worrying about what the devil is doing, it's time you made a switch. It's time you put that devil under your feet.

Jesus has already given you all the power and authority you need to do it. He's given you the keys of the kingdom. He's promised you that whatever you declare locked on earth is locked in heaven and whatever you declare unlocked on earth is unlocked in the heavenlies (Matt. 16:19). That means you can speak the Word and bind wicked spirits. You can speak the Word and loose the angelic forces of God to work in your behalf.

What's more, you've been given the power of attorney that enables you to use the mighty name of Jesus. A name that's above every other name. A name which will cause every knee to bow—in heaven, in earth, and under the earth! (Phil. 2:9,10).

So don't waste time worrying about the devil. Take authority over him. Bind the evil spirits that are trying to destroy your home, your church, and your nation. Loose God's Word in the earth and enforce it with the name of Jesus.

You hold the keys. Learn to use them and before long the devil will be wringing his hands worrying about *you!*

SCRIPTURE READING: Matthew 16:13-27

Christ in You!

"To whom God would make known what is
the riches of the glory of this mystery among the Gentiles;
which is Christ in you, the hope of glory." **(Colossians 1:27)**

Some years back, I was praying and walking the floor of our little house in Tulsa, Oklahoma. I was walking up and down confessing 1 John 4:4, "Greater is He that is in me, than he that is in the world." Greater is He.... Greater is He.... Suddenly, revelation knowledge welled up in me and I knew, *Oh! God is in me!*

It hit me like somebody walked up and slapped me with a wet rag. It just shook me awake. I started to stomp grandly around that old house. All of a sudden, I wasn't just a poor preacher living in a shack anymore! I was the dwelling place of the Most High God! That changed my thinking about so many things. I looked at my hands and it hit me. *His fingers are in my fingers!* I looked at my legs. *His legs are in my legs. His feet are in my feet! If I walk into danger, He walks into danger.*

Now, when I hear people say, "Brother Copeland, my prayers aren't getting any higher than the ceiling," I want to say, "Higher than the ceiling? They don't need to get any higher than your nose! *He's inside you!* The Author of your prayers, the Author of your faith, Jesus of Nazareth has taken residency inside you. Hallelujah!"

Some people think you don't get filled with the Spirit until you receive the baptism of the Holy Ghost. But that's not so. The Holy Spirit came into you when you made Jesus Lord of your life. He came into you when you were born again. Getting baptized in the Holy Spirit is another thing. It's when the power of the Holy Ghost comes upon you to empower you for service (Acts 1:8).

That means even if you've just been born again two seconds, Jesus is in you! He's living there, and He will be from now on. Can you fathom that? No, probably not. If you'll spend some time thinking about it and meditating on it, you can receive revelation of it just like I did. It will start growing in your spirit, and if you'll let it, it will eventually change your whole life.

"As God hath said, I will dwell in them, and walk in them; and I will be their God, and they shall be my people" (2 Cor. 6:16). Jesus is in you. That's the most glorious truth in the Word of God. Let that truth come alive in you today.

SCRIPTURE READING: Colossians 1:13-27

God Wants You Well

"For I will restore health unto thee,
and I will heal thee of thy wounds, saith the Lord." **(Jeremiah 30:17)**

God wants you well! Did you know that? He wants you healthy and strong in every single area of your life.

He wants you to be spiritually strong. Strong in faith. Strong in the Word. Strong in redemption. Strong in the love of God.

He wants you to be well in your mind, to be strong and stable emotionally.

He wants you to have a healthy will, a will that's aligned with His will.

He wants your body to be well. He wants you free from the bondages of pain, sickness, and care. Free from the worries and woes of this earthly life.

Your heavenly Father wants you well!

What's more, in this day and hour, He *needs* you well. He needs you living in victory and healing so that you can teach others how to do it too. We're stepping into a time when that kind of knowledge is an absolute necessity. There's no more time for the Body of Christ to limp along, uninformed and unprepared for the devil's attacks.

In fact, here's what the Lord has told me:

The further you go, the more dangerous things in the earth will become. People will have to grow in the realities of redemption and the "how to's" of living by faith in order to live in the great, overcoming way I have planned for them.

Jesus gave Himself in death so that we could be well. He was raised in life, ever making intercession for us *now* so that we can be well. And He wants us to be healthy and strong as a witness in these last days to a world that's filled with terror—a witness of His love, His grace, and His power.

Receive Jesus' healing power in every area of your life. Start applying it by faith right now. Commit yourself to getting well and growing strong in every area of your life today!

SCRIPTURE READING: Psalm 107

Don't Be Stony Ground

"And these are they likewise which are sown on stony ground;
who, when they have heard the word, immediately receive it with
gladness; And have no root in themselves, and so endure but for
a time: afterward, when affliction or persecution ariseth for the
word's sake, immediately they are offended." **(Mark 4:16,17)**

There seems to be an abundance of "Stony Ground" Christians these days. Initially, they get excited about the Word of God. They'll hear a message on prosperity, for instance, and they'll go home saying, "Hallelujah! I'm going to prosper in the name of Jesus!" But then, somehow, things don't work out like they thought they should.

Their bank balance doesn't double overnight. They go through some disappointments. They suffer some criticism. Then, before you know it, their faith has withered away.

If you don't want that to happen to you, make up your mind right now that you're not going to let the rough times defeat you. Decide now that you're going to hang on to the Word even when the persecutions and afflictions come—because, I can guarantee you, they *will* come.

When you decide to walk by faith, you don't get rid of trials. You learn to overcome them.

When you let the Word of God get down in your heart, you're going to learn more about the devil than you ever wanted to know because he's going to do his best to see to it that the Word is unfruitful in you. He's going to be trying to mess you up every time you turn around. You'll have problems, but the difference is *now* you have the answer—the Word of God.

Thank God, however, through Christ Jesus you have the power to defeat him. When he brings problems and disappointments your way, you don't have to lie down and let them steamroll over you. Just keep fighting the good fight of faith until you win.

Sure, you'll get knocked down sometimes. But when you do, get back up and say, "Look here, devil, I'm not going to let you steal the Word out of my heart. It's in there and I'm meditating on it; I'm saying it with my mouth; and I'm acting on it until God's blessings overtake me. If you don't believe me, just hide and watch!"

If you'll take that attitude, no matter what that devil does, he'll never make a "Stony Ground" Christian out of you!

SCRIPTURE READING: 2 Corinthians 4:6-18

Just Do It

"And the ruler of the synagogue answered with indignation, because that Jesus had healed on the sabbath day, and said unto the people, There are six days in which men ought to work: in them therefore come and be healed, and not on the sabbath day." **(Luke 13:14)**

Religion is dangerous. Religion would rather debate about healing than see somebody healed. Religion would rather argue about deliverance than see somebody set free.

You can see an example of that in the thirteenth chapter of Luke. There Jesus had healed a woman who had been bowed over for 18 years. Think of it, a dear old woman—*a daughter of Abraham* Jesus called her—set free after being bound by the devil for nearly two decades. You'd think the temple rulers would have been rejoicing at what Jesus had done. But, no! They were angry because He'd done it on the wrong day.

Do you know what's worse? Those very same religious leaders who criticized Jesus for healing on the Sabbath could have ministered healing to that woman themselves on any of the other six days of the week if they'd cared enough to do it.

That's why Jesus was so indignant with them. They had the same covenant of Abraham that Jesus was ministering on. But their religion had kept that woman bound instead of setting her free. It always does.

Remember that next time someone tries to get you sidetracked into a religious debate about healing or deliverance. If someone needs to be delivered from a demon, just do it! Don't get all hung up on theological questions about where the demon is. "Is it in his body? Or his brain? Or his spirit? Or his pocket?" While you're arguing about questions like that, the demon will be driving the poor guy up the wall.

The question isn't, "Where is the demon?" The question is, "Why haven't we gotten this man delivered? He's our blood brother in the name of Jesus and he ought to be free!"

Once you start asking that question, you won't care whether that demon is inside or outside, hovering over or sitting under. All you'll care about is getting that person free!

That's the difference between religion and the love of God. Religion argues. Love acts. Choose love today.

SCRIPTURE READING: Luke 13:11-17

Make His Word the Last Word

"I am Alpha and Omega,
the beginning and the ending, saith the Lord, which is,
and which was, and which is to come, the Almighty."

(Revelation 1:8)

Jesus is the beginning and the ending. He is the Almighty. When He told us that in the Book of Revelation, He wasn't just giving us a general piece of information about Himself. He was giving us a powerful truth we can apply now, today!

Let me show you how. He said He is the beginning. So no matter what challenge or situation you may be facing right now, you need to start with Him. John 1:1 says Jesus is the Word. That means, if you're going to start with Jesus, you're going to start with the Word. Don't do anything until you find out what the Word has to say about it.

Then, stay on the Word. As Colossians 1:23 says, "Continue in the faith grounded and settled, and be not moved away from the hope of the gospel, which ye have heard." Continue in the faith. The only way the devil can defeat you is to pressure you into throwing away the Word. Everything he does, every challenge he brings you is intended to make you doubt the Word of God. So don't let go of the Word, no matter what may happen. Settle it with God in prayer and stay with it forever. It is written!

Then end with the Word. Jesus said He was the first and *the last*. That means the word of your doctor is not the last word. Even the word of your pastor is not the last word. The Word of Jesus is the last Word!

Remember this: You are now what the Word says you are. You can do what the Word says you can do. And you can have what the Word says you can have. Begin to believe that. Begin to say it out loud in faith.

Now shout the victory. Yes, *now*! You don't have to wait to *see* the outcome to celebrate. You have Jesus' Word on the matter, so you know beyond any doubt that your breakthrough is coming. Once you've settled yourself on Him, you can be assured that He will have the last word!

SCRIPTURE READING: Proverbs 1:1-9

Four Words That Work

"Therefore I say unto you, What things soever ye desire, when ye pray, believe that ye receive them, and ye shall have them." **(Mark 11:24)**

Believing. That's the key to everything in the kingdom of God. It's the way we tap into the very power of Almighty God. Most all of us know that. But few of us are sure exactly how to do that kind of believing. We don't know how to put it into action.

Actually it's so simple, it's startling. It's as simple as saying, "I believe I receive."

Something happens in your spirit when you say those words. I don't understand how, but it does. I don't understand how my digestive system knows what to do when I swallow something, but it does. All I have to do is take a bite of food and it goes to work. I don't have to make it happen. I don't have to feel it happen. It just happens. That's the way the body is made.

In much the same way, when you feed on God's precious promises and "swallow" them into your spirit by saying, "I believe I receive," faith is released. You don't have to make it happen. You don't have to feel it happen. It just happens. The reborn spirit is made that way.

When you constantly say with your mouth, "I believe I receive my healing" or "I believe I receive my financial needs met," and then quote the scriptures that back those things, faith is released to bring power to bear on those needs.

As Dr. Kenneth Hagin says, you need to "keep the switch of faith turned on." And Gloria and I have discovered that speaking out that phrase, "I believe I receive," is one way to do it. We say it when we pray. We say it when we praise God. We say it when we read the Word.

We especially say it in the face of darkness when it looks like we're not receiving. When everything looks the worst, we say it the loudest. *I believe I receive!*

Do you want to activate your faith today? Then make these four key words the most important words in your vocabulary. Use them every day. You'll soon discover, just as we did... they work!

SCRIPTURE READING: Mark 11:12-24

Hit Him With the Rock

"The Lord is my shepherd; I shall not want.
He maketh me to lie down in green pastures: he leadeth me
beside the still waters." **(Psalm 23:1,2)**

Have you ever thought about David and wondered how a shepherd boy could become a man after God's own heart? A man so strong in spirit that God chose him to be king of Israel? I have.

In fact, I asked God about it, and He showed me that revelation was what turned David into such a spiritual powerhouse—revelation that came to him through hours of thinking about the things of God. I imagine the day he wrote the Twenty-third Psalm he was just sitting and singing praises to God and meditating on His goodness. Just fellowshipping with Him when suddenly the anointing of the Lord came upon him and he said, "The Lord is *my* Shepherd!"

Suddenly he thought about the sheep he watched over as a boy. "I faced death for those sheep. I led them where pastures were green and waters were cool, clean, deep, and peaceful." He kept on meditating on that until it started to thrill him. When the lion and the bear came, didn't He prepare a table before me in the presence of those enemies? He gave me victory.

"My God! My God will fight for me. The *Lord* is my Shepherd! I shall not want!"

That revelation welled up in David so strong that the devil couldn't beat it out of him. So when Goliath tried to make a fool out of Israel, David went after him. Goliath was able to scare off everyone else, but he couldn't shake David because he had a revelation inside him that said, "Yea, though I walk through the valley of the shadow of death, I will fear no evil: for my God is with me." That revelation enabled David to say, "I come against you in the name of the Lord of Hosts" and to send a rock sailing into that giant's brain.

Is the devil out to destroy you? Do what David did. Meditate on God and His Word. Sing praises to your King. Fellowship with Him until the revelation of who He is in you starts to thrill your soul. Then tell the devil, "You're not going to kill me. The Lord is my Shepherd!" Hit him with the rock of revelation knowledge, and you'll knock him flat every time.

SCRIPTURE READING: Psalm 23

Thank You, Lord

"In every thing give thanks: for this is the will
of God in Christ Jesus concerning you." **(1 Thessalonians 5:18)**

Notice that this scripture instructs us to give thanks "in" all things, not "for" all things. When tragedy or temptation strikes, we are not to thank God for them. He is not their author. He's the One who provides our way of escape from them. And *that's* what we're to thank Him for.

If you read the four Gospels, you'll find that Jesus never gave thanks for sickness or death. Instead, when He encountered them, His response was to overcome them by God's power. So give thanks as Jesus gave thanks—not for Satan's activities but for the victory God has given you over them.

SCRIPTURE READING: John 11:1-48

Out of the Shadow

"The next day John seeth Jesus coming unto him, and saith,
Behold the Lamb of God, which taketh away the sin of the world."
(John 1:29)

Jesus came to *take away* sin. Do you realize what that means? It means that God, through the blood of Jesus, has so completely done away with the power of sin that you, as a born-again believer, can live as if it never existed. You can step out from under its shadow once and for all.

Understand now, stepping out from under sin's shadow doesn't mean living a perfect life. You're still going to miss it sometimes. There will be times when you stumble and fall into sin. (You don't have to but probably will!) But you have a promise from God, sworn in the blood of Jesus, that says when you confess that sin, He's faithful and just to forgive you of it and cleanse you from all unrighteousness.

You don't have to live under the shadow of that sin five seconds if you have sense enough to repent and receive God's forgiveness.

"Oh, but Brother Copeland, I just feel so bad about it!"

It doesn't make any difference how you feel about it. Do it by faith. Learn to be quick to repent. Then stand up and laugh in the devil's face.

I remember one time in particular when I was in that spot. I'd missed it something awful, and I was supposed to go preach that night. I felt so guilty that I just told the Lord I wasn't going to go. "Lord, You'll just have to get Yourself another preacher tonight because I'm not going over there to that service."

Suddenly the Spirit spoke up inside me. "Did you confess that sin before Me, Kenneth?"

"Yes, I did."

"Do you account the blood by which you're sanctified as an unholy thing?"

"Oh, dear God, no!" I answered.

"That's what you're standing there doing," He said. "I gave you My Word that when you confess your sin before Me, I would not only forgive you of it, but I'd cleanse it and cast it into a sea of forgetfulness. Now it's not good taste for you to keep bringing it up."

I'm telling you, I dropped the matter right then and marched into that service and preached for two and a half hours on the forgiveness of God!

Don't let feelings of guilt and unworthiness rob you of the power of Jesus' blood. Repent and step out by faith from under the shadow of sin into the mighty light of God's forgiveness today!

SCRIPTURE READING: John 1:1-34

Let Peace Rule

"And let the peace (soul harmony which comes) from the Christ rule
(act as umpire continually) in your hearts — deciding and settling with finality
all questions that arise in your minds.... And be thankful — appreciative,
giving praise to God always." **(Colossians 3:15, AMP)**

Have you been praying that God will let you know whether a certain action you want to take is agreeable to His will or not? Let this peace of Christ be your guide. Let it help you settle the issue. If you start to take that action and you realize you don't have peace about it, don't do it.

Remember, though, that this inner leading of the Holy Spirit, this subtle sense of uneasiness or peace He gives you, is something you have to watch and listen for carefully. He generally won't just come up and knock you out of bed one morning and tell you what you need to do. The primary way He speaks to you is by what the Bible calls an inward witness.

So, you have to listen. You can't just stay busy about the things of the world all the time. You have to give Him time and attention.

Also, watch out for strife. When you're irritated and upset about things in your life, it's very hard to receive that quiet guidance from the Holy Spirit. So take heed to the instructions at the end of this scripture and "be thankful...appreciative, giving praise to God always." Maintain a thankful, grateful heart. You'll find it much easier to hear the "umpire of peace" when He makes a call.

SCRIPTURE READING: Psalm 95:1-7

Uncommon Protection

"The thief cometh not, but for to steal, and to kill, and to destroy."
(John 10:10)

Considering how much the devil hates people and how dead set he is on destroying them, it's no wonder we see so much tragedy and disaster in the world. In fact, it's amazing that we don't see *more*!

I asked the Lord about that one time and He told me it takes the realm of darkness a long time to set up major disasters. Take the aviation industry, for example. It's highly regulated and works hard at policing itself because safety is its product. You take a highly regulated system like that and the devil has to work terribly hard to cause disasters.

He can't just come roaring in and rip things up anytime he wants to. If he could, he'd knock every plane out of the sky tonight. But he can't do it.

Why? Because he's bound. The Bible says he's bound to things that are common to man. He has to line up certain things in this natural, human realm before he can lay a finger on you. He has to use people to get his work done.

But, bless God, we're not bound to what's common to man. We're free to use what's *common* to God! We fight our warfare with uncommon weapons. What does that mean? It means you ought to have the devil wrapped up and sewed up. You ought to put him in a sack with a ribbon on top.

The devil can't cause disaster in your life unless he has been given place. He can't come in and start destroying and stealing from you unless he can get you into a place of sin, doubt, ignorance, or disobedience. So if he's been giving you trouble, ask the Holy Spirit to show you where you've let those things in. Then repent and get rid of them.

Once you've done that, pull out the weapons God has given you and fire away with both barrels. Pull out the Word. Pull out prayer. Pull out faith and use it to tie the devil in knots. Use the uncommon power of God to keep him bound and he won't be able to put anything over on you.

SCRIPTURE READING: Ephesians 6:10-18

Your Final Authority

"I am the Lord, I change not." **(Malachi 3:6)**

The world's order of things is unsure and indefinite. Desperate words of uncertainty are crying out daily from radio, television, and newspapers. Everything around us seems to be in turmoil.

But, praise God, if you're a believer you have something you can depend on: The unchanging Word of God!

God has no double standard. He doesn't say one thing today and something else tomorrow. He is the same yesterday, today, and forever.

If you will make that Word the final authority in your life, it will give you stability when everything else around you gives way. If you'll let what God says settle the issues of life, you'll be confident when others are confused, peaceful when others are under pressure. You'll be overcoming when others are being overcome!

What does it mean to make God's Word the final authority? It means believing what He says instead of believing what people say. It means believing what He says instead of what Satan says. It means believing what He says instead of what the circumstances say.

Determine in your heart to do that today. Make up your mind to live by faith, not by sight. Fearlessly commit yourself to the authority of God's Word and there won't be anything in this old, unstable world that can steal your security from you.

SCRIPTURE READING: Psalm 9:1-10

Thank God Instead

"If possible, as far as it depends on you,
live at peace with every one." **(Romans 12:18, AMP)**

When I was a new Christian, it was almost impossible for me to live at peace with *anyone*! Almost every time I opened my mouth, I said something ugly. I was constantly hurting the people I was close to. In fact, I spoke more harshly to them than to anyone else.

I criticized Gloria's driving so much that she nearly refused to drive while I was with her. I criticized my children so much that they began to avoid me. I didn't want to be so insensitive, but I couldn't help it. I had a well-developed habit of speaking harshly and didn't know how to change it.

Then I found Ephesians 5:4. It said, "[Let there be] no coarse, stupid, or flippant talk; these things are out of place; you should rather be thanking God" (*New English Bible*). When I read that, I realized that what I needed to do was replace the words I was used to saying with words of thanksgiving. That would solve my problem. After all, I couldn't speak harshly and thank God at the same time. I couldn't criticize those around me if I had a thankful attitude about them.

I immediately decided to put this principle to work in my life. Rushing into my son's room one day ready to lambaste him about something he had done, I recognized my old behavior pattern. I just stopped and said to myself, "The Word says this kind of behavior is out of place, so I am going to stop and thank God." I wasn't nearly as angry after I spent a few minutes praising and thanking the Lord.

If you've developed the habit of speaking harshly, start changing that habit today. When someone crosses you on the job, at school, or wherever, and you're tempted to tear into them with cruel words, stop! Then take a few moments to give thanks and praise to God. Once you begin thinking about how good God is, more often than not, those harsh, angry words will just slip away unspoken.

Instead of using your tongue to tear people down, train it to lift God's praises up. Then living at peace with others will come easily to you!

SCRIPTURE READING: Ephesians 4:26-32, Ephesians 5:1-4

Tithe With Joy

"And it shall be, when thou art come in unto the land
which the Lord thy God giveth thee for an inheritance...That thou shalt take
of the first of all the fruit of the earth...and shalt go unto the place which the
Lord thy God shall choose to place his name there." **(Deuteronomy 26:1,2)**

Tithing. Most Christians aren't very excited about it. But they should be—and they *would* be if they understood how to do it properly.

Scriptural tithing stirs up faith. It activates the power of God in our lives when we do it in gratitude and joy, expecting our needs to be met abundantly.

In Deuteronomy 26:8,9, God told the Israelites exactly what to say when they brought their tithes. He instructed them to acknowledge the fact that He had brought them out of the bondage of Egypt and to say:

The Lord brought us forth out of Egypt with a mighty hand, and with an outstretched arm, and with great terribleness, and with signs, and with wonders:

And he hath brought us into this place, and hath given us this land, even a land that floweth with milk and honey.

What does that have to do with you and me? God has done the same thing for us! He's brought us out of a life of bondage and poverty into a life that flows with the abundance of God.

So when you bring your tithe to the Lord, follow the example set by the Israelites. Make it a time of rejoicing. Make it a time of realizing anew the wonderful things Jesus Christ has done for you.

Thank Him for delivering you from a land of darkness and scarcity and bringing you into His promised land of plenty. Thank Him that it is a land of mercy, a land of joy, a land of peace, and a land of prosperity.

Tithe in faith, expecting the rich blessings of that land to be multiplied to you. You may soon find it to be one of the most exciting things you can do.

SCRIPTURE READING: Deuteronomy 26

Called to Intercession

"Blessed are they that mourn: for they shall be comforted."

(Matthew 5:4)

Do you know what Jesus was really talking about when He said those words? He was talking about the mourning of the intercessor. He was teaching about the comfort that comes to the intercessor when he is assured by the Holy Spirit that he has *prayed through*.

To *pray through* means "to break through the barriers that have stopped the work of God in the lives of others." It means using your spiritual armor to push back the forces of darkness that surround them.

There's a desperate need for believers who are willing to do that today. There's a need for intercessors who will go before God and reach out for His mercy and compassion for the sinner, for the sick, and for this downcast world. For prayer warriors who will stick with it until they have the assurance inside, in their spirits, that every barrier is broken and every area of bondage has been abolished.

God is looking for intercessors like that—and there are certain things that won't happen on this earth until He

finds them. There are blessings and moves of God that won't come until someone gives birth to those things by prayer.

Even the Lord Jesus Himself was ushered into the earth by intercession. Remember Simeon and Anna? They were both intercessors, prayer warriors of God. They'd spent years in spiritual mourning, praying for the Messiah to come. But when they were done, they experienced the comfort of the Holy Spirit. For when they saw Jesus as a tiny baby in the temple, they recognized Him and rejoiced.

If you're wondering if you're one of those who's been called to intercession, then you probably are. God is calling believers everywhere to experience that unique kind of mourning and comfort that only the intercessor knows. He's calling you to lay down your life for others through prayer.

Somewhere in the world, someone needs you to pray them through. Spend some time on your knees today.

SCRIPTURE READING: Luke 2:1-38

Punch a Hole in the Dam

"So [Israel] came up to Baal-perazim,
and David smote the [Philistines] there. Then David said,
God has broken my enemies by my hand, like the bursting forth of waters;
therefore they called the name of that place Baal-perazim
(Lord of breaking through)." **(1 Chronicles 14:11, AMP)**

ike the bursting forth of waters. I love that phrase! It paints such a powerful and accurate picture of a breakthrough.

Do you remember the story of the little boy who saw a leak in the dam and plugged up the hole with his finger? He knew that the force of the water flowing through that one tiny hole would have enlarged the leak with every second that passed. And, as the dam gave way to the pressure, that tiny trickle would have quickly become a raging flood.

If you'll reach out your hand in faith, expecting God to "break in upon your enemies" just like He did for David, that's how your breakthrough will come...'like the bursting forth of waters!"

All you have to do is punch one little hole in that wall of problems, in that devilish dam that's been holding you back. Dig one tiny hole in it with your faith and with the Word of God.

Then keep tearing away at that hole by speaking out that faith day after day. Don't quit! Because God's forces are backed up behind you like an ocean of spiritual water. Each time you speak a word of faith, they leak through. The more you speak and the more you pray, the bigger that leak will get.

Begin your breakthrough right now. Say, "Lord Jesus, I rejoice today that You are Lord of my breakthrough. I thank You that the flood of Your power is about to sweep through my life. I know there is no problem that can stand against it. Poverty can't stand against it. Family problems can't stand against it. Nothing the devil can do can stop my victory. I praise You for it *NOW!* Amen."

Keep praying that. Keep believing that. And before long, the forces of God will come bursting through, demolishing every obstacle in their path!

SCRIPTURE READING: 1 Chronicles 14:8-17

Beyond What You Can Ask or Think

"I thank my God, I speak with tongues more than ye all."

(1 Corinthians 14:18)

Few things in the Bible have created more fuss than the issue of speaking in tongues. Churches have split over it. People have been persecuted for doing it. People have even been killed for it.

Who's behind all the trouble? Satan, himself. He's so frightened of our ability to pray in tongues that he's continually trying to steal it from us through persecution and strife.

You see, the devil knows (even if *we* don't) that praying in tongues is the only way you and I can pray beyond what we know. It's the tool God has given us to use to tap into the mind of the Spirit.

When we pray in tongues, we activate the Holy Spirit within us and He begins to teach us and enlighten us. If you want to see an example of what praying in tongues can do, look at the apostle Paul. He said he prayed in tongues more than anyone in the whole Corinthian church and he was responsible for writing most of the New Testament!

Another example is the first church at Jerusalem. They didn't yet have any of the New Testament to read. They couldn't turn to Ephesians and find out what God's plan was for them.

They just had to pray in tongues until the revelation light of God dawned in their hearts. That's all the equipment they had. So they used it and turned the world upside down.

Some years ago God began directing me to spend an hour a day praying in tongues. After I did it awhile, I began to talk to other Christians who'd been directed to do the same thing. God was speaking to believers all over the world to spend time praying in the Spirit.

If you haven't made a commitment to spend some time each day praying in tongues, make one now. Set aside all the disagreements and confusion the devil has stirred up about it and just say, "Lord, I'm going to do it. I don't care what the devil says. I don't care what any man says. I know You have plans for me that are so good my human mind hasn't even conceived them—things that are beyond what I can ask or think. And by praying in the Spirit, I'm going to receive them."

Don't let the distractions of the devil disturb you. Tap into the mind of God. Speak forth His wisdom. Pray in the Spirit today.

SCRIPTURE READING: Isaiah 28:9-12

Weary of Worry

"Now thanks be unto God, which always causeth us to triumph in Christ, and maketh manifest the savour of his knowledge by us in every place."
(2 Corinthians 2:14)

As you fight the good fight of faith today, remember this: Your mind is where the battle will take place. Whatever you allow to captivate your mind will rule your life. Will it be the Word of God or the lies of Satan?

The decision is yours.

If you want the Word to reign, make up your mind now to resist the devil when he comes to plant doubts within you. Refuse to surrender to the circumstantial pressure he brings your way. Decide at the onset that you will not succumb to this trial. Dig your heels in and stand immovable upon the promises of God.

When thoughts come that are contrary to God's will, cast them down. And above all, don't worry. Worrying is meditating the thoughts of Satan.

When you recognize you are worrying, stop it immediately. Replace worried, fearful, and doubtful thoughts with the Word.

Be assured, Satan will continually try to tell you that your situation is hopeless. He will persistently peddle doubt, defeat, and discouragement. But if you won't allow him to sell you his goods, his commission will be zero. If you don't buy his lies, he can't cause them to come to pass in your life.

God has promised that He will *always* cause you to triumph in Christ. You are guaranteed victory over the adversity you are facing today. Make up your mind right now to be a winner and you'll spread the knowledge of victory in Christ everywhere you go.

SCRIPTURE READING: Philippians 4:1-9

You Can Open That Door

"Ask, and it shall be given to you; seek, and ye shall find; knock, and it shall be opened unto you." **(Matthew 7:7)**

How long has it been since you were backed into a corner, hemmed in by a seemingly insurmountable problem? If you're anything like most folks, it hasn't been very long. Some of us spend years trying to work our way out of financial binds only to end up more bound by debt than ever. Others work frantically on marriages that despite their best efforts deteriorate from year to year. Still others fight losing battles against fear or depression, drug addiction or disease.

Deep within our hearts, each of us knows there must be an answer to the problem we face. But often it seems to be out of reach, hidden behind a door that's locked tightly against us.

What I want you to know today, however, is this: WE CAN OPEN THAT DOOR! Jesus Himself has given us the keys.

Right now you may be facing a situation that looks utterly hopeless, but God has a key ring full of keys that will unlock *any* situation. He has the keys that open doors for you spiritually and physically, financially and emotionally. No matter how hard the devil tries to trap you, if you'll get hold of that key, you can find your way out.

God's Word is full of keys of kingdom principles—keys to bind the devil's operations and keys to loose yourself from his snares. God has a key that will unravel any knot that the devil can tie. He also has a key that will lock up the devil's operation so tightly that he won't be able to move.

Remember this: There's no situation so dark and so cleverly designed by the forces of darkness that there is not a kingdom key that will unlock it with kingdom power.

There *is* an answer to your situation. So keep digging for it. If you've been digging in the Word of God in one spot and haven't found your answer, then look at another chapter, a different verse. Keep digging until you find the keys. Keep knocking at every door until you find the one that opens.

SCRIPTURE READING: Psalm 63

Love is the Power Charge

"This is my commandment, That ye love one another,
as I have loved you. Greater love hath no man than this, that a man
lay down his life for his friends." **(John 15:12,13)**

Love. It is the first and foremost command Jesus gave us, yet all too many believers neglect to follow it.

I'm talking about believers who can quote tremendous amounts of scripture and who may speak the name of Jesus 35 or 40 times a day, yet they're rough and insensitive to the needs of their friends and family. They're so busy "serving God," they don't have time to serve people. Strife is their hallmark.

You may have been saved 45 years; you may talk in tongues all day long; but if you have strife in your heart and you're not living by the love commandment of Jesus, spiritual things are foolishness to you.

When you're in that condition, the name of Jesus won't work. Faith won't work because the Bible says that faith works by love. In fact, none of the gifts of the Spirit will work if you don't have love. First Corinthians 13 says so.

Do you want to see the incredible power of God released through your life? Then start putting the love command in action. Start loving those around you.

Love is the power charge, friend. God's power package just won't work without it. That's why we've seen so many power failures in the Body of Christ. Starting today, you and I can turn those failures around. We can make up our minds to let the Word dwell richly within us. We can set our hearts on keeping the commands of Jesus and speak His name with confidence and authority. And, most important of all, we can begin to love one another.

Then we will truly see the power of God begin to flow.

SCRIPTURE READING: 1 Corinthians 13:1-8

A Proven Success

"And the son said unto him,
Father, I have sinned against heaven, and in thy sight,
and am no more worthy to be called thy son. But the father said
to his servants, Bring forth the best robe, and put it on him;
and put a ring on his hand, and shoes on his feet....
For this my son...was lost, and is found." **(Luke 15:21,22,24)**

Prove yourself. In today's world, that's what you constantly have to do, right? On the job, among friends, even at home you're always working to win the approval you need. Working to convince those around you that you deserve the salary, the friendship, and even the love they give you.

Is there any escape?

You better believe there is! It's called grace. Unearned and undeserved favor and acceptance. And there's only one place you can find it—in the heart of God Himself.

There's no better picture of God's grace in action than in the story of the prodigal son. Few of us today can really feel the impact of that story like those first Jewish listeners Jesus told it to. You see, by their standards the prodigal son had committed some of the most despicable acts possible. He'd not only taken advantage of his father and spent his inheritance in riotous living, he'd left the nation of Israel and made covenant with a foreigner—a pig farmer! That was as low as you could get.

In their eyes, that boy's rebellion was so serious his father's only recourse was to disown him.

But that's not what this father did! He welcomed his repentant son home with open arms. He offered him grace—unmerited favor—that was based on the father's love rather than the son's performance.

Next time you catch yourself struggling to make up to God for something you've done wrong, working to win His approval, let the story of the prodigal son set you free. Let it remind you that, in spite of your sins, your Father has received you with open arms. He's put a robe of righteousness on your back and His signet ring on your hand. He's put the shoes of sonship on your feet!

Do you feel unworthy of all that? Sure you do. You *were* unworthy of it. But God hasn't based His relationship with you on your worthiness. He's based it on His love and on *Jesus'* worthiness. You don't have to struggle to prove yourself to Him. As far as He's concerned, you're a proven success.

SCRIPTURE READING: Luke 15:11-32

A Hidden Treasure

"The sower soweth the word." **(Mark 4:14)**

Right now, at this very moment, you have hidden within you a treasure that can change the world. A treasure that can change a man's eternal destiny, that can take him to heaven and save him from hell. A treasure that can turn a person's poverty into prosperity, his sickness into health, his sorrow into joy.

You have within you the all-powerful Word of God.

Don't keep it to yourself. Plant it wherever you go! Sow it into the hearts of those you meet. Share it at every opportunity.

"But I don't know how!" you may say.

Then start learning. Let these three steps help guide the way.

One: Make a decision. Make up your mind and heart today that you *are* going to share the Word with others no matter what! Determine right now that it's the most important thing you'll ever do. Commit to it. Once you've done that, you'll find the rest is easy.

Two: Prepare yourself. Spend time meditating in the Word each day. Allow the Holy Spirit to minister to you. That will make it easy for you to minister to others. You'll be sensitive to the Holy Spirit and be able to hear His voice. He'll help you know what to say in each situation.

Three: Stay in faith. Once you've shared the Word with someone, trust God for the results. The Word of God does not return void. Even if they seem indifferent to you, even if it appears the Word had no effect, keep believing. Your faith will keep that Word alive inside them, and eventually, it will do its transforming work.

You have, hidden within you, a treasure that can change the world. What are you going to do with it today?

SCRIPTURE READING: 2 Corinthians 4:1-7

Welcome to the Big League

"Blessed are ye, when men shall revile you,
and persecute you, and shall say all manner of evil
against you falsely, for my sake. Rejoice, and be exceeding glad:
for great is your reward in heaven: for so persecuted they
the prophets which were before you." **(Matthew 5:11,12)**

When persecution comes, don't sit around whining about it. Don't waste your time feeling sorry for yourself. Despite what you may think, that persecution hasn't come because the devil gets his kicks out of picking on you. It comes because you've become a threat to him. It comes because you've put the Word in your heart, and he knows that if he doesn't get it out, you're going to cause him more trouble than he can handle.

So rejoice! Heavy duty persecution means you've made it to the big league. It means the devil is taking you so seriously that he's sending in his best players in an effort to get you out of the game!

The players that make it to the Superbowl don't look for some way out of it, do they? They don't say, "Boy, I sure wish I didn't have to be in that Superbowl game. Those guys are the biggest, meanest players in the country. Maybe I'll get sick and I won't have to play." No! They relish the opportunity. "Let me at 'em," they say. "I've worked all my life to get here and now I'm going to prove I'm the best!"

That's how you should be when the devil challenges you. You should accept that challenge with joy, *knowing* you're going to come out a winner. After all, your God is sufficient to see you through. He never stops and wonders if He's going to have enough resources to get poor little you over your problems this time. He knows He can beat anything the devil brings against you.

So, when persecution comes, trust Him and rejoice, knowing that you've made it to the big leagues now!

SCRIPTURE READING: 1 Peter 4:12-19

Sin Stained...or Blood Washed?

"This is the covenant that I will make with them
after those days, saith the Lord, I will put my laws into their hearts,
and in their minds will I write them; And their sins and iniquities
will I remember no more." **(Hebrews 10:16,17)**

The Bible tells us that under Levitical law, an animal had to be offered every year to *atone* for the sins of the people. That word *atone* means "to cover" and it's used continually throughout the Old Testament.

But let me tell you something exciting. It's never used in the New Testament. The Greek word used to describe what Jesus did for us on the cross is a different word altogether. It doesn't just mean "to cover"—it means "to remit; to do completely away with something."

Do you know what that means? It means there is no longer a sin problem. Jesus solved it!

When you made Him your Lord, He didn't just cover your sins, He put you into right standing with God and recreated you by the Spirit of God as if sin had *never* existed.

But, if you're like many believers, you haven't fully grasped that magnificent truth. You're caught up in what I call a "sin consciousness." You keep thinking of yourself as sin stained instead of blood washed.

"Well, after all Brother Copeland, I'm just an old sinner saved by grace."

No, you're not. You *were* an old sinner, but grace changed you forever into the very righteousness of God. You are now His workmanship, created in Christ Jesus! As far as God is concerned, your past life is forgotten. It died the death of the cross.

Think about that. Let it sink into your consciousness until you can rise up boldly and receive the freedom from sin that's yours in Christ Jesus. Receive the righteousness that only the Lamb of God can give.

SCRIPTURE READING: Hebrews 9:11-26

Put the Word First

"Get wisdom, get understanding: forget it not;
neither decline from the words of my mouth. Forsake her not,
and she shall preserve thee: love her, and she shall keep thee."
(Proverbs 4:5,6)

Recently, God has been raising up ever-growing numbers of people who are hungry. Hungry to know their Lord in a deeper way. Hungry to serve Him—in pulpits, on mission fields, in homes, in office buildings, and anywhere else He might choose to send them.

They are people who simply aren't content to find the path of least resistance and coast their way into heaven. No. They're determined to run the race...to run, as the apostle Paul said, to obtain the prize. Spiritually speaking, they are on the road to excellence.

Are you among them?

If so, I want to share four simple words that, I believe, will enable you to run the race like a winner.

Put the Word first.

Whether your goal is to be an excellent evangelist or a first-rate engineer in the service of the Lord, it is the wisdom that comes from the Word of God that will get you there.

Jesus said it this way: "Seek ye first the kingdom of God, and his righteousness; and all these things shall be added unto you" (Matt. 6:33).

So commit yourself right now to do whatever it takes to totally saturate yourself with the Word of God. Use every available moment to read, study, listen to, and meditate on it.

I know it won't be easy, but if you've made a definite decision to amount to something in the ministry of Jesus Christ and you are determined to take the Great Commission seriously, then be diligent. Put the Word first and there will surely be glorious victories ahead.

SCRIPTURE READING: Proverbs 4:1-18

Joy: A Very Real Force

"The joy of the Lord is your strength." **(Nehemiah 8:10)**

Joy. It's not a warm, happy feeling you're supposed to have now and then when things are going well. It's much more than that. Joy is one of the most powerful spiritual forces in the world.

Look again at Nehemiah 8:10 and I'll show you why. If you were to diagram that scripture and remove the phrase, "of the Lord," you'd find what it's truly saying is this: Joy is strength. The two are interchangeable.

That's what makes joy so crucial. You can't live a life of faith without being strong in the Lord—and when God wants to make you strong, joy is what He uses to do the job!

Joy is not just a state of mind. It is not a fleeting emotion. Joy is a very real force, and the devil doesn't have *anything* that can stand up against it. Just as fear has to yield to faith, discouragement has to yield to joy.

Since joy is one of the fruits of the Holy Spirit, you already have it residing within you. But you must develop it, confess it, and live by it if you want to enjoy its power.

Whatever circumstances you are facing today, you *can* be full of joy. You can be strong in the Lord. You can draw on the supply of the Holy Spirit within you and come out on top.

Rejoice!

SCRIPTURE READING: Psalm 18:28-50

Behold the Lord

"And be not conformed to this world: but be ye transformed
by the renewing of your mind." **(Romans 12:2)**

Inside, you're perfect—born again in the image of Jesus Himself. But outwardly you find yourself falling frustratingly short of that perfection. Is there a solution? Yes! The secret lies in "the renewing of your mind."

Romans 12:2 tells us that, if you'll renew your mind, you can actually be "transformed." That word "transformed" is translated from the Greek word from which we get the term "metamorphosis." It's used in the Scripture in two other places.

One of those places is when Jesus was *transfigured* on the Mount as He spoke with Moses and Elijah. The other is found in 2 Corinthians 3:18. It says, "But we all, with open face beholding as in a glass the glory of the Lord, are *changed* into the same image from glory to glory, even as by the Spirit of the Lord."

Changed, transformed, transfigured! Those are powerful, exciting words, and they describe what will happen to you as you spend time beholding the Lord in the Word and in prayer. As you spend time renewing your mind, your outer being will be transformed in much the same way as a caterpillar is changed into a butterfly. Instead of conforming to the image of the world, you'll begin to conform to the image of the reborn spirit within you which is created in righteousness and true holiness.

Take time to get away from the world and study God's Word. Meditate on it and let it change you from the inside out. Be transformed by the renewing of your mind and release the beautiful spiritual butterfly that's living in you!

SCRIPTURE READING: 2 Corinthians 3:6-18

Be Willing to Wait

"He who guards his mouth and his tongue keeps himself from troubles."
(Proverbs 21:23, AMP)

There's just no two ways about it. If you want to live a life of blessing, you're going to have to make your words agree with what God says. Not just for a few hours or a few days, but all the time.

And, if you've ever done that, you know it's not easy. As time wears on and the circumstances around you appear to be stubbornly determined to stay in the same miserable condition they've always been in, it's hard to keep on speaking God's Word. But you have to do it if you ever want your harvest of blessing to come in.

When Kenneth started preaching prosperity, I sat out there and listened to him with holes in the bottom of my shoes. We had terrible financial problems. But we knew those problems didn't change what the Word of God said. We knew His prosperity promises were true even if we hadn't been able to tap into them yet. So, even though we felt foolish at times, we just kept on talking about God's generous provision for us.

I realized later that that Word went to work for us from the first day we began to believe it and speak it and order our lives according to it. Our prosperity crop began to grow the moment we started putting seeds in the ground. It just took time for them to come up.

The problem is, most believers don't last that long. They start planting well enough, but then when they don't see immediate results, when the bank account gets low and rent is past due, they get discouraged and begin to speak words of lack and defeat. They tear up their crop with the words of their own mouth, and they never get to enjoy the fruit of it.

The next time you strike out on faith, whether it's in the financial realm or any other area, keep that in mind. Determine from the beginning that you're not going to let that waiting period discourage you. Then hang on until the Word of God is manifested in your life. Put patience to work and keep your words in line. You *will* receive your harvest.

SCRIPTURE READING: Proverbs 18:4-8,20,21

Don't Stop at the Gate

"Let us therefore come boldly unto the throne of grace,
that we may obtain mercy, and find grace to help in time of need."

(Hebrews 4:16)

When you made Jesus the Lord of your life, one of the privileges you received was the right to come to the throne room of God any time you want to. Think about that! You have the right to go boldly before God and obtain whatever you need.

Even though that's clearly what the Bible says, most people don't act like they believe it. They don't go boldly into the throne room. Instead they think, "I could never go in to where God is. I'll just stand out here and yell and hope He hears me." I used to be guilty of that myself.

I remember one day I was in prayer, begging and pleading, bombarding the gates of heaven for revival. After I'd been at it a little while, the Lord spoke to me. "What are you doing?" He said.

"I'm bombarding the gates of heaven with prayer for revival," I answered.

"Kenneth, how big is My city?" He asked me.

"As far as I can tell from what the Bible says, it's about 1200 cubits or somewhere around 1500 miles square and 1500 miles high."

"Then why are you bombarding the *gates?* Assuming that My throne is in the middle of the city that leaves you about 750 miles short! And, by the way," He added, "those gates aren't locked. Why don't you quit bombarding them and just come on in?"

After I repented for mimicking old traditional prayers without thinking, I remembered that the Word says, "Come boldly *to the throne*" and I've been coming boldly ever since.

Do you need to receive something from God today? Don't waste time standing around outside heaven's gates. Through Jesus you belong in the very throne room of God. So come right on in. The door is always open for you.

SCRIPTURE READING: Hebrews 4:14-16, Hebrews 5:1-9

Peace at Home

"For where envying and strife is, there is confusion and every evil work."

(James 3:16)

Have you ever noticed that the easiest place to remain self-centered is at home? There's an incentive to be lovely with others, but with your family you are tempted to allow yourself more selfish privileges as if it didn't count there.

Before I was a Christian, I was more courteous and nicer to friends than to my own family. I was more demanding and less forgiving with those dearest to me than with anyone else.

But after I made Jesus Lord of my life, I realized all that had to change.

Gloria and I began to learn through the Word how important harmony is within our family. We learned that if we wanted the power of agreement (see Matthew 18:19) to work in our lives, we could not allow strife in our home.

Strife drops the shield of faith, stops prayer results, and invites Satan and his cohorts into your midst. Discord is deadly. It paralyzes the power of God in your life.

Don't allow the enemy to stop you at your own front door by allowing strife in your home. If you do, you'll be no threat to him anywhere else.

Put the power of harmony to work in your family.

Determine that.

SCRIPTURE READING: Philippians 2:1-13

The Choice is Yours

"Choose you this day whom ye will serve." **(Joshua 24:15)**

Choosing to side with God's Word is a continual challenge. It's not something you do just once. It's a process of choosing to believe and act upon the Word of God over and over in every circumstance.

That's what everyone has to do. Years ago I decided I was going to choose Jesus. Since then I've had to choose Him again and again in situations every day. I've chosen Him as my Lord and Savior. I've chosen Him as my Healer. I've chosen Him as my Financier. I've chosen Him as head of my household. I've chosen Him as head of this ministry. And I still have to choose Him moment by moment.

Sometimes that choice gets tough, but God has promised it will never get too tough. In 1 Corinthians 10:13, He says, "There hath no temptation taken you but such as is common to man:

but God is faithful, who will not suffer you to be tempted above that ye are able." What the Lord is saying is that He will not allow you to be subjected to a temptation you're unable to overcome. With every temptation, He'll make a way of escape. He'll ALWAYS make sure you have a choice.

The devil doesn't come tempt you while God is off somewhere else, unaware of what is happening to you. The Spirit of God is constantly there with you, providing you with the way to overcome. In other words, God matches even the toughest temptations with the weapons and power you need to conquer them. He always makes it possible for you to choose life.

So choose to walk in love. Choose to walk by faith. Choose to live by the Word. Jesus is the Way! Choose Him!

SCRIPTURE READING: Joshua 24:14-24

His Extravagant Love

"And all these blessings shall come on thee, and overtake thee,
if thou shalt hearken unto the voice of the Lord thy God." **(Deuteronomy 28:2)**

Some people have very low expectations of what God will provide for them materially. They trust Him to feed and clothe them, but they don't trust Him to feed and clothe them very *well!*

Somehow they've gotten the idea that God's an old miser who will do little more than put rags on their backs and beans on their tables. But that's not what Jesus told us. He said in Matthew 6 that God would clothe us better than He clothed Solomon. That one statement alone proves that God wants to do more than just meet our basic needs. He wants to bless us abundantly. I know that from personal experience.

A few years ago I came home and found two expensive automobiles parked in my driveway. They'd been given to me to use by men who'd been blessed by the Lord through my ministry.

I was baffled. "Lord," I said, "I didn't *need* these cars. I hadn't asked You for them, and I wasn't believing for them. What are they doing here?"

Then the Lord spoke up on the inside of me. "Have you ever read the scripture in Deuteronomy that says blessings shall come on and overtake those who hearken to My voice?"

"Yes," I answered.

"Well, son," He said, "you've just been overtaken."

Am I saying God gave me those expensive cars just so I could enjoy them? Yes. That's exactly what I'm saying.

First Timothy 6:17 says, "He giveth us richly all things to enjoy." God is a loving Father. He gets great pleasure from blessing His children. He's extravagant where we're concerned. But don't let that worry you. He can afford it.

Once you truly believe that and begin to hearken to His voice, it won't be long before His blessings will be overtaking you.

SCRIPTURE READING: 1 Kings 10:1-24

Better Things to Come

"But [God's grace] is now made manifest
by the appearing of our Saviour Jesus Christ,
who hath abolished death, and hath brought life and immortality
to light through the gospel." **(2 Timothy 1:10)**

Have you ever wondered what it will be like when your body dies and you go on to heaven? Well, according to the Word, when that time comes, this flesh and blood tent you live in will die, but you won't feel a thing. You'll just take off the cloak of your flesh, lay it down, and go to a better place.

Believers who have died and come back say that they have no sensation of loss—no sting. Their minds stay intact, and they even have arms and legs, but they are spirit and not flesh. One man said he couldn't even tell he wasn't in his body until he tried to grasp something. His hand would just go right through the material object. He was spirit and not flesh.

According to the apostle Paul, to be absent from the body is to be present with God (2 Cor. 5:1). So, when God calls you home, you'll just abandon your fleshly body and go to be with Him forever.

It's interesting though. God doesn't even refer to our old, abandoned bodies as being *dead*. He says they're just *asleep*. Why? Because He knows that just as sleep is temporary, so is the death of the body. He's planned a day when our sleeping bodies will be awakened and raised up in glory just like Jesus' was.

Hallelujah! There's coming a day when not only our spirits have victory over death, our physical bodies do too!

Death is not the "end" for you. It's only a change to a better place!

SCRIPTURE READING: 2 Corinthians 5:1-9

He Will Lead You

"This I say then, Walk in the Spirit,
and ye shall not fulfil the lust of the flesh." **(Galatians 5:16)**

Walking in the Spirit. That's the key to overcoming the flesh. If you follow the promptings of the Spirit of God within you, you won't be dominated by the pressure your flesh tries to put on you.

As you listen to the written Word and the Holy Spirit telling you what to do, you'll be constantly making little adjustments in your life according to what He says. And those little adjustments will keep darkness from overtaking you.

You see, God knows just what you need. He can look ahead in your life and see the traps and pressures the devil is laying for you. So follow the Holy Spirit's leading and He will maneuver you safely around them to victory.

SCRIPTURE READING: 1 Corinthians 10:1-14

Let God Rub Off on You

"For those whom He foreknew — of whom He was aware
and loved beforehand — He also destined from the beginning...
to be molded into the image of His Son [and share inwardly
His likeness]." **(Romans 8:29, AMP)**

As a believer, you're destined to be molded into the image of Jesus, to grow in spirit until you look just like Him. God's supernatural power began that process the moment you were born again. You were changed on the inside instantly. How successful you are in allowing this change to progress to the outer man is mostly up to you. We grow up spiritually just like we grow up physically.

What can you do to speed this "growing" process along?

Spend more time pursuing the things of the Spirit than you spend pursuing the things of the flesh. Become dedicated to the Word of God and to fellowship with Him. Be willing to pull aside from the busy things of life and get alone with Him, so He can guide you, teach you, and share His likeness with you.

Have you ever noticed that if you spend time around people who have strong personalities, you will automatically be affected by them? You'll find yourself doing the things they do. Their mannerisms will rub off on you. You can't help it. They just influence you, especially if they are people you respect and admire.

The same thing is true in your relationship with God. If you spend enough time with Him, He's going to rub off on you! His ways will become your ways.

So make yourself available to Him by praying in the Spirit and worshiping and loving Him. Hang around His Word and the people who love His Word and live it.

Before you know it, you'll begin to notice yourself changing. You'll find your character becoming more like His. You'll begin to think like He does and talk like He does and even act like He does. His image will begin to shine forth in you!

SCRIPTURE READING: 1 Corinthians 3:5-18

Defeat Your Giant

"Who is this uncircumcised Philistine, that he should defy the armies of the living God?" (1 Samuel 17:26)

You may be facing a giant today. He may be a giant of sickness or failure, of financial shortage or another kind of trouble. But don't let him scare you. You have a secret weapon. A weapon that once turned a shepherd boy into a bear-busting, lion-killing, giant-slaying champion. That weapon was a blood covenant with Almighty God.

Back in David's day, circumcision was the sign of that covenant. So, when he called Goliath uncircumcised, David was saying: *This guy may be a giant; he may be strong; but he has no covenant with God and that's why I can kill him.*

Just like David, you, too, have a covenant. But yours is better. You see, the covenant David had, offered a wealth of blessings to those who kept it, but it also included curses for those who broke it.

Yours doesn't. Yours is a New Covenant that Jesus bought with His own blood. It doesn't depend on your ability. It depends on Him and what He has already done. He has done it all! All you have to do is believe it and receive it.

Right now, read Deuteronomy 28:16-68. That's a list of the curses Christ has freed you from. You might even call it a list of the giants Jesus has already slain for you. It contains every diabolical thing the devil could ever use to destroy you.

Read them and rejoice. Those are the things God has healed you of and delivered you from!

Don't let any giant intimidate you. You have a blood covenant with Almighty God. There's no uncircumcised circumstance on the face of this earth that can take your victory away from you.

SCRIPTURE READING: Galatians 3:13-29

Called to Be Peculiar

"I pray not that thou shouldest take them out of the world,
but that thou shouldest keep them from the evil. They are not of
the world, even as I am not of the world." (John 17:15,16)

Being peculiar. That's not something most of us work to achieve, is it? But, you know, we should.

God has called us to be peculiar (1 Pet. 2:9). To stand out from the rest of the world as living proof of His power and His love.

He doesn't, for example, *want* us to share the ailments of the world. He doesn't want us to share their sickness and poverty and failure. He's never wanted that for His people.

He gave us a physical illustration of that during the time the nation of Israel was held captive in Egypt. Pharaoh had refused to set the Israelites free, so God had allowed a thick darkness to cover the whole land. The darkness was so dreadful throughout Egypt that no one moved for three days.

"But," says Exodus 10:23, "all the children of Israel had light in their dwellings."

What a thrilling example of how God wants us to live. We should be glorifying God by the miraculously victorious lives we lead. We should constantly have people telling us, "I've heard how God healed you," or "I've heard how God prospered you and saved your children!"

So don't hold back. Put the Word of God to work in your life and dare to receive the rich blessings that belong to those who believe. Start using the Word to draw boundaries around your life, to paint spiritual warning signs for the devil. Signs that say:

Off Limits! According to God's Word, I don't belong to you anymore. My family doesn't belong to you. My health doesn't belong to you. My money doesn't belong to you. My ministry doesn't belong to you. I belong to a different kingdom. Now, back off in Jesus' name!

Does that sound a little peculiar? Good. That's exactly what God's called you to be!

SCRIPTURE READING: Exodus 10:20-29

Let the Revelations Begin

"For this is good and acceptable
in the sight of God our Saviour; Who will have all men to be saved,
and to come unto the knowledge of the truth." **(1 Timothy 2:3,4)**

People go to great lengths trying to wring knowledge from God when all they need to do is go to the Bible. God's not holding Himself out from anybody. It's His will for every man and woman to walk in revelation of Him.

"Well now, Brother Copeland," some say, "God's not going to give all these sinners out here a revelation." Really? Why do you think He sends evangelists to preach to them? Why do you think He sent His Word? To reveal the truth!

So, if you want to know that truth, just open the Book and read it. All of it...not just the parts that are in red. Those aren't the only parts Jesus said. He said everything in Genesis. He said everything in Exodus. He said everything in Numbers. He said everything in Deuteronomy. He said everything in Leviticus. He said everything in Matthew, Mark, Luke, and John. He said everything in Romans. He said everything in the Book. He *is* the Word!

In fact, if you'll read the third chapter of Galatians, you'll discover that every promise made to Abraham was *for Jesus*! It was the promises that brought Him. It was the promises that enabled Him to heal and deliver people. He didn't minister by some special power nobody else could have. He based His ministry on the revelations He'd received through faith in the written Word of God.

When the devil came to tempt Him, He didn't fight him off with a special legion of angels who'd been assigned to protect Him because He was God's Son. He fought him off with the phrase, "It is written."

God has equipped you to do the same. He's given you His written Word, and He's given you His Holy Spirit to help you understand it. He's more than ready to give you the knowledge you need. You don't have to wring it out of Him—just open the Book and let the revelations begin.

SCRIPTURE READING: John 16:7-15

Be Consistent

"Jesus Christ the same yesterday, and to day, and for ever."

(Hebrews 13:8)

Years ago, God spoke a phrase to Gloria's heart that I've never forgotten. She'd been asking Him to teach her to walk in the Spirit, to operate more fully in the supernatural power of God.

"In consistency lies the power," He said.

That revelation was tough for me. In the natural I'm anything *but* consistent. My human nature tends to be up one day and down the next. But, praise God, I don't have to depend on my human nature to get me by. I have Jesus Christ living within me and He's the same yesterday, today, and forever!

Jesus isn't fickle. He doesn't change His mind from one day to another. He's constant, and if you'll press into Him, He can cause you to be that way too.

Most believers don't do that. That's why there are so many "faith failures"

around. They stand on the Word one day and fall off of it the next.

What we need to do is "continue." Jesus said if we'd *continue* in His Word, then we'd be His disciples. He said if we'd *continue*, we'd know the truth and that truth would make us free (John 8:31,32). There's a revelation of God that comes from consistency that the inconsistent person will never see.

Determine today to be consistent. Don't try to base today on yesterday's Bible study. Base today on *today's* Bible study. Start with the Word today, stay on the Word all day, and end the day with the Word. Then tomorrow get up and do it all again!

There's power in constant consistency. So don't be an "off again, on again" Christian. *Continue* in the Word every day.

SCRIPTURE READING: Colossians 1:14-23

Victorious Praise

"When he had consulted with the people,
he appointed singers to sing to the Lord and praise Him
in their holy [priestly] garments as they went out before the army,
saying, Give thanks to the Lord, for His mercy and loving-kindness
endure forever!" **(2 Chronicles 20:21, AMP)**

Praise precedes victory!

You can see a graphic example of that in 2 Chronicles 20. There, the Bible tells us that a *multitude* of forces were marching against Israel. The army of Israel was so outnumbered, they literally didn't know what to do. So they fasted and prayed until they received a word from God. "Be not afraid or dismayed at this great multitude; for the battle is not yours but God's."

Do you know what they did in response to that word? They put together a praise choir! That's right. They appointed singers and praisers and sent them out *in front of the army!* And when that choir began to sing, the Word tells us that "the Lord set ambushments against the men...who had come against Judah, and they were slaughtered."

When it was all over, not one Israelite had fallen—and not one of their enemies had escaped. What's more, when they came to take the spoil, they found so many cattle, goods, garments, and other precious things, it took them three whole days to haul it all home.

Now *that's* victory! And it all began with praise.

Are you looking for that kind of victory today? Then stand up and shout, "Glory!" After all, you're in the same situation those Israelites were in. You have an army marching against you, but Jesus has already defeated it. He won that battle for you on Resurrection Morning.

All that's left for you to do is trust Him and begin to praise. Sound out those praises today. Speak them, sing them, declare them in the face of your enemy. Once he hears them, he'll know he doesn't even stand a chance.

SCRIPTURE READING: 2 Chronicles 20:1-22

Expect to Hear His Voice

"The sheep that are My own hear and are listening to My voice, and I know them and they follow Me." **(John 10:27, AMP)**

So many believers are unsure of their ability to hear God or know His voice. They're always afraid that they won't be able to tell when the Spirit of God is talking to them.

What they don't realize is this: Hearing the voice of the Spirit is a privilege that the Bible says belongs to every believer (Rom. 8:14). All we have to do to exercise that privilege is to receive it by faith and put ourselves in a position to hear.

Next time the devil tries to tell you that you can't hear God's voice, remember that.

Jesus said His sheep will know His voice and a stranger's voice they will not follow. That is a promise of God to you today. You see, the Spirit of God will never guide you in opposition to the written Word of God (John 16:13).

So, if you're not familiar with what the Word says, you'll find it more difficult to discern His leading.

Get familiar with God's voice by meditating and studying the Word of God. Follow God's instruction to Joshua and meditate on it day and night. Act on what you find in the Word, not just when it's easy but every time. Be obedient even in the slightest things.

That continual obedience to the written Word will bring you into maturity and tune your inward ear to the voice of the Spirit. You'll soon be able to recognize it as easily as you recognize the voice of your dearest friend.

So, instead of wondering about it, start expecting to hear from Him.

Then start sharpening your spiritual ears by spending time in the Word.

SCRIPTURE READING: John 10:1-9

Meet the Living Word

"For the word of God is quick, and powerful,
and sharper than any twoedged sword, piercing even to the dividing
asunder of soul and spirit, and of the joints and marrow, and is a discerner
of the thoughts and intents of the heart." **(Hebrews 4:12)**

The living Word of Almighty God is the only power strong enough to discipline your flesh. It's the only power that can cause you to think, look, talk, and act like a born-again man.

When I became a Christian, I was dominated by a horrible smoking habit. I tried to quit every way I could think of but nothing worked. After months of struggling and failing, I decided to attend some meetings in Hilton Sutton's church in Houston, Texas. Before I went into those meetings, I tucked my cigarettes above the sun visor in my car and left them there.

Up to that time, I hadn't learned much of anything about the Word and had never been exposed to the power of God. So when I began to hear those preachers there preach under the anointing of the Holy Spirit, it captivated my mind. I was caught up in the living Word. My desires changed. All I wanted was more of God. For the first time in my life, the Scriptures came alive.

When those meetings ended and I started driving back home, I found those old, stale cigarettes tucked up in my sun visor and realized I hadn't even missed them.

What happened? The Word separated me from the desire to smoke. The Word empowered me to discipline this flesh of mine. When I saw Jesus in the Word and under the anointing of Almighty God, I was totally set free, not only of the habit but of the desire!

Get caught up in the living Word today and discover the power that can set you forever free.

SCRIPTURE READING: Psalm 119:1-9

The Habit of Holiness

"He that hath my commandments, and keepeth them,
he it is that loveth me: and he that loveth me shall be loved of my
Father, and I will love him, and will manifest myself to him."

(John 14:21)

There's a dimension of living you can only experience when you make a decision to please the Father in every activity of your life. In that dimension, Jesus becomes real to you and manifests Himself to you.

Just after the turn of the century, God poured out His Spirit and started a revival on Azusa Street. It was an awesome time, a time when people's entire lives were turned inside out. Everything else in their world seemed to lose importance. Supernatural things were happening. God was manifesting Himself in their presence.

The people involved in that revival soon began to be known to the world as "holiness" people. They got that title because they were so obviously different from everyone else. They'd let go of anything they thought didn't please God. They were so caught up in the power of the spiritual realm, they lost interest in natural things.

Few believers today even know what "holiness" means. Even fewer understand the outpouring of God that comes to those who dare to step into it.

Holiness simply means separated to God. It's what you do with your life day by day. It's ordering your conduct according to the Word of God and the promptings of the Spirit. Holiness is the habit of being one mind with God, of turning away from the ways of the world and...living instead in agreement with Him. Holiness doesn't happen to anyone by accident. It requires a decision of the will. Make that decision today.

Love God with all your heart by keeping His commandments. He'll show His love to you by manifesting Himself to you in powerful new ways. He'll pour Himself out on you just like He did on those believers at Azusa Street—and revival will truly begin in you.

SCRIPTURE READING: 1 Thessalonians 4:1-8

Watch Your Language

"In a multitude of words transgression is not lacking,
but he who restrains his lips is prudent." **(Proverbs 10:19, AMP)**

We believers need to start watching our language! We need to quit throwing words around like they weren't important and start using them like our lives depended on it—because, according to the Word of God, they do! (Prov. 18:21).

Too many of us have what Proverbs 19:1 calls a *perverted mouth*. Having a perverted mouth means more than lying and using profanity. It means having a disobedient mouth. It means saying things that are out of line with the Word of God.

All of us have done that at one time or another. We'll say, for instance, that we're believing God for our healing and then we'll turn right around to someone and make a statement like, "This pain is about to *kill* me!"

That's perverted! It's backwards from what God's Word says.

"Oh well, Brother Copeland, I know I said that, but it's not really what I meant."

Listen, the world of the spirit doesn't operate on what you mean. It operates on what you say. Mark 11:23 tells us that "whosoever shall say unto this mountain, Be thou removed, and be thou cast into the sea; and shall not doubt in his heart, but shall believe that those things which he saith shall come to pass; he shall have whatsoever he saith."

Take note. That verse didn't say you shall have whatsoever you *mean*. It says you'll have what you say. It's what you say that counts.

Now, I'm not suggesting you should be tied up in knots all the time worrying about what your next phrase might be. Just use the wisdom God has given you. Train your mouth to be obedient to His Word. Then, when you need it most, you'll find that Word dwelling richly in you.

SCRIPTURE READING: Proverbs 10:11-21

A Covenant of Love

"For God so loved the world,
that he gave his only begotten Son." **(John 3:16)**

For God so loved the world that He gave...and He gave...and He gave.

That is the message the Bible brings us from beginning to end. It sounds simple enough. Yet few of us really comprehend it.

We can understand the idea of a God of power. We can understand a God who desires to be served. But an Almighty God who loves us so much that He desires, above all, to give to us? That's hard to believe.

For thousands of years, God has been working to drop the revelation of His love into the hearts of men. He's made loving promises of blessing and protection. But He's always faced that same obstacle—human beings who just couldn't bring themselves to believe those promises were true.

The story of Abram is a perfect example. He wasn't accustomed to the idea of a God who gives. After all, he'd grown up as a worshiper of the moon, and the moon had certainly never seemed interested in doing anything for him. Then he encountered El Shaddai, the greatest Being of all. The one Almighty God. And the first thing this El Shaddai wanted to do was *give* to him.

God's promises so astounded Abram that he couldn't believe them. "Lord," he asked, "how can I know I'm really going to receive these things?" (Gen. 15:8).

Do you know how God answered him? By cutting a blood-covenant with him. That covenant settled forever any question Abram could ever have about God's love and loyalty. Once blood had been shed, he knew God meant what He said.

God did the same thing for you. He cut a blood covenant with you. And He sacrificed His own Son to do it. Jesus' broken body and shed blood have become the eternal proof of God's love for you. Through Communion, He's urged you to remember them again and again so that when your faith in His promises begins to waver, you "might have a strong consolation" (Heb. 6:18).

Get a revelation of God's love for you by meditating on the covenant He's made with you. Get out the bread and the cup. Go before the Lord with them and take Communion thinking about the body and blood of Jesus that enables you to be a blood covenant member of the family of Almighty God. Let them settle forever the question of God's love for you. You'll never again have to doubt His promises once you believe in His love.

SCRIPTURE READING: Genesis 15

As Your Soul Prospers

"Beloved, I wish above all things that thou mayest prosper and be in health, even as thy soul prospereth." **(3 John 1:2)**

Once you begin to believe it's God's will to prosper you, you can't help but wonder how He's going to do it. Is He going to put a check in the mail? Or start floating twenty dollar bills down from the trees?

No. He's going to do it by prospering your soul. He's going to plant the seeds of prosperity in your mind, will, and emotions, and as they grow, they'll produce a great financial harvest.

Go to the Book of Genesis and read the story of Joseph. It's a perfect demonstration of what I'm talking about.

When Joseph was sold as a slave to the Egyptians, he didn't have a dime to his name. He didn't even have his freedom. He'd been sold as a slave. But, right in the middle of his slavery, God gave Joseph such wisdom and ability that he made his owner prosper. As a result, the man put Joseph in charge of all his possessions.

Later, Joseph was put in prison. There's *really* not much opportunity for advancement in prison, is there?

But God gave him insight that no other man in Egypt had. That insight landed him a position on Pharaoh's staff. Not as a slave but as the most honored man in the entire country next to Pharaoh himself.

He rode along in a chariot and people literally bowed down before him. During a worldwide famine, Joseph was in charge of *all* the food. Now that's prosperity!

How did God accomplish all that? By prospering Joseph's soul. No matter how dismal his situation became, no matter how impossible his problems, God was able to reveal the spiritual secrets that would open the door of success for him.

That's what makes God's method of prospering so exciting. It works anywhere and everywhere. It will work in the poorest countries on the face of this earth just like it works here in the United States. And you can be sure that it will work for you!

SCRIPTURE READING: Genesis 39

Living by Faith – It's a Life-Style

"Endure hardness, as a good soldier of Jesus Christ."

(2 Timothy 2:3)

Times of hardness are inevitable. You need to know that. It's true that we've been redeemed from the curse, and there's nothing Satan can do to reverse that, but he *is* going to challenge you on it.

So don't be surprised when things get tough. Times will come when you have to stand strictly by faith, when you'll have to speak and act as though what God says is true even when you can't feel it or see it happening around you. There will be times when everything looks terrible. That's when you must endure hardness as a good soldier.

So many people hear the word of faith about healing or prosperity and they think, "Hey! I'm going to try that." Then when the hard times come, they give up and cave in.

Let me warn you, living by faith is not something you try. It's a life-style. You do it when it's hard. You do it when it's easy. You do it all the time because you're not doing it just to get in on the benefits. You're doing it because you know that faith pleases God (Heb. 11:6).

Things may get a little rough at times, but let me assure you, you'll always come out on top if you endure hardness as a good soldier. If you refuse to faint and fall away, you *will* have the victory. The only defeated Christian is the one who quits!

SCRIPTURE READING: Numbers 14:1-24

Activate the Power

"Now unto him that is able to do exceeding abundantly above all that we ask or think, according to the power that worketh in us." **(Ephesians 3:20)**

As a believer, you have the power of the Holy Spirit inside you. But that power won't go to work until you put it to work!

The Holy Spirit won't just muscle in on you. He won't come in and turn down the television set and jerk you up off the couch and say, "Now you listen to me."

No, He's a gentleman. He's sent to help you to do the will of God, to strengthen you, to counsel you...but He won't do a thing until He's asked.

That's why the Book of James says if you're in trouble or afflicted, pray. It's prayer that puts the power within you to work.

Just think about that. The Spirit of Almighty God. The Spirit that hovered over the face of the deep and carried out God's Word at creation, that same Spirit is inside you—waiting for you to call on Him!

I'll tell you, if Jesus came into your house and sat down at your table, you'd put aside everything to talk to Him, wouldn't you? You wouldn't just rush through and say, "Jesus, I'm so glad to see you. I wish I had the energy to talk to You, but You wouldn't believe what kind of a day I had today. I mean, everything in the world went wrong

and now I'm just too tired to do anything but lay here and watch TV. Maybe we can spend some time together later."

You wouldn't do that, would you? No! If Jesus were sitting there in your room where you could see Him, you'd fall on your face and begin to worship Him. You wouldn't care how tired you were or what kind of day you had. You'd jump at the opportunity to fellowship with Him.

Well, listen, the Holy Ghost is in you. He's waiting on you. He's ready any time of the day or night. He's saying, "I'm here to help you and strengthen you. I want to comfort you today. You know that problem you've been having? I want to help you get that out of your life."

The Holy Spirit has some things He wants to show you—things you've been beating your head against the wall trying to figure out. He's waiting there with the power to overcome every obstacle in your life. Take time to pray. Pray in the Spirit. Pray with understanding. Pray and activate the power that worketh within you today.

SCRIPTURE READING: Ephesians 3:16-21

The Heart of the Matter

"For the Lord seeth not as man seeth; for man looketh
on the outward appearance, but the Lord looketh on the heart."

(1 Samuel 16:7)

Too often we ask God to fix the problems *around* us when what He really wants to do is solve the problem *within* us. I did that myself for years where my weight was concerned. I prayed and prayed for God to help me lose weight. Yet I experienced repeated failure. I lost literally hundreds of pounds, only to gain them right back again.

Finally one day, I made a firm decision. I told God, "I am not going one step further until I find out what to do about this!" Then I went on a fast, shut myself away from everyone, and determined to hear from God.

During that fast the Lord revealed the real source of my problem. He showed me that I wanted to lose weight, but I didn't want to permanently change my eating habits. I was like an alcoholic who wants to be able to drink constantly and not be affected by it. I wanted to eat nine times a day and still weigh 166 pounds!

Suddenly I realized God wasn't content simply to rid me of the extra pounds on the outside of me, He wanted to rid me of the sin of gluttony on the inside of me. So I repented of that sin right then and there. (It was then that I realized just how hard it is for a man who drinks to face the fact that he's an alcoholic. It hurts to admit something like that.) Then instead of asking God for deliverance from my weight problem, I asked Him for deliverance from my food problem.

Sure enough, He did it.

If your prayers don't seem to be changing the problems around you, maybe it's time to take a look inside. Maybe it's time to ask God to go to work on the heart of the matter.

SCRIPTURE READING: Psalm 139:1-10,23,24

Train Your Senses

"For every one that useth milk is unskilful in the word of righteousness:
for he is a babe. But strong meat belongeth to them that are of full age, even
those who by reason of use have their senses exercised
to discern both good and evil." **(Hebrews 5:13,14)**

You're spiritually "grown-up" or mature when, through *practice*, you have trained your senses to discern between good and evil. You've practiced walking in the Spirit and renewing your mind by the Word of God until even your flesh habitually goes God's way instead of the world's way.

Stop and think for a moment. Aren't there some things your old flesh used to pressure you to do before you made Jesus Lord of your life that you don't even want to do anymore?

There are for me. For example, I used to smoke tobacco, and I felt sorry for all those Christians who couldn't. But you know what? Now that I'm a believer, I have no desire for tobacco anymore. It is not even part of my thoughts much less my life-style.

That's the kind of thing that happens as you feed and renew your mind on the Word of God. It doesn't necessarily happen quickly or easily. Your flesh may fight and buck for a while because it's been trained to go the way of the world so long. But if you stick with the Word and keep growing, your flesh can develop habits of righteousness just like it developed the habit of unrighteousness.

Don't starve your spirit by trying to get by on just a little spiritual milk now and then. Develop the habit of feeding on the solid food Word every day and find out what real maturity is all about.

SCRIPTURE READING: Hebrews 5:11-14, 6:1-3

Start Planting

"Being born again, not of corruptible seed, but of incorruptible,
by the word of God, which liveth and abideth for ever." **(1 Peter 1:23)**

You won't really get excited about the Word of God until you realize that it's more than just a collection of divinely-inspired promises. It's a living force that literally carries within it the power to make those promises become a reality in your life.

Is it tough for you to believe such a thing is possible?

It shouldn't be. You see it happen in the natural world all the time.

If I were to put a tomato seed into your hand and tell you that within that tiny, dry seed lies the power to produce a stalk thousands of times bigger than the seed, to produce leaves and roots and round, red tomatoes, you wouldn't have any trouble believing that, would you? You know from experience that even though that scrawny seed doesn't look like a tomato factory, somehow, given the right environment, it will become one.

Jesus says the Word of God works by that same principle. There's miraculous power within it. It is a seed that, once planted by faith in a human heart, will produce more blessings than you can imagine.

Once you grasp that, you'll get extremely excited about the Word of God. That's what happened to me.

Over 20 years ago, I caught a glimpse of what that Word could do. I caught a glimpse of the power within it. Before long, I had a Bible in every room of my house, a Bible in my car, and a tape player going nearly all the time.

I spent every possible moment in the Word of God because I wanted the power of that Word inside me more than I wanted anything else in the world. I knew it would blow the limits off my life, limits that had held me back and kept me down for years. I knew that when I read it, I wasn't just reading, I was planting seeds. Seeds of prosperity, seeds of health, seeds of protection, and seeds of victory for every area of my life.

Don't treat the Word of God like a book. It's not! It's spiritual seed that has the supernatural power within it to produce the harvest of a lifetime. Get excited about it and start planting today!

SCRIPTURE READING: Mark 4:23-32

Nothing to Be Afraid Of

"He hath said, I will never leave thee, nor forsake thee.
So that we may boldly say, The Lord is my helper, and I will not fear
what man shall do unto me." **(Hebrews 13:5,6)**

Self-consciousness is a major problem in the Body of Christ today. It keeps us from doing the things God tells us to do. Instead of simply obeying Him, it makes us start to wonder, "Now what will people think of me if I do that? What if I command that person to get out of the wheelchair and he doesn't get up? What if I start believing for prosperity and go broke? What about that, God? I won't look too good, will I?"

If you've ever been through that, let me tell you something: It doesn't *matter* how you look! It's that you obey God that counts. When it comes to obeying God, your own reputation doesn't count; and the sooner you forget it, the better off you'll be.

But you know what's ironic? Once you do that, your reputation gets better.

It's a funny thing. When you lose that desire to protect your image, your image will improve. Why? Because then when people look at you, instead of seeing that puny little image you have of yourself, they'll see the image of the Lord Jesus coming through.

So put aside that old self-consciousness and develop God-consciousness instead. Stop being dominated by the fear of man and start being motivated by faith in what Jesus can do.

After all, He has promised He will never leave you or forsake you. Grab hold of that. Believe it. Act on it. Once you do, you'll realize there's really nothing to be afraid of anymore!

SCRIPTURE READING: Romans 8:29-39

Stand Against the Devil's Strategies!

"Leave no room or foothold for the devil — give no opportunity to him."
(Ephesians 4:27, AMP)

If you give the devil place, he will take it. You have to stay alert and keep your shield of faith high because if you don't, he'll turn around and steal back from you the ground you just took.

There have been people who have received their healing and have fallen back into their old thinking patterns of sickness. They let their faith down and gave the devil an opening. When he came along with an old symptom, they weren't ready for him. They fell victim to his counterattack.

You can stand successfully against the devil's strategies! But before you do, you're going to have to make three quality decisions.

First, you must make the Word of God the final authority in your life. Line up your thinking with whatever the Word says.

Next, you must decide to live your life by faith in what God has said.

The Bible says, "Faith comes by hearing, and hearing by the Word of God."

Finally, you must decide to live by the love of God because faith works by love. Without love, your faith won't function. Without the Word, you can't have faith. So don't try to make one of these decisions without the other two. You need to make all three of them. This life-style of the Word, faith, and love keeps you in a place of resistance to the devil!

I suggest you get alone with God and pray:

In the name of Jesus, I commit myself from this day forward to live by the Word of God, to live by my faith, and to live by the love of God.

Decide today to give the devil no place!

SCRIPTURE READING: John 15:7-12

Be Clothed With Humility

"And be clothed with humility: for God
resisteth the proud, and giveth grace to the humble." **(1 Peter 5:5)**

Most believers don't know anything about true humility. If you tell them they're the righteousness of God, they'll fight to keep from believing it. You can give them scripture references to prove it, and they'll still argue.

"Oh no," they'll say, "I'm not righteous. I'm just an old sinner saved by grace." They're making a sincere attempt to be humble. But they're sincerely wrong. They're so afraid of being exalted by pride that they've let Satan trick them into falling right into it.

Let me show you what I mean. According to 1 Peter 5:5,6, to be truly humble is to submit to God. That means when God says something, you believe it no matter how foreign to your "religious" thinking it may be. When He says you've been made the righteousness of God in Christ Jesus, you say that too. In fact, you wouldn't dare say anything else because to do so would be to dare to disagree with God. And, when you get right down to it, that's the ultimate form of pride, isn't it?

Don't let Satan keep you groveling in the dust of false humility. Agree with God. Find out what His Word says about you, then be bold enough to say it yourself. Banish pride by submitting to His truth. Clothe yourself in true humility. It's sure to look good on you.

SCRIPTURE READING: 1 Peter 5:5-11

Are Angels Just for Kids?

"Are they not all ministering spirits, sent forth to minister for them who shall be heirs of salvation?" **(Hebrews 1:14)**

Most of us heard about our guardian angel when we were just children; and, in those days, it was a comforting thought. With monsters lurking behind the closet door and creepy things crawling beneath the bed, it was good to know that someone was there to protect us when the light was out.

But, as the years passed, we outgrew our childhood fears. The imaginary creatures that had once seemed so real disappeared from our minds—and sadly enough, for most of us, the angels did too.

But angels are not just kid stuff. They're powerful spirits sent forth to minister for us who are heirs of salvation.

The word "salvation" in Hebrews 1:14 is from the Greek word "soteria" meaning "deliverance, preservation of material, and temporal deliverance." Just think about that! God has created vast numbers of gloriously powerful spiritual beings for the express purpose of protecting us and delivering us from the evils of this world.

And remember, according to Psalm 103:20, the Word of God is what puts those angels in action. So when you're in trouble, don't cower and cry about how awful things are. Speak the Word! Give your angels something to respond to. Then be patient and let them have time to work. They'll get their job done.

SCRIPTURE READING: Psalm 103:17-22

Healing Always Comes

"And these signs shall follow them that believe...
they shall lay hands on the sick, and they shall recover." **(Mark 16:17,18)**

I used to get upset over people I'd lay hands on who wouldn't get well. I was praying one day and seeking God about it when He spoke to my spirit and said, "Healing always comes."

I remember I said, "What do You mean, *Healing always comes?* Not everybody gets healed."

"I didn't say they all received it," He answered. Then He spoke very sternly to me. "I do My part. And I said they would recover!"

Those words hit me like a ton of bricks. *He* said they would recover. He never lies. So if He said they would recover, then that means healing always comes. It's not God who's holding back. It's the receivers who aren't receiving.

Since then, I've never had any trouble laying hands on people and believing for them to be healed. Whether they walk away well or not, I just keep standing in faith for them. In fact, I know that if that fellow who went away still sick ever lines his faith up with God and me—I don't care if it's five years from now—he'll be healed.

If you've laid hands on someone who didn't receive their healing, don't cut off the flow of God's power by withdrawing your faith. Stand fast. Keep believing that "healing always comes" and somewhere down the line that poor sick fellow may just decide to stand up and agree with you!

SCRIPTURE READING: Mark 10:46-52

Coming Together

"Till we all come in the unity of the faith, and of the
knowledge of the Son of God, unto a perfect man, unto the
measure of the stature of the fulness of Christ."

(Ephesians 4:13)

If you know how to listen to the voice of God, you can hear Him calling throughout the Body of Christ today. He is calling for unity. He's calling us to lay down our disagreements and come together in preparation for Jesus' return.

Just the thought of that scares some believers. "How can I unify with someone from another denomination?" they say. "I'm not going to give up my doctrines and agree with theirs just for unity's sake!"

What they don't realize is this: Scriptural unity isn't based on doctrine.

Winds of doctrine, according to Ephesians 4:14, are childish. Winds of doctrine don't unify. They divide and blow people in every direction. The Word doesn't say anything about us coming into the unity of our doctrines. It says we'll come into the unity of the *faith*.

In the past, we've failed to understand that and tried to demand doctrinal unity from each other anyway.

"If you don't agree with me on the issue of tongues," we've said, "or on the timing of the rapture...or on the proper depth for baptismal waters, I won't accept you as a brother in the Lord. I'll break fellowship with you."

But that's not God's way of doing things. He doesn't have a long list of doctrinal demands for us to meet. His requirements are simple. First John 3:23 tells us what they are: *to believe on the name of His Son, Jesus Christ, and love one another.*

Once you and I come to a place where we keep those requirements and quit worrying about the rest, we'll be able to forget our denominational squabbles and come together in the unity of faith. We'll grow so strong together that the winds of doctrine won't be able to drive us apart.

When that happens, the devil's going to panic because the unity of the faith of God's people is a staggering thing. It's the most unlimited, powerful thing on earth.

Right now all over the world, the Spirit is calling the Church of the living God to unite. Hear Him and obey, and you can be a part of one of the most magnificent moves of God this world has ever seen.

SCRIPTURE READING: Psalms 132:13-18; 133

Obey Today

"He who being often reproved hardens his neck, shall suddenly be destroyed, and that without remedy." **(Proverbs 29:1, AMP)**

Some people have the mistaken idea that when the direction of the Holy Spirit comes to them, they can just ignore it for a while if they want to and then obey Him later in their own good time. They think to themselves, "I know what I'm doing is wrong. I know my life-style isn't right, but I'm just going to do it a while longer. Then I'll get things straightened out with the Lord."

Let me warn you, that is an extremely dangerous thing to do. Because God says that when you refuse His guidance, your heart grows hard. It's not that God's grace doesn't extend to you anymore. It's not that He wouldn't forgive you if you turned to Him. It's just that sin will callous your heart to the point where you can't hear Him calling.

That's what happened to the children of Israel. God would tell them what to do and they wouldn't do it. When He was trying to bring them into the Promised Land and He told them to go in and possess it, they flatly refused.

Of course, they thought they had good reasons for refusing. They were so full of fear and unbelief that they actually thought if they did what God said, they'd be destroyed. But, you know, it doesn't matter how good your reasons are for disobeying God. That disobedience will still cost you. It will still harden your heart.

The children of Israel ignored God's leading so often that He finally just sent them into the wilderness. They were so stiff-necked, He couldn't lead them into the blessings He'd planned for them, and He had to just let them wander around until all but two of them had died off. He had to raise up a whole new generation of softer-hearted people before He could take them into the land.

Take a lesson from that and don't play around with sin. When God tells you what you need to do, don't put Him off thinking it will be easier to do it later. It won't be. It will be harder!

When the Spirit of God comes to correct you, follow His instructions—and follow them quickly. Keep your heart tender. Obey the Lord!

SCRIPTURE READING: Nehemiah 9:6-37

Come Alive Today

"Therefore if any man be in Christ,
he is a new creature: old things are passed away; behold,
all things are become new." **(2 Corinthians 5:17)**

Resurrection. What do you think of when you hear that word? Most people think of the past. Of a stone rolled away. An empty tomb. And a risen Lord.

Praise God, Jesus is alive today, isn't He?

What we don't fully understand is this: He's not the only One who's been resurrected. We've been resurrected too!

We were spiritually resurrected the day we made the Lord Jesus Christ the Lord of our lives. That day we passed from death to life. The greater part of your resurrection has *already* happened!

Think about it. When you made Jesus Christ the Lord of your life, the Spirit of God hovered over you. The glory of the Lord came into your being. And that glory consumed the old, sinful man that you were. That old man died. And in his place a new creature was born.

Oh yes, there *will* be a day when the earthly body you live in will be raised and glorified—but you don't have to wait until then to be free from sin and from the sickness and poverty and failure that goes with this natural world. You're free from all that right now!

You may be sitting there thinking, "Well, if I'm so free, why can't I quit smoking? Why can't I lose this weight? Why am I always sick?"

Because you've let Satan convince you that you're still under his power. You've let him talk you into living as if you're still spiritually dead!

So, today I want you to begin considering yourself alive! Begin thinking of yourself as one who already has the life of God instead of an earthly being who's waiting for the Resurrection. Consider yourself dead to sin and alive to the power of Jesus. You'll find yourself living a whole new life *today*!

SCRIPTURE READING: Romans 8:1-14

Ambassador for Christ

"Now then we are ambassadors for Christ...." **(2 Corinthians 5:20)**

You are an ambassador for Christ! If you have made Jesus Christ the Lord of your life, you have been sent to act as a representative for Him in this world. Just as nations send ambassadors to represent their interests in other countries, you've been sent here to look after the interests of the kingdom of God.

Think about that. Everywhere you go you are representing the King of Kings and the Lord of Lords. That's a very high honor. It may also seem like a rather tall bill to fill. But God has equipped you to do it. He's given you His name and the power of His Word. He's even put His very own Spirit inside you. And He's given you the ability to hear and obey the directions of that Spirit.

I heard a prophecy years ago that said there would come a time when men on the earth would walk and talk and act like God. They'd be motivated by His power and His Spirit so strongly that people would say of them, "Look at those believers. They think they're God." "No," the Holy Spirit said, "they are not God. They are agents of God, children of God, ambassadors of God, sent to do the works of God."

I believe we're living in the day and hour that prophecy was talking about. We're seeing that army of light begin to grow.

This is no time to be half-consecrated and half-dedicated. This is the time to go all the way with God, to give Him your whole life. If you'll do that, He'll give you back such anointing and such power and such glory and goodness that you'll shine for Him, as Philippians 2:15 says, as lights in the midst of a crooked and perverse generation.

Begin to think about yourself today, not as just another ordinary man or woman but as an ambassador of Almighty God. Let the interests of His kingdom be foremost in your mind and heart. Submit yourself to Him and say, "Lord, show me how to be Your representative in everything I do."

You *are* an ambassador for Christ. Begin to live like it today.

SCRIPTURE READING: 2 Corinthians 5:10-21

From Believing to Perceiving

"Nay, in all these things we are more than conquerors
through him that loved us." **(Romans 8:37)**

The Bible calls us kings and priests (Rev. 1:6) and world overcomers (1 John 5:4). But for most of us, those are just phrases. They haven't become real to us. That's why the devil's been able to hoodwink us into living lives of defeat. It hasn't actually dawned on us who we really are.

If you'll look in 1 Chronicles, chapter 14, you'll see that David had a similar problem. He'd been anointed king by the prophet Samuel when he was just a teenager. He'd known for years that someday he'd rule over Israel. Yet somehow, it hadn't really sunk in.

But look what happens in verse 2. "And David perceived that the Lord had confirmed him king over Israel, for his kingdom was lifted up on high, because of his people Israel." Finally, it dawned on him! David perceived that the Lord had confirmed him king. I can just imagine David saying to himself, "I'm king. I'm actually king! I AM KING!" At that moment, being king ceased to be something David had only thought about. It became something he really was. He could see himself king.

What does that have to do with you and me? Just this. Much like David, you and I have been given a royal office. We're just having a hard time believing it. But until we do, we cannot exercise the power or authority that goes with that office.

Say, for example, you're sick. You can yell, "By His stripes I'm healed," 50 times a day. You can hope for healing. You can try to believe for healing till your hair turns gray. But if you don't really perceive yourself as whole and healthy in Christ Jesus, if you don't see yourself as "the healed" instead of "the sick," you won't get any supernatural help. Yet once that realization hits you that you are, in fact, "the healed," no one—not even the devil himself—will be able to keep you from getting well.

Don't let the devil hoodwink you any longer. Step over the line from trying to believe to actually perceiving by dwelling on the Word of God. Read it and think about it. Practice seeing yourself through the eyes of the Word until the reality of your royalty in Christ finally dawns on you!

SCRIPTURE READING: Ephesians 1:3-23

Turn Your Losses Around

"But God's free gift is not at all to be compared
to the trespass...For if many died through one man's falling away—
his lapse, his offense—much more profusely did God's grace and the free
gift [that comes] through...Jesus Christ, abound and overflow to
and for [the benefit of] many." **(Romans 5:15, AMP)**

If you're ever on a losing streak and need someone to tell you how to turn things around, go to God. He's an expert on the subject. He's suffered more losses than anyone who's ever lived.

Just think about it. He lost Lucifer, His top-ranked, most anointed angel. And when Lucifer fell, He lost at least a third of His other angels as well. Then He lost the man and the woman He had created; and because He'd given them dominion over the earth, when He lost them, He lost it too. Any way you figure it, that's a lot of real estate down the drain!

Yet, in spite of all that, God is no loser. He's the greatest winner of all time. Do you know why? Because He knows how to turn the losses around. He knows how to use the law of giving and receiving to transform losses into gains.

"Give, and it shall be given unto you; good measure, pressed down, and shaken together, and running over" (Luke 6:38). That's the powerful principle that breaks losing streaks.

Isn't that staggering? He had every option that exists to choose from to redeem the things He'd lost. He had all wisdom and all power available to Him. Out of all that, the law of giving is what He chose to use.

He gave the most irreplaceable thing He had: His only Son. Then He backed that gift with His own faith. And when the law of giving and receiving had done its work, the Almighty Father God received not only His first begotten Son, but millions of other sons as well.

Don't despair over your losses. Redeem them the same way God redeemed His. Give and put the most powerful principle in the universe to work for you.

SCRIPTURE READING: John 3:12-21

That Your Prayers May Not Be Hindered

"But if we [really] are living and walking in the Light
as He [Himself] is in the Light, we have [true, unbroken] fellowship
with one another." **(1 John 1:7, AMP)**

One area of our lives we believers have particularly neglected is the area of our relationships. We simply haven't heeded the Word of God where they're concerned. We've fussed with one another and criticized one another so much that we've hindered the forces that God has given us to make us successful in this world. That's right! Strife causes trouble in the spirit realm.

It opens the door to the devil. It keeps our prayers from being answered. It even keeps our angels from moving on our behalf!

Peter wrote to husbands in 1 Peter 3:7 to live considerately with their wives. He said, "...bestowing honor on the woman as the weaker sex, since you are joint-heirs of the grace of life, in order that your prayers may not be hindered." Husbands and wives. Parents and children. Co-workers. Fellow church members. All of us need to wake up to the danger of strife and start walking in love.

Shed the light of God's Word on your relationships. Dig into and get a revelation of the fact that we are all part of each other. Recognize that, as Ephesians tells us, we are one Body and one Spirit, and be eager and strive earnestly to guard and keep the harmony and oneness of that Spirit (Eph. 4:3,4).

Let the power of God flow in all of your relationships. Learn to walk in the light!

SCRIPTURE READING: Romans 15:1-7

Dig Into Your Covenant

"This cup is the new covenant [ratified and established] in My blood."

(1 Corinthians 11:25, AMP)

New Covenant. It's a familiar phrase to most of us. But do we really know what it means?

No, we don't. Because if we did, every one of us would be faith giants. Instead of struggling, "trying" to believe the promises of God, we'd be like Abraham. "Strong in faith...fully persuaded that, what God has promised, he is able to perform!" (Rom. 4:20,21).

That's the kind of confidence that welled up in Abraham when God cut the covenant with him. It was an inferior covenant to ours, made with the blood of animals. Yet it transformed a doubting Abraham into the very father of faith. Why? Because, unlike those of us today, Abraham understood the significance of it.

He knew that entering into the Covenant of Blood meant you were totally and forever giving yourself away to someone else. Once you did it, nothing would ever be exclusively yours again. All that you were, all that you had or ever would have became the equal property of your covenant partner.

During the covenant ceremony in Abraham's day, the partners exchanged coats, each one giving their authority to the other. They exchanged weapons as a way of saying, "Your enemies are now my enemies. I'll fight your fights

as if they were my own." They walked through the blood of slain animals, pronouncing their loyalty to one another, even to the death.

When God made covenant with him, Abraham knew there was no longer any room for doubt. God had proven how intensely He desired to be God to him. He'd given him everything He had and bound Himself to Abraham in a relationship that could not be desolved. Abraham comprehended the gravity of a covenant agreement. It convinced him once and for all that God's promises could be trusted. It became an anchor to his soul.

Do you want to be a faith giant like Father Abraham? Then dig into the covenant you have with God. Study it out in the Word. Let the Holy Spirit show you what really happened when Jesus became the sacrifice that ratified your covenant with God. Let Him show you what it meant when He gave you His name (John 16:23), His authority (Matt. 28:18-20), His armor and weapons (Eph. 6:10-17).

Once you realize what Jesus actually meant when He said, "This is the New Covenant established in My blood," your life will never be the same again.

SCRIPTURE READING: Hebrews 10:1-23

From Sons to Servants

"And on my servants and on my handmaidens
I will pour out in those days of my Spirit; and they shall prophesy:
And I will shew wonders in heaven above, and signs in the earth
beneath; blood, and fire, and vapour of smoke." **(Acts 2:18,19)**

You and I are living in the most exciting days this earth has ever seen. All around us God is pouring out His Spirit in preparation for the end-time revival that will bring this whole age to a glorious close.

Some of God's children are just standing by as spectators, watching Him work. Others, however, have become a vital part of it all. They've volunteered for service in this great end-time army. They've become what the Bible calls *the servants and handmaidens of God*.

Who are those servants and handmaidens? They're those who have committed themselves totally to their Lord. They're those who instead of being content simply to be born-again *children* of God, have gone even further, stepping into *servanthood* out of love for the Father.

The servants and handmaidens of God are those who've said, "I want to be involved in what God is doing in this hour. I want to be His bond slave, available to do His bidding 24 hours a day."

Those who make that powerful decision are the ones who are experiencing the great outpouring of God's Spirit that Peter spoke of in Acts 2. They are the ones whose Spirit-inspired words of prophecy and prayer are releasing the power of God upon the earth. They are the ones whose words are opening the way for the signs and wonders.

Do you want to be among them? You can be. God *wants* you to be. In fact, He *needs* you to be!

He needs those who will cut every cord that binds them to this natural world. He needs people He can call on in the middle of the night for intercession. People who will get up and do it no matter how tired they may be.

That's the quality and depth of dedication servanthood requires. It's a demanding role but its rewards are rich. For those who are willing to fill that role will be God's mouthpiece here on the earth in these final days. They will be vehicles of His Spirit and of His mighty powers. They will be key players in the Holy Spirit's greatest earthly production.

Make a decision now to become one of them. Take the step of faith into servanthood today.

SCRIPTURE READING: Acts 2:1-21

Let Your Life Shout

"The fool hath said in his heart, There is no God. They are corrupt, they have done abominable works, there is none that doeth good." **(Psalm 14:1)**

Most of us would never dream this verse could apply to us. After all, we're *believers!* We'd never say that there is no God.

But maybe we should think again. It's true that with our mouths we would never say something like that... but don't we sometimes say it with our actions?

We say it by sinning just a little here and there and thinking it won't matter. We'll go to an immoral movie or have a gossip session about the pastor, ignoring God's command to the contrary.

With our actions we're saying, "There is no God."

Psalm 14:1 connects that kind of thing to corruption. Whether you realize it or not, the more you act that way, the more corrupt you're going to become.

Don't make the foolish mistake of publicly proclaiming Jesus as your Lord, and then privately denying Him with one little action at a time. Use wisdom in everything you do so that both your heart and your life shout loudly, "My God reigns!"

SCRIPTURE READING: Psalm 14:1-7, 15:1-5

What a Future!

"God hath raised us up together, and made us sit together
in heavenly places in Christ Jesus: That in the ages to come he
might shew the exceeding riches of his grace in his kindness
toward us through Christ Jesus." **(Ephesians 2:6,7)**

All my life people told me the reason God saved us was so that when we got to Glory, we could spend the rest of eternity loving Him and worshiping Him. But, you know, that's just not so.

It sounds pretty good, but it's just something somebody made up. God isn't selfish. He's just the opposite. He's the ultimate giver. The ultimate lover. He doesn't do anything just so He can get something in return.

Why then did He save us? The Word of God tells us He did it so that in the ages to come, He could show us the exceeding riches of His grace.

Think about that! God is going to spend eternity showing the riches of His grace to you and me.

That's why He sent Jesus into the world. He so loved the world that He gave His only begotten Son. God gave Jesus so that He *wouldn't be* His *only* son. He sent Jesus so He could have more sons to love and give to—and He plans to spend the eons of time doing just that.

As a believer, you have the most glorious future ahead of you that anyone could ever ask for. But you don't wait until you get to Glory to enjoy it. You can start right now. You've already been seated!

SCRIPTURE READING: Ephesians 2:1-8

Born Again!

"Jesus answered and said unto him, Verily, verily, I say unto thee,
Except a man be born again, he cannot see the kingdom of God." **(John 3:3)**

Born again. Do you know what Jesus had in mind when He said those two words to Nicodemus? He was talking covenant talk. He was telling Nicodemus what it meant to have a covenant with God.

Let me paint the picture I believe was in Jesus' mind. Imagine a baby, a little baby born of an unwed mother. No one knows who its daddy is and no one wants to know. He is a child that nobody wants. He doesn't belong to anyone.

Now, picture the best kind of family you can think of. A family that loves God. The man has a good job. They're blessed financially. They're givers and lovers of people, and they fall in love with this baby. Before long, they adopt it.

What's happened? That baby was reborn. He got a new set of parents. Through adoption, he has now become an heir. Why? Not because of anything the baby has done. Those parents didn't say, "I want you to look at that baby. I'm so impressed with all that that child has done for us. He has certainly earned our love and respect."

No, it's a baby. It couldn't have done anything to earn its new life. This man and this woman agreed together out of the love in their hearts and bestowed grace on that child. Now he has access to everything they have. When they offer him a bottle, he doesn't knock the bottle away and say, "I'm so humble and undeserving. Just give me water."

Of course not. That baby acts like part of the family—and not just part of the family but the best part of the family. Because in Jesus' day a covenant or adopted child had the same birthright as the firstborn son.

That's what Jesus was talking about when He said, "You must be born again." He was talking about grace. He was talking about a new relationship of favor. A new family. A new authority. A new power.

If you feel unworthy to receive the rich blessings God has for you today, think about that. Meditate on it, so instead of worrying about and struggling with the needs in your life, you can just walk boldly into the throne room of your Father and receive help to get those needs met.

Discover what it really means to be a blood-bought child of Almighty God with a big brother like Jesus. Discover what it means to be *born again*!

SCRIPTURE READING: John 3:1-8

Be Loyal

"...them that honour me I will honour, and they
that despise me shall be lightly esteemed." **(1 Samuel 2:30)**

God honors those who honor Him. He'll never forget the seeds of loyalty you sow. He'll multiply them and give them back to you in a harvest of blessing. And Malachi 3:17 says when He makes up His jewels, you'll be forever among them.

Forever. Think about that for a moment. By honoring God with your life and your lips, you're stepping into a realm of blessing that will literally take an eternity to explore.

Once you begin to get that kind of eternal perspective on things, you'll see that it's grossly immature to get mad at God when temporary things don't work out exactly how and when you want them to. You'll see that your loyalty must be first of all to God, that you must seek first His kingdom—even when things seem to be going wrong. The Bible says that if you'll do that, all these other things will be added unto you.

God never forgets. He'll never forget that in the heat of the battle, when others were giving up and saying, "Hey, this faith stuff doesn't work!" you were still honoring Him by standing firm and speaking His promises.

So determine in your heart today to be loyal toward God in every word you speak. Make up your mind once and for all that nothing in your life is as vital as honoring Him. Keep honoring Him and speaking words of faith.

It will work deliverance for you in this life, and in eternity you'll sure be glad you did.

SCRIPTURE READING: Psalm 61

We Need Each Other

"That they all may be one; as thou, Father,
art in me, and I in thee, that they also may be one in us: that the world
may believe that thou hast sent me." **(John 17:21)**

It's time we, as believers, began to enter into the oneness Jesus prayed for in John 17:21. It's time we held onto one another in good times as well as bad. It's time we realized that we need one another.

We do, you know. I need your faith as much as you need mine. Together, we can face anything and win in Jesus.

Let me show you why. In John 3:34, God says Jesus was given the Holy Spirit without measure. He was more powerful than *all* the demons of hell and *all* wicked spirits of *all* classes, including Satan himself. He was able to defeat their power combined.

Now consider this. We are His Body. Each of us has been given *the* measure of faith according to Romans 12:1-3. That measure is enough to take care of our own personal needs. However, there is more involved here than just our own personal lives.

We have a world to win! We are the end-time generation. *We need all the help we can get. But, thank God, we can get all the help we need!*

How? By joining together. Ephesians 4:13 says that when we all come together in the unity of the faith, we'll have "the measure of the stature of the fulness of Christ."

In other words, when the Body of Christ comes together and begins to function as one, we'll have the Holy Spirit without measure—just like Jesus did! We'll begin to see ministries functioning in the fullness of their callings. We'll begin to see manifestations of the Holy Spirit in full measure. We'll see Jesus in fullness as we've never seen Him before.

Then the world will know the Father sent Him.

Step into that oneness today. Start today making a daily effort to make yourself available to God to pray for others. Start your day by saying, "Holy Spirit, use me to pray for someone today. I offer You my measure of faith."

Once we truly join together in faith, all the demons of hell won't be able to overcome us. We'll march right over them in the fullness of the power of Jesus and bring the age to a glorious close!

SCRIPTURE READING: Ephesians 4:1-16

Sorrow Not!

"The redeemed of the Lord shall return,
and come with singing unto Zion; and everlasting joy
shall be upon their head: they shall obtain gladness and joy;
and sorrow and [grief] shall flee away." **(Isaiah 51:11)**

Did you know that as a believer you've been redeemed from the curse of grief and sorrow by the blood of Jesus Christ? You don't have to put up with them any more than you have to put up with sin or sickness or disease.

God started teaching me about this personally several months before my mother went home to be with Him in August 1988. Every time He'd show me something about it, I'd put it into practice. (You ought to do that with anything God is teaching you. Start practicing it now, and you can walk in it when the time comes!)

So, eight and a half months before my mother left, I began standing against grief and sorrow. I made a decision to "sorrow not." Immediately the devil began to attack my emotions.

But I'd say, "No. I won't receive that. I take authority over these feelings in Jesus' name. I've given my body as a sacrifice well-pleasing unto the Lord, and I won't partake of anything but His joy." Then I'd start speaking the Word and praising out loud.

I went through three rugged days of resisting until those sorry spirits were gone.

What I'm telling you is this: You're going to have to stand against grief and sorrow. It doesn't belong to you. It's not from your heavenly Father. You may have to walk the floor all night long. But instead of worrying and crying, walk the floor and quote the Word until that heavy spirit leaves and the joy of the Lord comes.

Remember who you are. You're the one who shall obtain gladness and joy. You're the one sorrow and grief shall flee away from. You *are* the redeemed!

SCRIPTURE READING: Psalm 97

Resurrection Life

"Now upon the first day of the week, very early
in the morning, they came unto the sepulchre, bringing the spices
which they had prepared, and certain others with them. And they found
the stone rolled away from the sepulchre. And they entered in,
and found not the body of the Lord Jesus." **(Luke 24:1-3)**

Truly, it's time for us to stop looking for the living among the dead. It's time for us to stop wandering around in the cemetery of sin, sickness, and failure and to step into resurrection life!

As a resurrected creature, you're no accident going somewhere to happen. Your life isn't just a loose web of events and circumstances. God has specific plans for you.

Maybe He intends for you to have the greatest healing ministry of this century. Or perhaps He wants to turn you into a tremendous preacher. Maybe He has a revelation prepared for you that will enable you to bless the whole world. But you'll never know what He has in store for you until you put your attention on Him.

That's why the devil works hard to keep you focusing on the problems of life. That's why he tries to keep your attention turned away from the living Word of God. He doesn't want you to know you're full of the resurrection life of Jesus. In fact, the prospect of it terrifies him.

Why? Because once you truly understand that you have the life of God inside you, you'll begin to act just like Jesus did. You'll lay hands on the sick and they'll recover. You'll cast out demons. You'll preach the gospel to every creature.

In short, you'll be just what God intended you to be. You'll be the Body of Christ on the earth.

Don't let Satan bind you with the grave clothes of yesterday's sin and defeat. You're not dead anymore. You've been raised with Jesus. Come out from the tombs and start living resurrection life!

SCRIPTURE READING: Acts 17:16-34

Get on the Right Road

"I call heaven and earth to record this day against you,
that I have set before you life and death, blessing and cursing:
therefore choose life, that both thou and thy seed may live."
(Deuteronomy 30:19)

God's going to get you for that! Most of us have said that kind of thing jokingly for years. We've somehow believed that God slaps us down with pain and punishment every time we sin. But that's just not true. There *are* deadly wages for sin, but *God* is not the one who's doling them out.

You see, the Bible tells us there's been a curse in effect for thousands of years. And the devil is the cause of it, not the Lord God. God gave warning of it in Deuteronomy 30:19. After describing in detail the blessings that fall upon those who followed God and the terrible suffering that would befall those who separated themselves from Him, He said, "I have set before you life and death, blessing and cursing: therefore choose life, that both thou and thy seed may live."

Think of it this way. Curseville is out there. God warned us about it and urged us not to travel the road that leads there. But He has promised to give us freedom, and He'll allow us to choose our own way. If we get on the road to Curseville and don't get off of it, we're going to wind up there. Is that because God sent us there? No! He urged us *not* to go.

The vital thing to realize is this: At any point of the journey—whether you're on the road to Curseville or living right in the middle of it—God will save you from it. He'll take you out of there and deliver you. He'll deliver you from diseases, addictions, or anything else that's been holding you captive.

Today if you find yourself on the wrong road and see destruction ahead, just repent and get on the right road. Just commit your way to Jesus and He'll deliver you from whatever may be holding you captive. You can begin by praying, "Lord Jesus, I've chosen the wrong road and right now I ask You to forgive me. Today I choose life by choosing Your way. Please deliver me from this bondage and fill me with Your Holy Spirit. Thank You, Lord!"

Remember this: No matter what you've done, God doesn't want to *get* you for it, He wants to *forgive* you of it. He doesn't want to slap you down, He wants to save you and lift you up. Trust Him and let Him put you on the road of *life* today!

SCRIPTURE READING: Deuteronomy 30

Leave the Past Behind

"But this one thing I do, forgetting those things which are behind,
and reaching forth unto those things which are before." **(Philippians 3:13)**

ailures and disappointments. Aches and pains from the past that just won't seem to go away. Most of us know what it's like to suffer from them but too few of us know just what to do about them. So we limp along, hoping somehow they'll magically stop hurting.

But it never happens that way. In fact, the passing of time often leaves us in worse condition—not better. Because, instead of putting those painful failures behind us, we often dwell on them until they become more real to us than the promises of God. We focus on them until we become bogged down in depression, frozen in our tracks by the fear that if we go on, we'll only fail again.

I used to get caught in that trap a lot. Then one day when I was right in the middle of a bout with depression, the Lord spoke up inside me and said:

"Kenneth, your problem is you're forming your thoughts off the past instead of the future. Don't do that! Unbelief looks at the past and says, 'See, it can't be done.' But faith looks at the future and says, 'It *can* be done, and according to the promises of God, it *is* done!' Then putting past failures behind it forever, faith steps out and acts like the victory's already been won."

If depression has driven you into a spiritual nosedive, break out of it by getting your eyes off the past and onto your future—a future that's been guaranteed by Christ Jesus through the great and precious promises in His Word.

Forget about those failures in the past! That's what God has done (Heb. 8:12). And if He doesn't remember them anymore, why should you?

The Bible says God's mercies are new every morning. So if you'll take God at His Word, you can wake up every morning to a brand-new world. You can live life totally unhindered by the past.

So, do it! Replace thoughts of yesterday's mistakes with scriptural promises about your future. As you do that, hope will start taking the place of depression. The spiritual aches and pains that have crippled you for so long will quickly disappear. Instead of looking behind you and saying, "I can't," you'll begin to look ahead and say, "I *can* do all things through Christ who strengthens me!"

SCRIPTURE READING: Philippians 3:1-14

Feed on the Word!

"Attend to my words; incline thine ear unto my sayings.
Let them not depart from thine eyes." **(Proverbs 4:20,21)**

Once you've made the Word of God final authority in your life, your first step to victory over the attacks of the enemy is to go to the Word and lay hold of God's promises concerning your situation.

Notice I said, "*Go* to the Word." It's good to have the Word committed to memory. But don't let that substitute for getting the Word before your eyes on a daily basis.

Think about it this way. It never did a hungry person any good to think about what a potato tastes like. Not even if he can remember it perfectly. The same thing is true with the Word of God. It's important to keep it in memory, but it's also necessary to go directly to it and feed your spirit with it. There is power in keeping the Word in front of your eyes and going into your ears. That's how it gets in your heart, so you can live by it.

So don't just think about the Word today, read it. Go to the promises that cover your situation. Feed on those promises and grow strong!

SCRIPTURE READING: Deuteronomy 6:1-9

It's Not Over Till It's Over

"Withstand (the devil); be firm in faith [against his onset] rooted, established, strong, immovable, and determined — knowing that the same (identical) sufferings are appointed to your brotherhood (the whole body of Christians) throughout the world. And after you have suffered a little while, the God of all grace...will Himself complete and make you what you ought to be, establish and ground you securely, and strengthen (and settle) you." **(1 Peter 5:9,10, AMP)**

No matter how long you've been living by faith, no matter how much you've learned about it, every once in a while you're going to suffer a setback. You're going to run into some circumstances that just don't turn out the way you expected them to.

When that happens, remember this. Those setbacks are just temporary. You may have lost a battle, but you're not going to lose the war. Just get up and go at it again.

"But I don't understand it," you say. "I did the best I could. I walked in all the truth I knew to walk in. Why didn't I get the victory?"

Because there was something you didn't know! It shouldn't shock you too much that there are things you don't know about the realm of the spirit. Ken and I have been in the ministry for 20 years. We've spent untold hours in the Word. Yet it seems like the more we learn, the more we realize we don't know.

So, when we get to a situation that we can't seem to get victory in, we have to ask God for more wisdom. If you'll look in 2 Samuel 21, you can see a time when King David had to do that. His country had been suffering from a famine for three years and David just didn't understand it, so he inquired of the Lord. You know what the Lord told him? He told him the famine had come because of something *Saul* had done! Isn't that amazing? Saul had been dead for years, yet what he'd put in motion in the realm of the spirit was still affecting his country.

David could have just given up when his usual confessions of faith and ways of praying didn't drive out that famine, but he didn't. He inquired of God for more wisdom. He used his temporary setback to cause him to seek more knowledge from God.

Follow his example! Overcome the habit of quitting because of temporary setbacks. Refuse to let them knock you out of the game. After all, this thing's not over till it's over. And the Bible says when it's all over, you'll have won. So just be steadfast in your faith. In the end your victory is guaranteed.

SCRIPTURE READING: 2 Samuel 21:1-6

Weapon of Praise

"I will praise thee, O Lord, with my whole heart;
I will shew forth all thy marvellous works. I will be glad and
rejoice in thee: I will sing praise to thy name, O thou most High.
When mine enemies are turned back, they shall fall
and perish at thy presence." **(Psalm 9:1-3)**

Never underestimate the importance of praise. It's one of the most powerful spiritual weapons you have.

Praise is more than a pleasant song or a few uplifting words about God. It does something. It releases the very presence of God Himself. And, when the presence of God comes on the scene, your enemies are turned back. Sickness and disease can't stay on your body. Poverty can't stay in your house.

Even physical weariness has to flee when it's faced with real joy-filled praise. I know that from experience. Years ago, when I first began conducting "Healing School," I had a real battle with fatigue. I'd minister and lay my hands on the sick for so many hours at a time that by the time the meeting had ended, I was sometimes too physically weak even to close the service.

Then, in one particular meeting, I discovered the power of praise. I had just finished praying for those in the prayer line, and as usual, I was exhausted. But instead of rest, the Spirit of the Lord impressed on me that what I needed was to rejoice in the Lord. So, I did. I began to praise the Lord with my whole heart, mind, and body. Do you know what happened? The tiredness left me. And I was energized with the presence of God!

The next time the devil tries to stifle your effectiveness, to drain you of the strength and wealth and victory that's yours in Jesus, turn him back with that powerful weapon. Lift your hands and your voice and whole heart to God. *Praise!*

SCRIPTURE READING: 2 Chronicles 20:1-22

Leaving the Pain Behind

"Love...is not touchy or fretful or resentful;
it takes no account of the evil done to it — pays no attention
to a suffered wrong." **(1 Corinthians 13:5, AMP)**

Have you ever tried to forgive someone...and found you simply couldn't do it? You've cried about it and prayed about it and asked God to help you, but those old feelings of resentment just failed to go away.

Put an end to those kinds of failures in the future by basing your forgiveness on faith rather than feelings. True forgiveness doesn't have anything at all to do with how you feel. It's an act of the will. It is based on obedience to God and on faith in Him.

That means once you've forgiven a person, you need to consider them permanently forgiven! When old feelings rise up within you and Satan tries to convince you that you haven't really forgiven them, resist him. Say, "No, I've already forgiven that person by faith. I refuse to dwell on those old feelings."

Then, according to 1 John 1:9, believe that you receive forgiveness and cleansing from the sin of unforgiveness and from all unrighteousness associated with it—*including any remembrance of having been wronged!*

Have you ever heard anyone say, "I may forgive, but I'll never forget!" That's a second-rate kind of forgiveness that you, as a believer, are never supposed to settle for. You're to forgive supernaturally "even as God for Christ's sake hath forgiven you" (Eph. 4:32).

You're to forgive as God forgives. To release that person from guilt permanently and unconditionally and to operate as if nothing bad ever happened between you. You're to purposely forget as well as forgive.

As you do that, something supernatural will happen within you. The pain once caused by that incident will disappear. The power of God will wash away the effects of it and you'll be able to leave it behind you once and for all.

Don't become an emotional bookkeeper, keeping careful accounts of the wrongs you have suffered. Learn to forgive and forget. It will open a whole new world of blessing for you.

SCRIPTURE READING: Luke 6:27-37

Use God's M.O.

"Through faith we understand that the worlds
were framed by the word of God, so that things which are seen
were not made of things which do appear." **(Hebrews 11:3)**

God uses words to create. He used His Word to "frame" the worlds. Just look in the first chapter of Genesis and count how many times you see the phrase, "And God said." "God said, Let there be light: and there was light.... God said, Let there be a firmament.... God said, Let the waters under the heaven be gathered together.... God said, Let the earth bring forth...."

God doesn't do anything without saying it first. That's His M.O., His method of operation. And, if you're smart, you'll use that method of operation too. You'll take His words and speak them out until they take on form and substance and become a reality in your life.

"Well, Brother Copeland, I tried that and it didn't work. I said, 'By His stripes I'm healed' four times and nothing happened."

Big deal. God started saying that Jesus was coming in the Garden of Eden. He said it again in Exodus. He said it again in Numbers and Deuteronomy. He said it in Isaiah and the other prophets. He said it all through the Old Testament, over and over again.

Then after about 7,000 years, the Book of John tells us, "The Word became flesh and dwelt among men."

So if you've said you're healed four times and nothing's happened, don't worry about it. Just keep saying it! You might think it's taking a long time to manifest, but I'll guarantee you, it won't take 7,000 years.

Do you want to operate in God's power? Then use His M.O. Speak out His words and let them frame a life full of blessing for you!

SCRIPTURE READING: Genesis 1

Live the Love Life

"But whoso keepeth his word, in him verily is the love of God perfected: hereby know we that we are in him. He that saith he abideth in him ought himself also so to walk, even as he walked." **(1 John 2:5,6)**

There is nothing—absolutely nothing—that is more important than learning to love. In fact, how accurately you perfect the love walk will determine how much of the perfect will of God you accomplish. That's because every other spiritual force derives its action from love. For example, the Bible teaches us that faith works by love. And answered prayer is almost an impossibility when a believer steps outside of love and refuses to forgive or is in strife with his brother.

Without love, your giving will not work. Tongues and prophecy will not work. Faith fails and knowledge is unfruitful. All the truths that you have learned from God's Word work by love.

They will profit you nothing unless you live the love of God.

First Corinthians 13:4-8 paints a perfect picture of how love behaves. It's patient and kind. It's not jealous or proud. It doesn't behave rudely or selfishly and it isn't touchy. Love "bears all things, believes all things, hopes all things, endures all things."

Sounds like a tall order, doesn't it? But don't despair. You are a love creature. God has recreated your spirit in the image of love. And He has sent His love Spirit to live in you and teach you how to love as He loves. You can live the love life. Begin today.

SCRIPTURE READING: 1 Corinthians 13:1-13

Take Some New Ground

"Again I say unto you, That if two of you shall agree on earth as touching any thing that they shall ask, it shall be done for them of my Father which is in heaven." **(Matthew 18:19)**

As believers, you and I are part of a conquering army, constantly claiming new ground for the kingdom of God. Right?

Well, yes, that's the way it should be. But just about the time the army tops the hill and is ready to advance, it seems that Satan pulls out his big gun—DIVISION—and scatters believers in every direction.

How can we strike back against the strategy of division? By launching an even more powerful attack of our own. By using one of the most powerful resources given us by the Lord Jesus: the prayer of agreement.

Jesus said that if any two of us would agree as touching *anything* we ask, *it shall be done!* That statement is so powerful that most people don't really believe it. If they did, you'd find little groups of Christians huddled up in every corner agreeing together in prayer.

Find someone to agree with in prayer this week. Be sure to base what you pray on the Word of God. You may have differing opinions about everything else, but you can be in agreement about the Word.

Also, be sure your agreement is total—spirit, soul, and body. Cast down arguments, theories, and imaginations that are contrary to the Word. Take every thought captive to the obedience of Christ. Keep a watch over your thoughts and your words.

Then get your body in line by speaking the thing you've agreed on. Act like you've already received the answer. Don't keep asking but thank God for it. Stay in agreement and take some new ground for the Lord!

SCRIPTURE READING: Acts 4:1-31

No Offense

"He that loveth his brother abideth in the light,
and there is none occasion of stumbling in him." **(1 John 2:10)**

Whenever you find yourself stumbling into failure or sin, check your love life. Sit down with the Lord and ask Him to show you if you're in strife with anyone or if you've taken offense. If you have, the devil can come in and trip you up.

As a preacher, I've seen that happen countless times. I'll be preaching about something and some believer will get upset with me about it. He'll decide I'm wrong and go off in a huff—and first thing you know, he's in trouble.

Mark 4:17 tells us the devil uses those kinds of offenses to steal the Word from our hearts. He causes us to get crosswise with each other. Then he's able to pull the plug right out of us and drain the Word like water from a bucket.

Don't ever let that happen to you. If you hear a preacher or another believer saying something that rubs you the wrong way and you catch yourself getting offended say, "Oh no you don't. You're not stealing the Word out of me, you lying devil." Then get right down on your knees and repent before God.

Search the Word and listen to the Spirit within you and find out what you should do. If you still feel what that person said to you was wrong, pray for him.

Remember, taking offense never comes from God. He says we're to be rooted and grounded in love. So reject those feelings of offense. Give yourself to that person in love and in prayer. You'll be able to walk right on through that situation without ever stumbling at all.

SCRIPTURE READING: 1 John 2:1-11

Throw Open the Door

"Jesus sat over against the treasury, and beheld
how the people cast money in.... And there came a certain
poor widow, and she threw in two mites.... And he called unto him
his disciples, and saith unto them...this poor widow hath cast
more in, than all they which have cast into the treasury: For all
they did cast in of their abundance; but she of her want did cast
in all that she had, even all her living." **(Mark 12:41-44)**

H ave you ever wanted to get God's attention? You can, you know. There's a certain kind of boldness, a certain kind of faith in giving that will get His attention every time. You can see that in Mark 12.

Read that chapter and just imagine the situation it describes. Jesus was sitting by the treasury watching as people put in their offerings. Don't you know there were some sanctimonious displays going on with Him there watching? There was bound to be plenty of pharisaical robe swishing as those wealthy leaders walked up to put in their gifts that day.

Right in the middle of it all, this poor widow walked up and threw in her offering. I can just see her in my mind's eye. I can hear her say to herself, "By the eternal Almighty God that liveth, I've had enough of this poverty. I'm fed up with having nothing but want. I may just be a poor widow now, but I'm not going to be a poor widow anymore. I'm going to be a *broke* widow if God doesn't do something here because I'm giving Him everything I've got!"

Then, wham! She threw that last little dab of money she had into the offering.

Do you know what? That got Jesus' attention. He said, "Listen, everybody. I want to talk to you about this woman," and He started to preach.

What moved Jesus wasn't just the fact that she gave. It was how she gave. She gave in faith—not in fear. She didn't stop and calculate what she didn't have and say, "Boy, if I do this, tomorrow I won't eat." She just boldly threw in all she had, expecting God to take care of her in return.

You and I need to catch hold of that same attitude. We need to start holding our offerings up to the Lord in confidence, throwing it boldly into His service, expecting His blessings in return.

If you have a need right now, get God's attention by giving with boldness like that widow woman did. Throw open the door of your household by throwing everything you have at Jesus. Let God know that He is your source. Before long, the abundance of God will come pouring in!

SCRIPTURE READING: Mark 12:28-44

Be of Good Cheer

"And now I exhort you to be of good cheer." **(Acts 27:22)**

What do you do when you're in a really perilous situation?

If you're like I used to be, you cry out to God in desperation. One afternoon when I was squalling to God about something, He interrupted me and said, "Kenneth, did you know I don't hear the cry of My children when they cry out in desperation?"

"What?" I said. "I thought you did."

He said, "No, I hear the desperation cry of a sinner because that's all he can cry about. But once you get born again, son, you ought to be crying out of faith. I hear the faith cry."

What is a faith cry? It's calling things that be not as though they were (Rom. 4:17). It's what the Bible means when it says, "Let the weak say, I am strong" (Joel 3:10).

The apostle Paul knew how to use the faith cry. That's why, in Acts 27, he exhorted the men on that battered, sinking ship to "be of good cheer." He was telling them to start acting by faith. Can't you imagine what those sailors thought when he said that? "Listen to that stupid preacher. We're sinking and he says be of good cheer.

We've thrown everything we have overboard and he says be of good cheer."

You may feel just like those sailors did, right now. You may feel like your ship's going down. You may feel like crying out in desperation. But don't do it. Instead, do what Paul said and *be of good cheer!*

Cry out to God in faith and say, "Lord, I'm not going to panic. I'm not going to despair. I'm going to be of good cheer because Your Word says You'll deliver me from this situation" (Ps. 34:19).

Then start being cheerful. It may take more determination than anything you've ever done before, but God will give you the strength to do it. He'll give you the power to be cheerful in the middle of the most ungodly darkness the devil can bring up.

Instead of crying out in desperation, take a faith stand. Sing and rejoice and praise God for your deliverance. Be of good cheer and you can be sure God will bring you through the storm just fine!

SCRIPTURE READING: Philippians 4:4-9

Be Supernatural God's Way

"And the Lord said unto Moses,
Wherefore criest thou unto me?... Lift thou up thy rod,
and stretch out thine hand over the sea, and divide it:
and the children of Israel shall go on dry ground
through the midst of the sea." **(Exodus 14:15,16)**

If you hang around God very much, it won't be long before you'll start wanting to do things the world considers supernatural. You'll start wanting to lay hands on the sick and have them recover. You'll start wanting to cast out demons. You'll start wanting to cast mountainous problems into the sea.

What's more, you can do it if you want to!

How? Not by jumping out and "trying" to do supernatural things, but by obeying God one step at a time. By doing the things He's already given you power to do.

That's how it happened with Moses. He didn't have the power to divide the Red Sea. But he did have the power to stretch his rod out over it. And when he did that in obedience to the Lord's command, the Holy Spirit did the rest.

It will be the same way with you. When you start doing your part, the Holy Spirit will do His and supernatural things will start happening around you.

What is your part? Feeding on the Word. Praying in the Spirit. Listening to what the Spirit of God says to you. As you do those things, as you begin to move as God impresses you to move and take your direction from Him, you'll flow in the supernatural as naturally as a bird flies in the air.

You won't struggle and strain and try to "part the sea." You'll just trust the Lord and stretch out your rod... and watch the miracles roll.

SCRIPTURE READING: Exodus 14

God of Your Trouble, God of Your Heart

"Thou art my hiding place; thou shalt preserve me from trouble;
thou shalt compass me about with songs of deliverance." **(Psalm 32:7)**

In this day and time, trouble seems to surround us on every side. If it's not a failing economy, it's a failing business, a failing marriage, or failing health. Yet, in the midst of seemingly overwhelming problems, God has promised to deliver us.

Let me give you a word of advice though. If you want God to be God of your trouble, then you must let Him be God in your heart. God honors those who honor Him. So, if you're facing some problems today, don't just start kicking and screaming and begging Him to save you from them. Honor Him by going to His Word and doing what He says you should do.

Psalm 34 is a good place to start. It says, for example, that you should seek God (verse 4). As you seek Him, He will deliver you from the things that threaten you.

Secondly, it instructs you to cry out to the Lord. He will save you out of ALL your troubles (verse 6).

Next it tells you to fear the Lord. If you don't know how to do that, verses 11 to 14 will tell you exactly what you need to know: You must keep from speaking evil and deceit; depart from evil and do good; seek peace and pursue it.

Remember, if you want God to be God of your trouble, let Him be God of your heart. When you do that, all of heaven will get involved in your deliverance—and your triumph will be guaranteed.

SCRIPTURE READING: Psalm 34

He Really Does Care for You

"Casting all your care upon him; for he careth for you." **(1 Peter 5:7)**

Do you know what it's like to face a problem so big it seems downright irresponsible not to worry about it? There may not be a thing you can do about it, but you feel like you need to at least be concerned. After all, *somebody* needs to! And no one else seems to be volunteering for the job.

I remember one time in particular I felt exactly that way. I was holding a series of meetings in Ruston, Louisiana. I had just discovered our budget was $800 short—and in those days, $800 might as well have been nine million! The devil was attacking my mind, telling me that no one cared about me or my ministry, telling me that I was facing this problem alone.

But instead of giving in to those thoughts, I got my Bible and turned to every scripture in the Word of God that guaranteed me my needs were met. Then I rolled the care of those expenses over on God. I promised God that with the Holy Spirit as my helper, I would not touch that problem with my thought life again.

That wasn't an easy promise to keep. I wanted to worry so badly! I went into the courtyard of the motel where I was staying and walked around the swimming pool. Every time I thought about the problem, I would say out loud, "No, I have rolled the care of that over on the Lord. I will not think about it. The budget is met."

After a while, a man drove up in the driveway and began to honk his horn. I tried to ignore him because I don't like to be interrupted when I'm praying, but he stuck his head out of the window and shouted, "Come here!" He said it with such authority that I obeyed.

He said to me, "Brother Copeland, I'm sorry to disturb you, but I'm committed to another obligation and will be late for the meeting tonight. I was afraid I would miss the offering." Then he handed me a check. When I went back to my room and looked at that check, I found it was for $500. Coupled with the offering in the service that night, it totaled the exact amount I needed to meet that budget.

Would you like to have people chasing you down to meet your needs? Then next time you're facing a problem, give it to God. Let *Him* be the one who's concerned about it. He's volunteered for the job and you can trust Him to do it well. After all, He really does care for you.

SCRIPTURE READING: Psalm 37:1-11

Oppose the Devil

"Submit yourselves therefore to God.
Resist the devil, and he will flee from you." **(James 4:7)**

If you've been crying and asking God to run the devil out of your life, STOP! The Bible says *you're* the one who's supposed to overcome the devil.

How? By resisting him. By rebelling against him when he tells you to do something and doing what God says instead! When Satan tells you some lie, contradict him with the Word of God. Oppose him. This verse says when you do that, he'll flee from you. He'll "run as in terror."

That means everywhere you go, as you walk in faith and oppose the devil, darkness is pushed back.

So start pushing back that darkness. You can do it! The life of God is within you. Jesus Himself is living inside you. Everywhere you go, He goes. Every problem that rises up against you, every evil spirit that tries to influence your life, is coming up against GOD when he comes up against you.

All you need to do is become conscious of that. Begin now living your life moment by moment, knowing that the light of God is in you. The Word of God is in you. The Spirit of God is in you.

Live knowing that Jesus, the Son of God, is in you. Then watch the devil run!

SCRIPTURE READING: Ephesians 6:10-18

Inside Out

"But we all, with open face beholding as in a glass
the glory of the Lord, are changed into the same image from glory
to glory, even as by the Spirit of the Lord." **(2 Corinthians 3:18)**

Have you ever thought about the fact that man is the only creature God created who has to wear clothing to cover himself? All the other creatures grow their own coverings. Some grow fur, some feathers, others scales, or leathery hide. But all are clothed from the inside out!

Most people don't realize it, but in the beginning, man was clothed that way too. He was made in the image of God. And, if you'll look in Ezekiel 8:2, you'll find that God is clothed in fire from the loins up and from the loins down. That fire is His glory emanating outward from His innermost being.

When man was first created, he was like that too. He was covered with the very glory of God. It radiated from his inner being outward. That's why he had no sense of nakedness until after he sinned and the glory departed from him.

It was a tragic day when man lost that glorious covering. But I want you to know something today. It's not lost forever. The Word of God says we can gain it back.

You see, when you put your faith in the blood of Jesus and were born again, the glory of God once again took up residence in you. It may be well-hidden right now, but believe me, it's in there.

And the Bible says that as you gaze into the Lord's face by studying the Word and fellowshipping with Him, as you renew your mind to understand who you are in Christ, you'll be changed into His image on the outside as well. As you learn to hear His voice and obey it, you'll start giving outward expression of the glory within you. Little by little, you'll be turned inside out!

Instead of simply staring into your closet every morning, spend some time gazing at Jesus and beholding His Word. Let Him clothe you in His radiant presence. Once His glory starts shining through, anything you wear will look beautiful on you.

SCRIPTURE READING: Psalm 8

It's Beginning to Rain

"Be glad then, ye children of Zion, and rejoice
in the Lord your God: for he hath given you the former rain moderately,
and he will cause to come down for you the rain, the former rain,
and the latter rain in the first month." **(Joel 2:23)**

There's a spiritual flood coming. God has promised it. He's promised us an outpouring of Holy Spirit power that will bring in the greatest harvest of souls any of us have ever seen.

As believers, we've been reading about it in the Word and hearing about it from the pulpit for years. We've been staring toward heaven so long, waiting for it to come, that we've gotten cricks in our spiritual necks. We've had this mental image of God pouring down His Spirit from some sort of big heavenly pitcher above us.

But you know what? We've been looking in the wrong direction!

The pitchers God is going to use to pour out His power are right here on earth. Jesus explained it this way. "He that believeth on me, as the scripture hath said, out of his belly shall flow rivers of living water" (John 7:38).

The end-time flood we've all been expecting is going to be composed of living waters that will pour forth from *believers*. The Holy Spirit within us will be the source of all the signs and wonders and miracles the prophets foretold. And when we begin to fervently pray the prayer of intercession, the flood of that power will begin to flow.

Zechariah 10:1 says, "Ask ye of the Lord rain in the time of the latter rain; so the Lord shall make bright clouds, and give them showers of rain, to every one grass in the field."

Our prayers, our intercession, is what will release the great outpouring of God's Spirit. As we begin to join together and cry out to God, the rivers of living water within each one of us will join together and become a flood of spiritual power in the earth.

So, ask, pray for a Holy Ghost gully-washer. Intercede for the outpouring. Make this mighty flood of spiritual power a priority in your prayer life.

Glory to God, it's already beginning to rain!

SCRIPTURE READING: Joel 2:23-32

Press on in Patience

"...be not slothful, but followers of them who
through faith and patience inherit the promises." **(Hebrews 6:12)**

You've been walking by faith. You've been believing God to meet your need. But what do you do when the results seem slow in coming and you are tempted to give up?

Be patient!

There is not much said about patience these days. But, when it comes to receiving from God, it is just as important as faith.

It will make the difference between success and failure for you.

Patience undergirds and sustains faith until the result is manifested. After you have meditated on the promises of God and have them in your spirit, patience will encourage you to hold steady. Patience is power. It has the courage to refuse the lie of Satan that says the Word is not working for you. It knows that God's Word has never failed. Patience will not draw back in fear but will press forward in faith until you have the answer.

When the results of your faith seem slow in coming, don't give up! Continue to put the Word first, with patience, and you will *surely* receive the promise of God!

SCRIPTURE READING: Hebrew 10:32-39

Obedience: No Small Thing

"But he that heareth, and doeth not, is like a man
that without a foundation built an house upon the earth; against which
the stream did beat vehemently, and immediately it fell;
and the ruin of that house was great." **(Luke 6:49)**

Do you ever have seasons in your life when it seems like every time you go to church and every time you spend time in prayer and every time you open the Bible, you receive a revelation from God? I do. Spiritually, everything will be going great. I'll be higher than a Georgia pine. Then, suddenly, something starts to happen. I start drying up in spiritual things.

It seems like it doesn't make any difference what I pray or how much I read the Word, I can't get anywhere spiritually. I'm so dry my spirit's creaking!

That used to baffle me. I didn't know what the cause was. I didn't have any sin in my life. I'd taken care of that. I was still praying. Still meditating. Still acting on and confessing the Word. But instead of getting results, I was getting nowhere. I'd stand in front of my mirror and confess faith over and over again and the only thing that happened was that my voice got tired!

If that's ever happened to you, may I make a suggestion? Backtrack and find the last thing God told you to do that you didn't do—and *do it!*

It's probably nothing big. Just a seemingly small thing. But, believe me, those minor disobediences will dry up the flow of the Spirit just like the major ones will.

Most of us don't realize that. We'll get on our knees and say, "Oh Lord, I want to go to China for You. I'll go to Africa. I'll go to Russia." But when God says, "Go next door," we just shrug it off.

"I can't do that," we'll say. "That guy next door doesn't like me. Besides, I want to be like Brother Schambach and get a big tent."

If you've done something like that, repent. Then pick up where you left off and do what God directed. And from now on, remember, no matter how insignificant God's instructions may seem, obeying them is no small thing! It's those simple acts of obedience that will make your spiritual house stand...or fall. All the small things combined become the direction of our lives.

SCRIPTURE READING: Luke 16:1-10

Follow Your Dream

"And Moses said unto God, Who am I,
that I should go unto Pharaoh, and that I should bring forth
the children of Israel out of Egypt? And he said,
Certainly I will be with thee." **(Exodus 3:11,12)**

Have you ever had a Holy Spirit-inspired dream, a dream of doing something really great for Jesus? A dream of being so prosperous, for instance, that you can finance a nationwide revival? A dream of leading thousands of people to the Lord?

At one time or another, you probably have, but you backed away from it. You thought, "Oh my, I couldn't do *that*. Satan's kept me defeated for so long I have a poor self-image."

If so, I have some good news for you. If you'll believe God, even a poor self-image won't keep you from success. Look in the Book of Exodus and you'll see a man who proved that. His name was Moses.

Moses didn't have a very good self-image. He'd made a terrible mistake early in his career. It was a mistake that drove him into the wilderness and kept him there for 40 years herding somebody else's sheep.

He'd once dreamed of being a deliverer of God's people, but no more. As far as he was concerned, he was finished...a failure...a flop!

But God didn't think so. In fact, when God came to Moses in that wilderness, He didn't ask for Moses' credentials. He didn't mention his shady history. He just told him to go see Pharaoh and tell him to let God's people go.

Moses, however, was still wrestling with his poor self-image. "Who am I that I should go to Pharaoh?" he stammered.

You know what God said in response? He just said, "Certainly, I will be with thee."

You see, it didn't matter who Moses was. What mattered was that the living God was with him. The same thing is true for you today. You don't need a history of successes behind you to answer God's call. You don't need a string of spiritual credentials. All you need is the presence of the Lord.

Think about that when the devil tells you you're a failure, when he says you'll never be able to do what God has put in your heart to do. Put him in his place. Tell him it doesn't matter who you are because the living God is with you.

Then dare to follow your dream!
SCRIPTURE READING: Exodus 3:1-14

Don't Let the Devil Put One Over on You

"When he [the devil] speaketh a lie, he speaketh of his own: for he is a liar, and the father of it." **(John 8:44)**

Some people find it difficult to believe God's promises because they've seen so many things in the natural world that seem to contradict them. They've seen faithful tithers go broke. They've seen sick Christians fail to receive their healing.

In reality, it would be more accurate to say that they *think* they've seen those things. Because, you see, there's a deceiver at work in the world. A deceiver who's busily doing the same thing he's been doing ever since the Garden of Eden: tricking mankind into believing God's Word isn't true.

And, after working on it for thousands of years, he's a master at it. Think about that the next time he tries to make things look as though God's Word is not going to work for you, when he makes it look like all hope is lost. Say, "I don't care about appearances. I believe the Word and I refuse to doubt it."

Let me show you what I mean. Have you ever seen a magic show where someone crawls inside a box and then is sawn in half? You can see it with your own two eyes. The guy's feet are sticking out one end of the box and his head is poking out the other, and the box is plainly cut in two. Then the magician slides the two halves back together and the sawed-apart fellow jumps out of the box in one piece.

Now tell me, did you really believe, even for a moment, that fellow was truly cut in half? Of course not! You knew that you'd seen a trick, a deception, something that appeared one way when, in reality, it was a different way altogether. You may not have known how it was done. You may not have been able to explain it. But you knew a person couldn't be sawn in half, then put back together, so you refused to believe your eyes.

That's exactly the way you need to be where the Word of God is concerned. You need to learn to trust it and rely on it to such an extent that when Satan shows you something in the natural world that appears to contradict it, you just say, "Well, I saw that, but I'm not going to be gullible enough to believe it. I'm just going to stick with the Word."

If you'll do that, the father of lies will never be able to put one over on you.

SCRIPTURE READING: Psalm 119:89-104

Be a Cheerful Giver

"Let each one [give] as he has made up his own mind
and purposed in his heart, not reluctantly or sorrowfully
or under compulsion, for God loves (that is, He takes pleasure in,
prizes above other things, and is unwilling to abandon or to do
without) a cheerful (joyous, prompt-to-do-it) giver.... And God
is able to make all grace (every favor and earthly blessing)
come to you in abundance." **(2 Corinthians 9:7,8, AMP)**

Some people say you need to "give till it hurts." Don't you believe it. God doesn't want gifts given in pain. He wants gifts given in joy! In fact, those are the only kinds of gifts that please Him.

That's why He tacked His promise of abundance onto His command about cheerful giving. The two are connected.

Cheerful, full of faith, even hilarious, giving—that is the key that unlocks the treasure house of God. Have you ever seen a group of people give that way? I have. I'll never forget it. I was at a camp meeting years ago when offering time turned into a spontaneous, supernatural celebration. Ken was singing "Cast your bread upon the waters," and the people were just dancing their way down the aisles to give their money. The joy in that place was wonderful. Great healings and miracles were done that night.

But what stood out to me above all was how joyously and hilariously the people brought their offerings to God. The offering wasn't extracted from them like a dentist extracts teeth. It was brought forth gladly.

Listen, the concept of "giving till it hurts" didn't come from God. He'd rather you give ten dollars with that kind of joy than twenty dollars grudgingly. In 2 Corinthians 8:11,12, the apostle Paul urges the church in Corinth to give with *eager willingness.* Eager willingness. That's what God looks for!

If you haven't given that way in the past, make a firm commitment to start. Repent for the times you've given grudgingly. Then spend some serious time with God and His Word in your prayer closet, so when you give again, you can give from a willing heart.

Put the "pain" of giving behind. Become a cheerful, joyous, prompt-to-do-it giver, and believe me, your blessings *will* abound!

SCRIPTURE READING: 2 Corinthians 9:6-15

Break Through the Wall

"I can do all things through Christ which strengtheneth me."

(Philippians 4:13)

You're running the race set before you, moving full speed ahead with God's blessing overtaking you at every step. Then suddenly, wham! You hit the wall. It may be a wall of sickness or financial trouble, of spiritual failure or family problems. But, regardless of the form it takes, the effect of "the wall" is always the same. It stops you cold.

The question is, once you hit a wall like that, what will you do? You'll be tempted to quit, to turn back in defeat. But don't do it. Because God will enable you to break through that wall and keep right on going.

I'm not going to tell you it's easy. The truth is, it's tough. But you have to push on through the tough times if you're ever going to have a breakthrough.

Ask any athlete. He'll tell you that! Because if he's a winner, he's been there. He's pushed his body to what seems to be the maximum. His side has hurt. His lungs have ached. He's had cramps in his legs and thighs. And just when he felt like he couldn't go on, he's heard some coach yell, "Come on! Move it!"

Athletes call that "hitting the wall." It's a time when the body says, "That's it. That's all I can do. I can't go any farther. I can't go any faster. I quit."

But the seasoned athlete knows that "the wall" isn't the end. It's a signal that he's on the verge of a breakthrough. If he'll toughen up and push himself a little more, he'll get a second wind. Suddenly, he'll go faster than before. He'll reach a level of excellence he couldn't have reached any other way.

When you feel the worst, when failure is breathing down your neck, press into the Word as never before. You may meditate on a particular scripture for days and even weeks sometimes, trying to get a revelation of it, seemingly without success. Then suddenly, like the dawn of the morning, light will come pouring in. You'll see the way to break through. All you have to do is punch one little hole in that wall of problems, dig one tiny hole in it with your faith and with the Word of God.

Then keep tearing away at that hole. Don't quit! And, before long, the forces of God will come bursting through, demolishing every obstacle in their path!

Once that happens you'll never be the same again. You'll be hooked. It will only take one breakthrough like that to make a never-dying, never-quitting champion out of you.

SCRIPTURE READING: 1 Corinthians 9:24-27

Train Your Spirit

"It [grace] has trained us to reject and renounce all
ungodliness (irreligion) and worldly (passionate) desires, to live
discreet (temperate, self-controlled), upright, devout (spiritually-
whole) lives in this present world." **(Titus 2:12, AMP)**

When an athlete goes into training, he practices to improve his skills. He works hard, repeating the same motions over and over until they become what we'd call "second nature" to him.

Most of us understand how crucial that kind of training is in the physical realm. We know that you simply can't be a winner without it. But did you know we can train ourselves that same way where spiritual things are concerned?

That's right! Hebrews 5:14 says we can *train* our senses to discern between good and evil. When you train, or practice, for something, you expose yourself daily to whatever it is you want to become. You practice it over and over until it becomes second nature to you. People who are lazy have practiced being lazy. People who are disciplined have practiced being disciplined.

Spending time with God is "spirit" practice. As you do it diligently, your spirit will grow stronger and will start to overcome the habits of the flesh.

If, for example, you have trouble getting up in the morning to spend time with God before the busyness of the day begins, if you've been giving in to your flesh and staying in bed, then you'll have to start practicing getting up. The more you practice it, the easier it will be.

Don't expect yourself to do it perfectly right from the beginning. Don't get discouraged when you stumble and fail. You're just out of practice. Get back on your feet and go at it again!

Become a spiritual athlete. Put yourself in training by practicing the things of God. Build your spirit muscles through fellowship with Him. You will be surprised to find just how much of a winner you can be.

SCRIPTURE READING: 2 Peter 1:2-11

Can He Count on You?

"And the Lord said, Who then is that faithful and wise steward,
whom his lord shall make ruler over his household, to give them their portion
of meat in due season?" **(Luke 12:42)**

We often praise God for His faithfulness. We're thankful that we can always count on Him to be there for us. But we rarely consider the fact that He needs us to be faithful too.

It's true. God needs people He can count on. He needs faithful and wise stewards He can trust over His household. In this final hour, He needs faithful believers to team up with, so He can manifest Himself in the earth more than ever before.

"Oh Gloria, God doesn't need *me!*"

Yes, He does. Ever since the Creation, when He gave man dominion over the earth, He's needed people to work with Him to get His will done here. You can see that all through the Bible. When the children of Israel were in bondage in Egypt and He wanted to lead them out, He teamed up with a man, Moses, to get the job done. Moses' responsibility was to stretch out his hand in the earth and command the will of God to be done.

Why did He choose Moses? Because He needed someone who was faithful and would dare to act on His Word. He needed someone He could count on, and He knew Moses was that kind of man.

Psalm 103:7 says, "He made known his ways unto Moses, his acts unto the children of Israel." If Moses hadn't been faithful to know God's ways, the children of Israel would never have seen God's acts!

God needs you just as He needed Moses. He needs *you* to be faithful and alert to spiritual things. He needs you to be someone He can trust to know His Word and be obedient to it. He needs you to be a steward who will stretch out his hand like Moses did so that He can perform signs and wonders before the people.

Will you be faithful? It's a decision you have to make. No one can do it for you. Right now, commit yourself to be that wise and faithful servant. Say in your heart and with your mouth, "God, You can count on me."

SCRIPTURE READING: Psalm 105:23-45

No More Surprises

"But God hath revealed them unto us by his Spirit:
for the Spirit searcheth all things, yea, the deep things of God."
(1 Corinthians 2:10)

God is *not* full of surprises. He's not an unpredictable being who likes to keep you guessing. Countless believers, however, have the idea He is.

"You just never know what God is going to do," they say. They base that idea on 1 Corinthians 2:9 which says, "Eye hath not seen, nor ear heard, neither have entered into the heart of man, the things which God hath prepared for them that love him." They interpret that scripture to mean that God is keeping secrets from His people.

But, praise God, He isn't!

In fact, verse 10 says He's given us His Spirit to *reveal* those secrets to us! He wants us to know everything that's on His heart.

If you're in the dark about God's will for you, you don't have to stay that way. He wants you to know about His plans and provisions for your life. He'll show them to you if you'll let Him.

So, don't depend on guesswork. Determine today that you're going to start receiving that revelation from the Holy Spirit. As you read the Word, pray in the Spirit and ask Him to reveal to you the reality of the Scriptures. Ask Him to shed His light on them and show you exactly how they apply to you.

Remember: God isn't in the business of keeping secrets from you. He's in the business of revealing them. Take time to listen to Him and you'll never have to settle for a life of uncertainty again.

SCRIPTURE READING: 2 Corinthians 2:1-16

Take Time to Listen

"If any of you lack wisdom, let him ask of God,
that giveth to all men liberally, and upbraideth not;
and it shall be given him." **(James 1:5)**

When you're facing a problem, the very first thing you should ask God for is wisdom. Not money. Not power. Not even healing. But wisdom.

God's wisdom is the key that will unlock every door in your life. It will turn your every failure into success. So, stop wasting your prayer power begging God for things you *think* you need and spend some time instead listening to what He has to say about your situation.

If you've never tried that before, practically speaking, here's what you need to do.

First: Lay out the entire problem before the Lord, not because He doesn't know what you're going through, but because laying it out helps you. It helps you see things from a more objective point of view.

I remember when I used to take my problems to my father, A. W. Copeland. Somehow, when I was explaining them to him, they began to look different to me. I'd get a new perspective, and as I talked, he'd point out areas I hadn't considered yet. Explaining your problems to God, point by point, will help you accomplish the same thing.

Second: Listen for the Spirit of God to advise you. Pay particular attention

to what He says through the written Word. Most likely, the care of your problem has choked the Word of God right out of your heart (Mark 4:18, 19). If so, you need to get the Bible and begin to put that Word back in again. Then the Holy Spirit will begin to speak to you through it.

As you're listening, be sure to remain teachable. Be ready to accept rebuke if necessary. Be very honest with God. Look for ways in which you've been wrong and confess them to Him. It's all right. Those sins won't come as any surprise to Him. He already knows about them. Confession just gives you the opportunity to get rid of them.

Third: Act on the wisdom God gives you. Let go of your own methods and put His methods into operation. Be obedient. If you don't, that wonderful wisdom won't do you any good at all.

As you pray today, set aside your own ideas and start seeking the wisdom of God. It's the only thing that can permanently solve the problems you've been facing. It's truly the most precious gift God has to give.

Seek wisdom.

SCRIPTURE READING: Proverbs 8:10-36

Put the Word Into Action

"Whosoever heareth these sayings of mine, and doeth them,
I will liken him unto a wise man,
which built his house upon a rock." **(Matthew 7:24)**

If you want your deeds to be blessed, if you want to see supernatural results in your life, you'll have to do more than simply read the Word of God. You'll have to put it into action.

That's what I did. Years ago when I realized that God was the one who had the answers to all my problems, that He was the one who could supply all my needs, I committed myself to do everything His Word told me to do. I made a quality decision to step out in faith on every command I saw there.

When I found out, for example, that God's Word instructed me to tithe, Gloria and I were already trying to stretch what little money we had further than it could possibly go. We were up to our necks in debt! We couldn't possibly afford to give away ten percent. But we did it anyway. We stepped out on faith and kept our commitment to do every command we saw. Before long we began to see financial increase. We've been increasing ever since.

Keep on reading and studying the Bible. Listen to teaching tapes. Go to church and hear the Word preached. But don't stop there. Go one crucial step further by taking the Word you've heard and put it into ACTION!

SCRIPTURE READING: Matthew 7:17-27

The Grace of Giving

"Therefore, as ye abound in every thing, in faith,
and utterance, and knowledge, and in all diligence, and in your love to us,
see that ye abound in this grace also." **(2 Corinthians 8:7)**

How do you give to the Lord? Do you just drop some money in the plate at church without much thinking about it? Or do you just write a check to God at the first of every month and pay Him like you pay all your other bills?

You need to think about that because how you give is a matter of deep concern to God. He's particular about how offerings are given. He won't receive just any old thing however you feel like giving it.

In Malachi, for example, God refused to receive Israel's offerings. They were bringing Him their defective animals, their blind calves, and the injured ones they couldn't do anything else with—and God said it offended Him. He told them, "You don't have any reverence or honor for Me, and I'm not going to accept your offering."

I'm sorry to say, but that kind of thing didn't die out after the Book of Malachi was written either. Many today don't have any reverence for God at offering time. People wait for the preacher to beat them over the head until they feel so guilty they have to reach down in their pocketbooks and get some money out.

But I want you to know, that's offensive to God. In fact, He spoke directly to a friend of mine about it. The statement He made to her so impressed me, I wrote it down word for word.

"It grieves Me when the Church takes offerings," He told her. "I said to worship Me. Don't take from the people, but let them bring their gifts and worship Me. Then they will see the fruits of their giving."

If you and I want God to be pleased with our offerings, we're going to have to do what the apostle Paul wrote about in 2 Corinthians 8:7. We're going to have to learn to "excel in this grace of giving." We're going to have to quit being casual about it and to learn to give with faith and reverence in worship.

Next time the offering plate is passed, don't just drop your gift carelessly in the plate as it goes by. Get serious. Determine to obey God. Worship Him with your money and be thankful. He'll do more than simply receive it, He'll open the windows of blessing for you.

SCRIPTURE READING: Malachi 1:1-14

Keep Quiet

"A fool uttereth all his mind: but a wise man keepeth it in till afterwards." **(Proverbs 29:11)**

One of the things that you and I as believers must learn if we want to be faithful servants in the kingdom of God is how to keep our mouths shut. Very few of us have mastered that skill.

When we get our backs up about something, we think we have to let everybody know about it. "I'm just going to give them a piece of my mind," we say.

Don't make that mistake. Nobody wants or needs a piece of your mind — and if you give it to them, you'll only end up alienating people and bringing harm to yourself. Learn, instead, to keep quiet.

This especially applies in the area of spiritual insight. When the Holy Spirit gives you discernment about a situation, don't go spreading it all over town. If you do, you'll come to the place where the Lord can't trust you with revelation and insight into things and situations.

I've seen that happen. I've known intercessors who've received revelations about someone's weaknesses or needs. They've been given insight into the problem in someone's life, so they could pray for that person. But, instead of keeping that information between themselves and God in prayer, they told others about it. As a result, they lost their effectiveness as an intercessor.

Don't let that happen to you. Develop the quiet art of the wise man, and the devil will find it increasingly difficult to harm your prayer life and ministry to others.

SCRIPTURE READING: James 3:1-13

The Father's Heart

"But when he was yet a great way off,
his father saw him, and had compassion, and ran,
and fell on his neck, and kissed him." **(Luke 15:20)**

How much love do you have for sinners?

That may sound like a strange question, but it's one I want you to think about today. All too often, once we get saved and get our lives cleaned up a little bit, we lose our compassion for those who are still lost. We look at the drunk stumbling down the street or the guy at the office who lies to the boss and tells dirty jokes and turn up our spiritual noses.

But if we ever truly understood the heart of our heavenly Father, we'd never do that again. Jesus told a story that can give us a glimpse of that heart. It's the story we call the prodigal son.

You've probably heard it many times, how the son rebelled and dishonored his father, and how the father, in spite of it all, received him home with joy when he repented. But there's one phrase in it I want to draw your attention to today. It's this one: "But when [the prodigal son] was yet a great way off, his father saw him."

That phrase gives such a moving glimpse of the heart of that loving father. It tells us that even before his boy had repented, even during those long days when he was up to his eyebrows in sin, that father was watching for him, longing for him to come home.

Every morning he scanned the horizon, hoping to see the silhouette of his returning son. And the last thing every night, he'd look again... straining his eyes in hope. His son was constantly on his mind, and his heart was always full of love for him. The kind of gut-wrenching love that, on the day his son came home, drove that father to run to him and kiss him.

That's the kind of heart our heavenly Father has for those who are lost. It's the kind of heart He had for you while you were still wandering in the world. It's the kind of heart that embraced you with open arms even when you were still covered with the grime of sin.

There's a whole world full of weary people out there who haven't yet found that embrace. They're more than just "sinners," they're our potential brothers...lost ones in desperate need of a loving heavenly Father. God forbid we should ever turn up our noses at them. May He help us instead to start bringing them home.

SCRIPTURE READING: John 8:1-11

Head for the Light

"We have also a more sure word of prophecy;
whereunto ye do well that ye take heed, as unto a light
that shineth in a dark place, until the day dawn, and
day star arise in your hearts." **(2 Peter 1:19)**

So many times when we need insight into a problem, we try to get it by focusing our attention on that problem. We study it. We ponder it. We examine it from every angle. But the apostle Peter gives us a different approach. He says we should take heed (or focus our attention) to the written Word of God until the answer to that problem dawns on us through the light of revelation.

We use the term "seeing the light" in the natural all of the time. We say, "Have you seen the light on that yet?" meaning, "Do you have insight into that situation?" Well, the entrance of God's Word into our hearts brings light (Ps. 119:130). It brings the insight we need.

Have you ever been in a dark room and tried to find your way out? Or lost outside in the night? What is the first thing you look for in these situations? Light!

It could be coming from under the door or shimmering from a lamp in a house far off. But either way, you head straight for it. You don't waste your time studying the darkness. You don't focus your attention on that. You fix your eyes on the light because you know its brightness will drive out the confusion of the darkness and orient you to your surroundings.

If you need insight on some problem or situation you're facing, pay attention to the Word. Head for the Light and the answer you need will dawn on you.

SCRIPTURE READING: John 1:1-9

Never Fall

"Study to shew thyself approved unto God,
a workman that needeth not to be ashamed." **(2 Timothy 2:15)**

A lot of people have been playing games when it comes to the Word. They claim to be faith people in public. But, in private, they never open the Bible at all. Then, when a time of trouble comes and they try to stand on the Word, they fall flat on their spiritual faces.

Well, the time for playing games is over. It's time for us to realize that real faith involves action. James 2:20 says faith without works [or corresponding action] is dead.

If you want the kind of faith that will keep you on your feet when others are falling around you, you need to take some action where the Word is concerned.

First, you need to *study*. You can study the Word in many ways. You can not only read it, you can dig deeply into it with concordances, Greek/Hebrew dictionaries, and other study guides. What's more, if you have a cassette player, you can walk around half the day listening to teaching tapes. It's only one way of study, but it is a powerful one.

The second thing you need to do is go where the Word is being preached.

When Romans 10:17 says "faith comes by hearing," it's talking about the preached Word.

Whenever I start feeling surrounded by problems and I'm having trouble hearing from God, I drop everything and find some place where I can hear the Word preached. I've received more answers from God that way than I can count. Even though the preacher may not have been preaching about anything even remotely connected with the issue I was struggling with, some word of scripture would suddenly start my thoughts in a certain direction. Then I'd realize, "That's the answer to that problem I've been dealing with for the past six weeks!"

Third, you need to start confessing the Word you've heard. Find the promise of God that covers your situation and then declare it out loud as if it had already come to pass in your life.

Get serious about the Word of God. Study it. Go hear it preached. Confess it. Become such a diligent workman that the devil himself will look at you with fear and say, "There's one believer who's not playing games anymore."

SCRIPTURE READING: 2 Peter 1:3-10

River of Revelation

"But be ye doers of the word,
and not hearers only, deceiving your own selves." **(James 1:22)**

Have you ever been in the position in the past where every time you opened the Bible you received a river of revelation? Does it seem lately that that river's run dry? If so, I strongly suggest that you backtrack to the last revelation God gave you. Back up and see if you acted on it, if you did what God showed you to do. If you didn't, start again, digging into that revelation and then putting it into action in your life. You'll soon find new revelations are beginning to flow.

You see, revelation is most prolific when you are acting on the Word. I've discovered that for myself again and again. The more I act on the Word, the more I see into it. That's why James 1:22 tells us to not only hear God's Word but to DO IT!

It may seem that the things God has revealed to you are very insignificant. They may not even make good sense to your natural mind. But do them anyway! If you had insight into the spirit realm, you'd see they're far more important than you think.

Open God's Word anew today. Come before Him with expectancy of a fresh revelation of the Scripture and commit to Him to follow it up with actions of obedience. Be a doer of God's revelations and not a hearer only and your river will *never* run dry.

SCRIPTURE READING: James 1:22-27

Take Your Place

"[For my determined purpose is] that I may know Him —
that I may progressively become more deeply and intimately
acquainted with Him, perceiving and recognizing and understanding
[the wonders of His Person] more strongly and more clearly. And that I
may in that same way come to know the power outflowing
from His resurrection." **(Philippians 3:10, AMP)**

The more you fellowship with God around His Word, the more you'll know the "power outflowing from His resurrection." You'll develop joy. You'll develop faith. You'll start developing God's own characteristics... just by fellowshipping with Him. You'll begin to understand who you really are in Jesus.

I remember one day I was reading the story of the woman with the issue of blood who touched the hem of Jesus' garment and was healed.

I'd read the story many times and pictured myself as almost everybody in the story...just experiencing how it would feel to be someone in the crowd or even the one who was healed.

Suddenly God spoke to my spirit and said, "Read that again and this time picture yourself as the one wearing the garment."

I was stunned. "Lord," I said, "how can I do that? I can't take Your place!"

"That's just what's wrong with the Body of Christ," He told me. "That's

the reason the world doesn't know anything about Jesus. You identify with everyone except Me. But I sent you to be MY witnesses, to imitate ME, to stand in MY place...not everybody else's!"

So, I read that story again. This time I pictured myself in the role of the one with the anointing of the Holy Ghost. Instead of crawling up to touch the hem of His garment, I was the one wearing the garment, freely giving what God had given me. After all, the Bible does say, "Clothe yourself with the Lord Jesus Christ."

Did you know who scares the devil most of all? Believers who've found out they can do that. Believers who, instead of begging for a little touch from Jesus, are letting His very life flow out to others.

Come on, give the devil a scare. Fellowship with your Father around the Word and start discovering who you really are today.

SCRIPTURE READING: Luke 8:40-48

Priorities of Prosperity

"No man can serve two masters:
for either he will hate the one, and love the other;
or else he will hold to the one, and despise the other.
Ye cannot serve God and mammon." **(Matthew 6:24)**

God isn't against your having money. He's against money having you. He's against your making it your priority and putting your trust in it instead of in Him.

Why? Because He knows money makes a lousy god. Its power is limited. It will only buy so much. It will only go so far.

If you need healing from an incurable disease, money won't help you at all. If your family is falling apart, money won't mend it. But if you'll seek God first, His prosperity will reach into every area of your life.

God is so generous that He desires you to have the best on this earth, just as you desire the best for your children. His plan is for you to have *all* of your needs met according to His riches in glory by Christ Jesus. Get in on that plan by keeping your priorities straight. Seek *Him* first and His righteousness.

Make pleasing God your number one priority. Set your eyes on Him above all else and all these things *will* be added unto you.

SCRIPTURE READING: Mark 10:17-27

Don't Forget the Joy

"Rejoice in the Lord alway: and again I say, Rejoice."

(Philippians 4:4)

Years ago, I decided I was going to walk by the Word of God. I told God that, as far as I was concerned, His Word was final and I'd confess it the rest of my life no matter what. That was the most important decision I've ever made.

Not too long after that, I decided that no matter what happened, whether I felt like it or not, I'd walk in love. Because the Bible clearly says "faith worketh by love." It won't work any other way.

Those two decisions—to operate by faith in the Word of God and to walk in love—are the two most important decisions I've ever made in my life.

Recently, though, God pointed out to me that there was something I'd been leaving out. The force of joy. He told me I have no right to walk by faith and love and just leave joy dormant in my spirit. It's too important. As He taught me about it, I soon came to realize that joy is an essential part of a life of victory. Without it, I might have an occasional triumph now and then, but I wouldn't be able to sustain them. They'd quickly slip away.

You see, joy is what gives you the strength (Neh. 8:10) to hold steady when the circumstances get rough. Joy gives you the ability to laugh in the devil's face when he starts trying to knock you off your faith. It gives you a kind of staying power that will make you a winner again and again.

So make a commitment to God that you're going to walk, not only in faith and in love but in joy as well. Make it a point to rejoice in the Lord *always*... and there won't be anything the devil can do or say to steal your victory from you!

SCRIPTURE READING: Psalm 84:1-7

Step Out of the Boat

"And Peter answered him and said, Lord,
if it be thou, bid me come unto thee on the water. And he said,
Come. And when Peter was come down out of the ship,
he walked on the water." **(Matthew 14:28,29)**

It's easy to be so afraid of making a mistake that you never get around to stepping out on faith. You can spend all your time wondering, "Is this faith? Or is it presumption? What if I exercise my faith for something and find out later I've missed God's will?"

Don't worry. God can handle any mistake you can make. I know because I've made plenty of them. When I did, I'd just go to the Lord and He'd tell me, "Stay on the Word, son. Together we'll overcome this thing." And we always did.

If you act on the Word out of the sincerity of your heart and you'll steadfastly stay with the Word, Jesus will never let you down...no matter how many dumb mistakes you make. He proved that the night Peter jumped out of the boat in the middle of the lake.

Have you ever stopped to think about that incident? Peter hadn't been praying or seeking God's will before he did that. On impulse he just blurted out, "Lord, if it's You bid me come."

What was Jesus supposed to say? He couldn't very well say, "It's not Me." I suppose He could have said, "Wait a minute now. You don't have the faith to get out here. You'd better stay in that boat or you're going to drown for sure."

But He didn't say that to Peter—and He won't say it to you. If you want to get out and walk by faith, He'll get out there with you and pick you up when you start sinking. He'll walk you back to the boat if He has to.

It's better to risk being presumptuous than to waste your life in the boat of unbelief! If you have to, just dive into the water and say, "God, help me!"

Don't let fear keep you from taking that step of faith. Come on, get out of the boat today!

SCRIPTURE READING: Matthew 14:22-33

Walk in the Light You Have

"But continue thou in the things which thou hast learned
and hast been assured of, knowing of whom thou hast learned them."

(2 Timothy 3:14)

If you're born again and have the Word of God in your heart, you can live in victory. You may not have all the answers. There may be a great many spiritual things you don't understand. But it's not those things that are most likely to destroy you. It's the things you know to do—but *don't*—that usually make you fall.

Just think about walking at night down a dark, unfamiliar path in the middle of a jungle. The guide up ahead has a flashlight to keep you on the right path. But then, you just decide to wander off into the darkness by yourself. What do you think will happen to you? You'll probably stumble and fall. Very likely, you'll get hurt.

That's exactly the same thing that can happen in your walk with the Lord. He knows what's ahead and He shines just enough light for you to take one step at a time. You have to continue walking in that light in order to get where you're going.

You may not know why He's leading you a certain way. You may not understand all the things involved. But God will make up for your ignorance by the Holy Spirit. He'll see to it that you have victory if you continue in what you know.

It's good to keep studying. It's good to keep learning. But, remember, it's not the great revelation you haven't yet had that will cause you the most trouble. It's failing to walk in the ones God has already given you. So be faithful in those things. Continue in them day after day after day. You'll make it through just fine!

SCRIPTURE READING: 2 Peter 1:2-11

He'll Be Listening

"And this is the confidence that we have in him,
that, if we ask any thing according to his will, he heareth us:
And if we know that he hear us, whatsoever we ask, we know
that we have the petitions that we desired of him."

(1 John 5:14,15)

Have you ever been in prayer and suddenly had the disturbing sensation that God simply isn't listening?

It's happened to all of us. But few of us know just what to do about it. We just limp along praying the same old prayers, half-hoping those prayers are heard and half-suspecting they're not.

Today I want to show you how to resolve that dilemma once and for all. But let me warn you, I'm not going to slap you on the back and assure you God will listen to any old doubtful, self-centered thing you say to Him. He won't. He's only promised to listen to prayers that are prayed *according to His will*. The apostle John says when you pray like that, you'll *know* that you have the "petitions" you desire of Him.

The word *petition* is defined as "a formal written request addressed to a sovereign superior of a particular right or grace," and that's exactly what you need when you're praying about something serious.

How do you put together a solid petition, one that's in line with the will of God?

First, you'll have to roll up your sleeves and dig into the written Word. Find scriptures that apply to your situation and make those the foundation for your petition.

Then get on your knees and consult with the Holy Spirit. Let Him help you develop your petition in detail. The best way to do that is to spend time praying in other tongues. (See Romans 8:26,27.) Expect God to reveal things from His heart to yours. He wants you to know His will. So, while you're praying, listen!

Last of all, write it down. Make a formal written request by writing down every scripture you found. Also, as you're listening to the Holy Spirit for the details, write down the impressions and ideas He gives you.

Take your time. Let the Spirit develop your prayer. Let the truth He reveals to you settle in and begin to work in you. Get your petition firmly in mind, then when you're ready, present it to God.

Believe me, He'll be listening.

SCRIPTURE READING: 1 John 5:1-15

Don't Waste Time Wondering

"Wherefore be ye not unwise, but understanding
what the will of the Lord is." **(Ephesians 5:17)**

So many believers wring their hands and worry about whether or not they're praying according to God's will. "Oh, dear me," they say, "I certainly can't expect God to do something for me that's outside His will." And they're absolutely right.

But they don't need to waste time standing around looking puzzled. They need to grab their Bibles and *find out* what the will of God is.

God has made some very specific promises in His Word and it's His will to fulfill every one of them in your life. In fact, those promises are divinely guaranteed by a contract that's been signed in the blood of Jesus.

Think of it this way. Your Bible is the last will and testament of Jesus Christ. It is a record of your inheritance. Everything that belongs to you has been written down in that book and the smartest thing you can do is to find out what is in it. Don't leave it lying on the coffee table and hit the floor crying, "Oh, God! Oh, God! I'm searching for the truth."

Pick your Bible up off the coffee table and find out what belongs to you! Find out how you need to change to get in line with God's will.

Most people don't do that. They try to change God instead. They'll go on and on trying to convince God just how badly they hurt or how poor they are. They'll beg and plead and wheedle, all the while acting as though they had to somehow change God's mind about the situation. Those folks are in for a long wait.

God is *never* going to change. The Bible says He's the same yesterday, today, and forever. His will is too. So don't waste your time wondering if your prayers are in line with it. Get the Book and base your prayers on it. Then you can rest assured the answer is on the way!

SCRIPTURE READING: Proverbs 2:1-12

Free From the Curse

"Christ hath redeemed us from the curse of the law,
being made a curse for us: for it is written, Cursed is every one
that hangeth on a tree." **(Galatians 3:13)**

You know the story. Satan came to Adam's wife in the form of a serpent and deceived her into disobeying God. Adam, although he was not deceived, followed suit.

When Satan came into the Garden that day, he didn't have any power at all. He had to come in like a sneak, not even talking to Adam directly but talking to his wife.

Now Adam was standing there, and he should have kicked him out right then. But he didn't. Instead, he set aside the command God had given him and did what Satan told him to do instead...and when he did that, he made Satan his lord.

In bowing his knee to Satan, he gave Satan the authority that God had given him. He made Satan the illegitimate ruler of the earth. Immediately things changed. Through one man's trespass, death passed to all men (Rom. 5:12).

The earth and everything in it was suddenly cursed.

"Okay," you say, "are we to live under this curse for the rest of our lives? Wasn't there anything God could do?"

He could and He did! He sent Jesus. Through Jesus, He set us free from the curse (Gal. 3:13).

The moment you made Jesus Christ Lord of your life, you were delivered from the lordship of Satan. You were redeemed from the curse. I didn't say the curse wasn't out there anymore. It is! You can see it all around you. But now you have a choice. You have authority over it in the name of Jesus, so you can stand against it.

God's done everything that love can do. He sent Jesus to redeem you from the curse. The rest is up to you. Now you must appropriate what has already been done for you.

SCRIPTURE READING: Romans 5:12-21

Possess Your Promised Land

"When ye are passed over Jordan into the land of Canaan;
Then ye shall drive out all the inhabitants of the land from before you...
and dwell therein: for I have given you the land to possess it."

(Numbers 33:51-53)

God has given you a Promised Land. It's a place flowing with milk and honey, where your every need can be met. A place where you can keep sin underfoot as you rule and reign with Christ. A place where no weapon formed against you will prosper. A place where you are seated with Christ in heavenly places, far above principalities and powers—far from oppression.

As you study the Word of God, you'll find that's an accurate description of the kind of victory you should be experiencing in Christ—not in the sweet by-and-by—but right here, right now.

You may say, "Yes, that sounds nice in theory, but I'm dealing with reality here. The rent is due, and all I see is sickness, oppression, and fear. This doesn't look like much of a Promised Land to me."

That's because you're still letting the devil live there! He's not just going to pack up and go home, you know, just because God has promised you victory. You have to kick him out.

But don't let that scare you. God has given you the power to do it.

Remember what Jesus said? He said, "Behold, I give unto you power to tread on serpents and scorpions, and over all the power of the enemy: and nothing shall by any means hurt you" (Luke 10:19).

What's more, the devil is totally unarmed! Colossians 2:15 says, "[God] disarmed the principalities and powers ranged against us and made a bold display and public example of them, in triumphing over them in...[the cross]" (AMP). You have absolutely no reason to cower before the devil. Jesus defeated and disarmed him through His death, burial, and resurrection. The devil can't defeat you unless you let him. All he can do is make empty threats.

But beware! Empty threats can stop you cold if you believe them. So don't. Believe the Word of God instead. Use the Word and the name of Jesus to drive the devil out of every last detail of your life.

Don't let him dwell in your territory. Force him to pack up and go home. Start possessing your Promised Land!

SCRIPTURE READING: Mark 16:17,18; James 5:7-9

Silence the Critics

"For so is the will of God, that with well doing
ye may put to silence the ignorance of foolish men." **(1 Peter 2:15)**

I know from personal experience that when people start to criticize you and persecute you because you live by faith, your natural human response is to want to strike back. You want to start dishing out a little criticism of your own. "Maybe if they get a taste of their own medicine, they'll shut their mouths," you think.

But you know what? They won't. Your words will just add fuel to their fire and they'll criticize you harder and louder than they did before.

According to the Word of God, however, there *is* a way to silence them. Not by arguing with them. Not by defending yourself. But by keeping quiet and continuing to do the good works God has called you to do.

Jesus was highly criticized by the religious establishment of His day. But He never fought back. Instead, Acts 10:38 says He simply went about doing good.

When people start riding you about living the faith life, be like Jesus and just keep on blessing people. Keep on praying for folks who are oppressed by the devil and get them delivered. Keep on laying hands on the sick and get them healed. Keep on doing what God has called you to do.

That will aggravate the devil because his primary purpose is to make you ineffective for the kingdom of God. He wants you to get wrapped up in the criticism. He wants to distract you, to get your mind off the job God has given you. He really wants you to quit.

Don't do it! Instead, follow the instructions in 2 Timothy 3:14 and "continue thou in the things which thou hast learned and hast been assured of." Silence the ignorant criticisms of men by continuing to do good and by continuing to live by faith. And when all their foolish words have faded away, you'll still be standing strong.

SCRIPTURE READING: Luke 23:1-9

The Bridegroom Cometh

"And at midnight there was a cry made,
Behold, the bridegroom cometh; go ye out to meet him." **(Matthew 25:6)**

The Spirit of God is delivering a vital message to you today: *Get ready for Jesus' return!* It's an old message. But there's a fresh urgency to it. An urgency you can't afford to ignore.

Some believers make the mistake of saying, "Oh well, I just don't think we're supposed to know about the Second Coming. It's supposed to come upon us like a thief in the night!"

But they're wrong. The Word of God says that as children of light we shouldn't be taken by surprise. We should be so keen in the Spirit that even though we don't know the day or the hour, we should sense that the season of Jesus' return has come.

First Corinthians 2:10 tells us that God reveals His plans to us through His Spirit. I suspect that those who are walking in the Spirit on the day the Lord comes again will actually begin to anticipate that something is about to happen.

Be like the five wise virgins in Matthew 25 who were prepared when the bridegroom's arrival was announced. Stay full of the oil of the Holy Spirit and with your light shining!

Don't get caught sleeping when Jesus returns. Wake up now to the Holy Spirit. Let Him put you on the inside track and get you ready for your Lord. Because just as Jesus foretold, there is a cry going out at midnight. The Spirit of the Lord is announcing His return.

Can you hear it in your spirit? Can you sense the Lord saying, "Get up and come out to meet Me. Fellowship with Me. Get in the light now, and at that crucial hour, you'll be on the inside of My plans."

Obey Him quickly. For, behold, the bridegroom cometh!

SCRIPTURE READING: Matthew 25:1-13

Sure to Win in Him

"Wherefore remember, that...at that time ye were
without Christ...having no hope, and without God in the world:
But now *in Christ Jesus* ye who sometimes were far off are
made nigh by the blood of Christ." **(Ephesians 2:11-13)**

Have you ever really thought about what it truly means to be *in Christ Jesus*? Have you ever gotten a clear revelation of that? Once you do, it will revolutionize your life.

You see, it's *in Him* that we're raised up from our sins. It's *in Him* that we're made to sit in heavenly places so that God can show us the exceeding riches of His grace. It's *in Him* that we're made the righteousness of God!

If you want that revelation to explode in you, start searching out scriptures that refer to being *in Christ*. Watch for the words *in Him, with Him, through Him,* or *in Whom.* Mark those and meditate on them until the truth of them gets down into your spirit man. They'll give you some powerful ammunition against the attacks of Satan.

When he tries to tell you, for instance, that you're just a sinner and God doesn't want to be bothered with your problems, you'll know he is lying. You'll be able to answer him boldly and say, "Thank God, I *was* a sinner, but now I'm the righteousness of God *in Christ* Jesus. I've been raised up to sit with Him in heavenly places. Now I'm *in Him* and you can't touch me at all!"

Be prepared the next time Satan comes at you with doubt, unbelief, and condemnation. Be ready to fight back with the scriptures about who you are in Jesus. You're sure to win once you truly know you're *in Him!*

SCRIPTURE READING: Ephesians 1:1-14

Awake to Righteousness

"Awake to righteousness, and sin not." **(1 Corinthians 15:34)**

When your alarm clock goes off tomorrow morning, don't just wake up to another day. Do what the Word says to do and "awake to righteousness!" Reawaken yourself to the glorious fact that you've been made the righteousness of God in Christ Jesus and given right-standing with Almighty God.

Why? Because tomorrow—and every other day of your life on this earth—Satan is going to try to convince you that you don't have any right to the things of God. He's going to try to bring you into bondage again to sin in order to control your life. But he won't be able to do it if you'll reawaken yourself every day to who you really are in Jesus.

Here's a prayerful confession to help that revelation come alive in you:

"Father, I confess anew Jesus Christ as my Lord and Savior today. Lord, You are the head of my life. I completely yield myself to You. My will is now Your will. My plans are now Your plans.

"As a new creation in Christ Jesus, I accept the gift of righteousness and all that gift includes: health, prosperity, peace, joy, and life abundant. I put aside every weight and the sin that so easily besets me. I now look unto Jesus, the Author and Finisher of my faith.

"According to Your Word, I can now reign in this life as a king. The power of sin and death in my life has been overcome. No longer am I ruled by the forces of evil but by the God above all gods. I am more than a conqueror through Him who loves me.

"I determine today to walk consciously of my right-standing with You, Lord, and with every step to draw closer and closer to You. Thank You for the gift of righteousness. Because of that gift, I can do all things through Christ Jesus who strengthens me.

"In Jesus' name. Amen!"

SCRIPTURE READING: Colossians 2:9-15

Discover What the Name Can Do

"Wherefore God also hath highly exalted him, and
given him a name which is above every name: That at the name
of Jesus every knee should bow, of things in heaven, and things in earth,
and things under the earth." **(Philippians 2:9,10)**

Once you make up your mind to keep the commands of Jesus and begin to allow the Word to dwell in you richly, the name of Jesus will become far more powerful to you. It will become more than just a word. It will become a force that will cause every circumstance and every demon that tries to stand in your way to bow its knee to your command.

I tell you, the name of Jesus works. There is far greater power in it than any of us have yet realized.

My faith is so set on the authority of the name of Jesus that there are times I just say, "In the name" and the power of God comes on the scene.

In fact, I've discovered that the name of Jesus—just the name alone—is effective when spoken by a Word-abiding believer. Revelation 19:13 says the name of Jesus is the Word of God! So, when an evil spirit is trying to bring sickness, poverty, depression, or any other garbage into my household, I don't have to quote every scripture I know to stop him. I can just point my finger at him and say, "Jesus!" That's like throwing the whole Word of God in his face at one time!

Discover for yourself what the exalted Name can do. Begin to speak it with confidence and authority. There is power in the name of Jesus.

SCRIPTURE READING: Acts 3:1-16

God Wants You Well

"If thou wilt diligently hearken to the voice
of the Lord thy God, and wilt do that which is right
in his sight, and wilt give ear to his commandments, and keep
all his statutes, I will put none of these diseases upon thee,
which I have brought upon the Egyptians: for I am
the Lord that healeth thee." **(Exodus 15:26)**

Has the devil ever tried to put you under condemnation by telling you that it's contrary to the principles of faith to use doctors and medicine when you need healing? If so, here are some encouraging words that I believe will help you put your heart at rest.

It *is* God's will to heal you. That's the first and most important thing for you to understand. If your faith is strong and you can believe the Word without wavering (regardless of what circumstances or symptoms come against you), then you'll be able to receive that healing by faith alone.

But that kind of faith takes more than just hearing a few sermons about healing. It takes a deep personal revelation of God's healing power. So, if you haven't yet developed that kind of faith, the doctor is your best friend.

If you're not certain whether your faith is strong enough or whether you need a doctor's help, follow the instructions of the apostle Paul (Col. 3:15) and let peace be your umpire.

If fear rises up within you when you think about doing without medical help, then go to a doctor. And go in faith! On the other hand, if you have a sure confidence within you that healing is yours strictly by faith, let your faith do its work and receive your healing directly. Whether or not you go to the doctor is not the issue. It is what you do with your faith.

Either way, you can rejoice knowing God is working with you, meeting you at the level of your faith. Thank God for your healing—however it comes!—and do not let Satan put you under condemnation. It is none of his business!

SCRIPTURE READING: Deuteronomy 7:8-15

Receive the Man of God

"Verily, verily, I say unto you, He that receiveth whomsoever I send receiveth me; and he that receiveth me receiveth him that sent me." **(John 13:20)**

I can't tell you how many born-again, Holy Ghost-filled Christians pick their pastor apart on Saturday night and then expect him to pray the prayer of faith for them Sunday morning! They'll constantly make critical comments about the evangelists and preachers that God has sent to minister to them and then wonder why the rain of the Spirit has all but dried up in their churches.

Most of those folks would never dream of criticizing the ministry of Jesus. Yet, according to the Word of God, that's precisely what they're doing. You see, Jesus said, "He that receiveth *whomsoever I send receiveth me.*"

I know ministers fail sometimes. I know they make mistakes. Jesus knew they would too. But, even so, He said, "If you receive them, you receive Me."

If you think some preacher's doctrine is wrong, then pray for him. Stop sitting under his ministry if necessary. But the scripture says, "Who are you to judge someone else's servant? To his own master he stands or falls. And he will stand, for the Lord is able to make him stand" (Rom. 14:4, NIV).

The ministers of the gospel are not your servants, they're God's servants. Whether they're right or whether they're wrong, love them and respect them if for no other reason than to honor the One who sent them.

Learn to receive the minister of God that Jesus sends to *you* with the same respect and the same honor that you would give Jesus Himself. You'll open the door for great spiritual power to be released. You'll clear the way for God to meet your needs. The anointing of God will be released through the man of God to you.

Refuse to let criticism hold back the anointing of the Holy Spirit. Then get ready to be blessed because, I guarantee, He won't hold out on you.

SCRIPTURE READING: Numbers 12:1-16

Don't Hesitate

"He that wavereth is like a wave of the sea
driven with the wind and tossed. For let not that man think
that he shall receive any thing of the Lord. A double minded man
is unstable in all his ways." **(James 1:6-8)**

W hat happens when you hesitate to do something God has told you to do? Your adversary takes the first step. The devil gets the jump on you.

If you want to live by faith, hesitation is one of the most hazardous habits you could ever have. It comes from being indecisive. The Bible says a man like that is "unstable and unreliable and uncertain about everything he thinks, feels, decides'" (AMP).

If you are double-minded, the decisions you make are split. You try to live by faith and protect your fear at the same time. You make faith statements like "I believe God is going to heal me." Then your fear whispers, "But I wouldn't want to say I'm well just yet." You're so busy going back and forth between faith and fear, you can't make any progress at all.

Kick the habit of hesitation today. Make a solid decision to trust in and act on the Word of God. Settle it forever. Resolve never to entertain doubts again. When doubt comes to your mind, cast it out quickly.

When God speaks, don't waste a moment. Step right out in faith. That way, you can always keep the devil a step behind you!

SCRIPTURE READING: James 1:1-8

Tell the Good News

"God was in Christ, reconciling the world unto himself,
not imputing their trespasses unto them; and hath committed
unto us the word of reconciliation." **(2 Corinthians 5:19)**

Very few unsaved people today have ever really heard the "Good News." Why? Because too many Christians are busy telling the world God is mad at them. And telling them that they're terrible and wrong. Some call that "good news," but it's not, and it's not what God has commissioned us to share.

He's given us the "word of reconciliation"!

He's sent us to tell the news that God has restored harmony and fellowship between Himself and men. *All* men. Not just believers. Not just the people in your church, but everyone!

That's right. The worst old reprobate sinner in the world is every bit as reconciled to God as you are. Look at Romans 5:10 and you'll see what I mean. It says that "when we were enemies, we were reconciled to God by the death of his Son."

Reconciled. That word is past tense. God has already restored fellowship between Himself and the world. He did it when there was not one person on earth except Jesus who believed in the new birth. He did it when the entire world was lying in sin.

Through the death and resurrection of Jesus, God has cleansed and forgiven and restored to Himself every man, woman, and child on the face of this earth. All any of us have to do now is receive it.

That's the good word God has given us. That's the word we need to share with those who are lost. If we'll do it, I can almost guarantee you, they won't stay lost very long.

SCRIPTURE READING: 2 Corinthians 5:10-21

Live in Power

"Therefore we are buried with him by baptism into death:
that like as Christ was raised up from the dead by the glory of the Father,
even so we also should walk in newness of life." **(Romans 6:4)**

As a believer, you actually have residing in you the same new life God gave Jesus when He raised Him up from the dead. The old sinner you once were has died. You've become a new creation on the inside.

You are full of the resurrection life of God!

But sin, disobedience, and living a selfish, carnal life will keep that resurrection life from flowing out. Sin will separate you from the power of God, even though you're born again. Resurrection life will lay dormant in you if you walk in sin.

You can't overcome sin by trying to stop sinning, however. You overcome it by walking after the new life God has put within you. By spending time in the Word and in prayer. As you do that, the Spirit of God will strengthen you and enable you to put that sin under your feet.

Remember, though, the Holy Spirit will not subdue those old fleshly habits of yours on His own. He'll wait on you to take the initiative. Then He will strengthen you to follow through with *your* decision. He will teach you how to walk in the new life that is on the inside of you.

Take the first step today by asking for His help. Say, "Lord, I desire to experience the power to live by this new life every day. By a decision of my heart, I put down the dictates of sin. I declare myself dead to it. In Jesus' name, I will spend time in prayer and in the Word today. As I do, I believe I'll receive a Holy Ghost refreshing in my life. I believe I'll begin to live out the resurrection power that You've placed in me!"

SCRIPTURE READING: Romans 7:1-6

The Great Escape

"Trust in the Lord with all thine heart;
and lean not unto thine own understanding. In all thy ways
acknowledge him, and he shall direct thy paths." **(Proverbs 3:5,6)**

Once you start stepping out in faith and walking in the Spirit, the devil will see to it that you have ample opportunity to fall flat on your spiritual face. He'll try to get you into some jams where there appears to be no way out.

But take it from me as one who's been there, if you'll look to God and trust His wisdom instead of your own, He'll always show you a way of escape (1 Cor. 10:13). Not only that, but He'll do it in such a way that He'll get the glory and you'll have the last laugh on the devil.

I remember one particular Wednesday night in Wichita Falls, Texas, where I was faced with just such a situation. I was preaching on the reality of the righteousness of God, and the anointing was really strong. Just as my message reached its climactic moment, a woman in the audience suddenly burst forth in tongues. I told her to stop three times, but she only continued to grow louder. By the time she hushed, the anointing had gone and the message was forgotten. So I looked at that woman sternly and began to correct her for being out of order.

Then a man sitting next to her spoke up and said, "Brother Copeland, she is stone deaf. She can't hear a word you're saying."

At that point, I had no idea what to do. Not only had my sermon been shattered, but the whole congregation was mad at me for getting onto that poor deaf woman. (I found out later the man next to her used her to disrupt services and run preachers out of town. When the service reached a high point, he'd punch her and tell her it was her turn to prophesy.)

So I just stopped a moment and got quiet and waited for the Lord to tell me what to do. Sure enough, He told me. He said, "Call her up and lay hands on her and I'll open her ears."

Talk about a turnaround! When God healed that woman's ears, He turned that disaster into one of the most powerfully anointed meetings I'd ever had. Everybody was blessed!

Next time the devil tries to back you in a corner, get quiet. Ask God to show you the way of escape. He'll bring you out in victory every time.

SCRIPTURE READING: Acts 14:8-22

Begin to Praise

"Rejoice in the Lord, O you [uncompromisingly] righteous
[you upright, in right standing with God]; for praise is becoming and
appropriate for those who are upright in heart." **(Psalm 33:1, AMP)**

Praise. According to the Word of God, that's the most appropriate, becoming thing that you as a believer can do.

Let me warn you though, God's idea of "appropriate" praise and your idea of appropriate praise may well be two very different things. The praise He calls for is joyous and uninhibited. And, at times, it's just plain loud!

If you don't believe it, look in the Bible and see the kind of praise that goes on in heaven. Read Isaiah 6 and find out how they act in the throne room. The seraphim shout in there until the doorposts shake! And when they do, the glory of the Lord fills the house.

When you get to heaven, you're going to be praising like that too. You're going to be leaping and praising God with every part of your being. But don't wait until then to start. Begin now.

Decide today that instead of praising God the way *you* like, you are going to start doing it the way *He* likes. Begin to release those praises joyously, uninhibitedly. Don't wait until you get to heaven to praise God with all your being. Do it now. He deserves it!

SCRIPTURE READING: Isaiah 6:1-8

Free From Fear

"For God hath not given us the spirit of fear;
but of power, and of love, and of a sound mind." **(2 Timothy 1:7)**

What would you think if I told you that you could live without fear? Would you believe me if I said that despite what you saw on the news tonight, you could be perfectly at peace? Impossible? Unrealistic? No!

You see, fear isn't just a reaction to external circumstances. It's a spiritual force. It begins inside of you. And it is totally destructive. In fact, fear is Satan's primary weapon. He moves in response to fear, the way God moves in response to faith. He challenges the promises of God with it.

An excellent example of this is found in the fourteenth chapter of Matthew's Gospel when Jesus invited Peter to come to Him on the water. "But when he [Peter] saw the wind boisterous, he was afraid; and beginning to sink, he cried, saying, Lord, save me" (verse 30).

What enabled Peter to walk on the water? His faith in the word of Jesus.

What caused Peter to sink? He saw the wind boisterous and he was afraid. It wasn't the wind that defeated him, it was his fear of it! He looked at his circumstances, gave in to the fear, and the result was defeat. If Peter had kept his focus on Jesus, his faith would never have wavered. All the blustering and blowing in the world couldn't have drawn him off course.

Faith is developed by meditating on God's Word. Fear is developed by meditating on Satan's lies. Such fearful meditation is called "worrying." Don't do it!

The Word of God is the sword of the Spirit. Use it to fight Satan every time he comes against you. Hold up your shield of faith and quench all of his fiery darts. Speak words of faith and fear will depart.

SCRIPTURE READING: Psalm 27

Strength Made Perfect

"And he said unto me, My grace is sufficient for thee: for my strength
is made perfect in weakness. Most gladly therefore will I rather glory in my
infirmities, that the power of Christ may rest upon me." **(2 Corinthians 12:9)**

When you run into an impossible situation, a situation you simply don't have the strength or the ability to handle, are you often tempted to simply give up and accept defeat? Don't! Instead shout, "Glory!" because the Word says God's strength is about to be made perfect in you.

The word translated "strength" in this scripture is *dunamis.* It means "God's miracle-working power." Just think about that. When your human strength ends, God has promised that His miraculous power will bring you through!

If you'll look in the Book of Acts, you can see that promise in action. There, in the fourteenth chapter, the scriptures say that the apostle Paul was stoned by a group of Jews, taken out of the city, and left for dead. Paul's human strength had ended. He was absolutely powerless.

But the disciples gathered around him and prayed and the Lord raised him up, and he went on his way. In other words, when Paul didn't have enough human strength to overcome, God's miracle-working power was sufficient for him. It enabled him to be an overcomer in spite of his weakness!

So, if you are facing a crisis today—

If you're sick and medicine has failed you—

If your finances are out of control—

If your family is falling apart—

If bad habits have you hopelessly bound—

If you've done absolutely all you know to do and you still haven't gotten results—

Then rejoice! *For when human strength ends, the power of God excels!*

Only believe!

God's grace is sufficient for you!

SCRIPTURE READING: Acts 14:1-22

Trust Him to Deliver You

"A thousand shall fall at thy side, and ten thousand at
thy right hand; but it shall not come nigh thee. There shall no evil
befall thee, neither shall any plague come nigh thy dwelling."

(Psalm 91:7,10)

Naturally speaking, this is a terrifying world we're living in today. A world that staggers from one disaster to another. Almost daily we hear about wars, about the dangers of nuclear weapons and chemical warfare, about oil spills and earthquakes and floods, about diseases on the rise, and crime sweeping through our cities.

But in the midst of it all, God is promising to be a refuge and a fortress to those who will trust and dwell in Him.

"But Gloria," you might say, "He made that promise thousands of years ago when things weren't in as desperate shape as they are today!"

That may be so, but you know what? That promise is right up to date. It was made for our generation. Just think about it. Back when Psalm 91 was written, man hadn't even invented weapons that could destroy ten thousand people at once. We're the generation that did that. So when He said, "No evil will befall you," He was including us.

No evil will befall you. My, what a statement! You need to catch hold of it and believe it today. Believe that God wants to be God in your life. He wants to be your protection. He wants to be

your security. He wants to be the first name you call when trouble comes your way. He wants to be the One that you trust in and look to, to keep you safe. And if you'll do that, He'll never, never let you down.

He can handle all the dangers that surround you. I don't care how bad they are, He can handle them! He proved that with Shadrach, Meshach, and Abednego. They were bound and thrown into a fiery furnace that was so hot that the men who threw them in were killed by the heat. Now you can't get in any more trouble than that. But God brought them through and when they came out, they didn't even smell like smoke. Hallelujah!

So, no matter how terrifying things around you seem to get, trust God. He'll always be faithful. He'll never be out doing something else when you need help. He'll be right there to deliver you from any problem, any catastrophe, any kind of devastation.

Let Him prove in your life what He proved in the lives of Shadrach, Meshach, and Abednego: No other can deliver like Him!

SCRIPTURE READING: Daniel 3

High Priest of Your Confession

"Wherefore, holy brethren, partakers of
the heavenly calling, consider the Apostle and High Priest of our profession
[or confession], Christ Jesus." **(Hebrews 3:1)**

Very few believers today understand the mystery of the apostleship and priesthood of Jesus. We think that an apostle is some kind of supersaint. But "apostle" actually means "sent one." So, Jesus has been sent from God to do something for us.

He's been sent to serve as our High Priest. Again, many believers don't have the first idea what a high priest does. They picture a person walking around in strange clothes performing religious rituals.

In reality, a high priest is much more than that. He is one who is authorized to administer, to execute, to implement, and to carry into effect. Now, you may wonder what it is that Jesus is authorized to administer, execute, or carry out on your behalf. Hebrews 3:1 says that Jesus is the High Priest of our confession. He's been sent to put into effect, to execute, to carry out the words that you say.

But, chances are, you've been speaking what you feel, instead of speaking words of faith. If, for example, you're speaking sickness, what's He going to do with that? He's not High Priest over sickness. He can't execute that. If you're saying, "I'm so weak, I'm so tired," He can't carry that out. The Bible says, "Let the weak say, I am strong!" The minute you say that, Jesus can administer STRENGTH.

Jesus is not going to administer sickness or disease or poverty or sin. He's defeated all that. He is High Priest over deliverance and righteousness and freedom.

Consider that. Then as you come before Jesus, don't speak words of defeat. Speak words He can implement— words of victory. That's what He's been ordained by God to bring to pass in your life.

SCRIPTURE READING: Hebrews 7:20-28

Put the Rumor to Rest

"And Moses stretched forth his hand toward heaven; and there was a thick darkness in all the land of Egypt...but all the children of Israel had light in their dwellings." **(Exodus 10:22,23)**

Years ago Satan started a rumor. He told a few Christians that they had to live like the world, sharing all the same misfortune, defeats, poverty, and failure with those around them. Well, the word spread. You may have heard the rumor yourself. But I am telling you right now that it is a crafty lie.

The Word of God says in Psalm 91, verse 10, that evil can't even come near your house if you are abiding in Him.

In the gospel of John, chapter 16, Jesus Himself says He has deprived the world of power to harm you. And Exodus 10:23 says that when thick darkness surrounded the Egyptians, the children of Israel had light in their dwellings.

By these and other scriptures, you can see that God never intended you to experience all of the junk that the world suffers. He's always wanted His children to live above it, to stand out as light in a dark world.

In the Old Testament, God's fame was established because of the miracles He had worked for His children.

That same thing should be true today with you and me. We should be glorifying God by the miraculously victorious lives we live. People should be coming up to us and saying things like, "I've heard how God healed you." Or, "I've heard how your children were delivered from drugs," or, "God has really brought you out of a financial crisis."

Can you see now why Satan would spread a rumor that would make you believe you have to suffer with the world instead of live as victor over it? He doesn't want people running after you asking where you get your power, your peace, and your health or prosperity.

But that's exactly what God wants to happen. So put the Word of God to work and dare to receive the blessings He has promised to you. Let the light of God's power in your life put the devil's dark rumors to rest!

SCRIPTURE READING: Philippians 2:1-16

Addicted to the Word

"Ye know the house of Stephanas...and that they have
addicted themselves to the ministry of the saints." **(1 Corinthians 16:15)**

I want you to begin to develop an addiction today—an addiction to the Word of God. That may sound odd to you, especially if you don't have much of an interest in the Word right now. But, believe me, it's possible. I've done it myself and I've seen others do it, time and again.

All you have to do is make a decision to give yourself to it. To focus your time and attention on it. The more you give yourself to it, the more your desire for it will grow. Eventually, it will consume your thinking.

Surprised? You shouldn't be. That happens with anything you totally give yourself to. It happens, for example, with people who give themselves to pornography. As they focus their attention on it, the spirit behind it moves in on their consciousness and eventually draws them from mental activity on into physical activity. Finally, they come to a place where they can't be satisfied. They can't get enough.

That same principle works on the positive side when you begin to give yourself to God's Word. You can give yourself to it to the point where it totally consumes your mental and physical life. The more of it you get, the more you want. The Spirit behind the Word, the Holy Spirit, will draw you and lead you closer to Jesus than you ever imagined possible.

I've never yet met anybody walking in faith and power who at sometime hadn't developed that kind of addiction by giving themselves totally to the Word for an extended time. I don't mean just a few minutes here and there either. I'm talking about some serious time.

So determine to do that. Determine to become a "Word addict." Once you do, you'll never be willing to live without it again.

SCRIPTURE READING: Hebrews 4:1-12

Grace is Enough

"And lest I should be exalted above measure through the abundance of the revelations, there was given to me a thorn in the flesh, the messenger of Satan to buffet me." (2 Corinthians 12:7)

The devil has used the traditional teaching of Paul's thorn in the flesh to talk believers out of the blessings of God for years, to convince us to settle for everything from sickness to sin—and to do it of our own free will.

It is perhaps the most destructive and the most widely accepted misinterpretation of scripture that exists in the Body of Christ today. I've gone into countries to preach to people who hardly had any knowledge of the Word at all and still I have found that somehow they'd been taught about Paul's thorn.

And most of them have been taught wrongly.

Tradition says that God gave Paul the thorn in the flesh. What's more, tradition makes the "thorn" into some great mystery. But the scripture doesn't say that at all!

It says that the thorn in the flesh was a messenger of Satan. Not God—Satan! The thorn was quite literally just what Paul says it was—a "messenger sent from Satan."

You see, everywhere Paul went, he preached the gospel and every time he preached, he destroyed a little more of Satan's kingdom. So, Satan sent a messenger, an evil spirit, to stop him.

When Paul sought the Lord concerning this thorn (look at 2 Corinthians 12:8-10), God didn't answer Paul in the negative. God said, "My grace (or, My favor) is enough. It is sufficient for you. For My strength is made perfect in your weakness (inability to produce results)" (*W.E. Vine's Expository Dictionary*).

In other words, when Paul didn't have enough human strength to overcome, God's miracle-working power was sufficient for him. It enabled him to be an overcomer in spite of his weakness.

Don't allow the devil to talk you out of your victory. Throw tradition aside and dare to believe the Word of God. Fight the fight of faith, and just like the apostle Paul, you will see the salvation of the Lord!

SCRIPTURE READING: 2 Corinthians 12:1-10

Develop the Love

"And what this love consists in is this,
that we live and walk in accordance with and guided by His
commandments — His orders, ordinances, precepts, teaching. This is the
commandment, as you have heard from the beginning, that you continue
to walk in love — guided by it and following it." **(2 John 1:6, AMP)**

Quite simply, God says love is keeping His commandments. That brings love out of the indefinite into something explicit. But God has done more than define love for you. He's given you instructions so that you can know how to love as He loves. By giving you His Word, God has given you His love manual in black and white. All you have to do is follow it and you'll be walking in love.

If you've made Jesus Christ the Lord of your life, you've already taken the first step of obedience. The love of God has been born within you. But, unless you take steps to develop it, that love will remain hidden within you. Love works in much the same way as the force of faith. Like faith, love becomes active through knowledge of the Word.

Become love conscious by confessing and acting on God's Word today. As you meditate these scriptures, see yourself living the love life. See yourself walking in accordance with and guided by the commandments of Jesus. Develop the love He has hidden in you.

SCRIPTURE READING: 1 John 2:3-11

From Desperation to Devotion

"Set your affection on things above,
not on things on the earth." **(Colossians 3:2)**

Things, things, things! A better job. A bigger house. New clothes for the kids. Tomorrow's luncheon date. A better television. Get the picture?

Many of us have learned to believe God to prosper us to such a degree that we have too much to keep up with. We end up spending so much time and energy taking care of the legitimate "things" of life that we unconsciously give the attention and affections of our heart over to this natural world instead of to God.

When Kenneth and I first heard about living by faith, we were in desperate circumstances. We were sick and broke, so it was easy for us to dedicate ourselves to prayer and to the Word. But as we honored God's Word, He honored and prospered us. We came to the place where we were no longer desperate. Then came the real test of our faith. Would we serve God out of our love for Him instead of our desperation?

Well, praise God, we did. But in the process we found out one thing: It takes a lot more dedication to serve God when you're prosperous than it takes when you're desperate! There's a constant temptation to get so caught up in the earthly things that your desire for the things of God fades into the background.

As the material blessings of God come your way, remember, God has not trained you in His Word so you can consume it on your own lusts. He has revealed His Word to you so you can walk in the Spirit and do the job He's called you to do.

Don't let the things of this world cause you to miss out on the glorious things of the Spirit. Get your priorities in line with God's Word. Set your mind on the things above, and you'll discover just how heavenly life was really meant to be!

SCRIPTURE READING: Colossians 3:1-16

Play to Win

"Who is he that overcometh the world,
but he that believeth that Jesus is the Son of God?" **(1 John 5:5)**

I've often heard people say, "It's not whether you win or lose, it's how you play the game." That's nonsense. If you play the game right, you'll win!

Any coach will tell you that part of playing the game right is having a winning attitude. That's what God wants us, as believers, to have. He wants us to have so much faith in Him that we *expect* to whip any obstacle the devil brings our way. He wants us to *expect* to win at the game of life.

But most of us don't come by that attitude easily. We're so accustomed to losing that we have to totally change our way of thinking if we want to have a winning mind-set. In Ephesians, the apostle Paul told the church to renew their minds. Like us, they needed to change their attitudes, to renew their minds to the fact that Jesus has overcome the world.

If you haven't already, you need to do that too! You need to develop a glorious sense of confidence that says, "Hey, devil, I'm going to be victorious and there's not a thing you can do to stop me!"

"But, Brother Copeland, you don't know the kinds of problems I'm facing."

I know I don't, but Jesus does and He said you should "cheer up" because He can give you peace in the midst of tribulation. He said that when Satan comes against you with everything he has, you should take heart because He's already beaten it— Jesus has already overcome it and so can you!

First John 5:5 puts it this way, "Who is he that overcometh the world, but he that believeth that Jesus is the Son of God?"

Do you know what that scripture means? It means that if you are a born-again believer, you have an absolute right to be a winner, to overcome every aspect of this evil world. Think about that. Meditate on it. Start developing a winning attitude today!

SCRIPTURE READING: Romans 8:29-39

Blessings by the Bushel

"And he said unto them, Take heed what ye hear:
with what measure ye mete, it shall be measured to you." **(Mark 4:24)**

How many blessings are you going to receive from the Word of God? It depends on how many you expect to receive. When God measures them out to you, He'll be using your measuring stick, not His own. He always works that way.

Two people can hear God's Word about healing, for example. One will measure it with faith. "Praise God, by His stripes I was healed!" he'll say. "I believe that with all my heart, and I'm going to keep on believing it until I receive my healing."

The other will measure it with skepticism. "I don't care what Bible verses he comes up with," he'll say. "I just don't trust that preacher. I'll give this healing stuff a try, but I doubt very much if anything's going to come of it."

Both of those people will get exactly what they expect. God will measure to them just as they measured the Word. One will get healed...the other won't.

I must warn you though, sometimes measuring the Word with faith is hard. Years ago, when Gloria first read the scripture, "Owe no man anything," it was tempting for her to measure it as a curse, not a blessing. We were living in a terrible little house at the time, and she wanted a new one more than just about anything.

How were we ever going to buy a decent house without borrowing? It didn't seem possible. So, to her, it was as if that scripture had said, "Gloria, you can't have a new house."

But she refused to measure it that way. She grabbed the devil by the throat and said, "Look here now, you're not going to cheat me out of my house." Then she started believing that somehow God could provide her with a house debt free. Sure enough, He did.

If you want to receive blessings by the bushel load, start going to the Word with a bushel basket. Put a big measure of faith in the hand of God. He'll fill it to overflowing and give it right back to you!

SCRIPTURE READING: Luke 8:1-18

Know God's Will

"Except the Lord build the house,
they labour in vain that build it." **(Psalm 127:1)**

What a time of monumental decisions and changes we're living in. If there ever was a day when you and I *must know* God's will and purpose for our lives, it's now.

In fact, nothing else is going to work! God is changing and rearranging things, lining them up for the end-time move of the Spirit. If you're going to keep up, you must know God's perfect plan for your life—*and* how to carry it out in His power!

How do you do that? Through prayer.

In fact, God has provided us a prayer in His Word that we can use to receive the wisdom and understanding we need for this critical time we live in. You'll find it in Colossians 1:9-11.

"For this cause we...do not cease to pray for you, and to desire that ye might be filled with the knowledge of [God's] will in all wisdom and spiritual understanding; That ye might walk worthy of the Lord unto all pleasing, being fruitful in every good work, and increasing in the knowledge of God; Strengthened with all might, according to his glorious power, unto

all patience and longsuffering with joyfulness."

In recent months, God has instructed Gloria and me to pray that prayer for our ministry partners and for ourselves every day. It's a powerful, Holy Ghost-inspired prayer that will not only enable you to know what God's will is, but to have the wisdom and understanding to carry it out.

That's where most failure comes in Christian endeavors. We get a glimpse of God's will for our lives in the Spirit, but then we mess things up by trying to carry it out in the flesh. Instead of letting the Lord build the house in His power, we try to build it ourselves and end up doing it all in vain.

Don't make that mistake in the days ahead. Instead, pray this prayer that God has given us. It was written in the New Testament for you. Put your name in it. It's a prayer you can be sure God will answer. Put it to work in your life daily and God *will* fill you with His knowledge and understanding!

SCRIPTURE READING: Colossians 1:9-22

Cast Your Cares on Him

"Humble yourselves therefore under the mighty hand of God, that he may exalt you in due time: Casting all your care upon him; for he careth for you." **(1 Peter 5:6)**

When I first learned to cast my cares on the Lord, I was down in south Texas preaching a meeting that nobody was coming to. I'm telling you, people were staying away from that meeting by the thousands; and after a service or two with just the preacher, one or two others and me in attendance, I was starting to sweat it. But the Lord said, "Cast that care on Me," so I did.

I started walking around grinning and whistling. I told the devil, "I'm not going to frown or have one worried thought. I came here to preach and that's what I'm going to do, and it's God's business whether anyone shows up or not. I couldn't care less!"

I went around so happy I felt downright foolish. The devil said, "What's the matter with you? Don't you even have sense enough to worry over something like this?" I suppose people were saying, "I guess he's too dumb to worry. I think it's because he's never been to seminary. He can't tell a landslide from a flop."

But I told the Lord, "I have my care rolled over on You, and if *nobody* shows up but that one dear old woman, she's going to be the most preached-up old woman in the state of Texas because I'm going to preach just the same as if there were a crowd."

I didn't realize then what was happening, but that carefreeness put me in a non-compromising position with the devil. He couldn't get to me anymore. He couldn't get me in fear and unbelief anymore. He couldn't pressure me and get me to compromise because I didn't care. I'd given all my care to God!

Are you ready to be free of care? If you are, just make this confession of faith:

I'm a believer. I'm not a doubter. The Word works in me; and at this moment, I humble myself under the mighty hand of God. I cast all my care over on Him. From this moment forward, I refuse to worry. Instead, I will pray. I will use my faith and believe, and He'll exalt me over the problem and over the devil. For I belong to Jesus and He cares for me!

SCRIPTURE READING: Psalm 55:16-22

Hang On

"So shall my word be that goeth forth out of my mouth:
it shall not return unto me void, but it shall accomplish that which I please,
and it shall prosper in the thing whereto I sent it." **(Isaiah 55:11)**

Did you know that the battleground for the problem you're facing right now is in your mind and on your lips? If you'll hit the devil with the Word and cast the care of the situation over on God, you'll win.

Let me warn you though, hanging onto the Word isn't always easy. The devil knows that if he doesn't steal it from you, you'll use it to enforce his defeat.

So don't be surprised when he sends an evil spirit to exalt itself against the Word of God. If you're sick, he'll begin to tell you, "You're not healed. You know that healing's not for today. Even if it were, it wouldn't work for you. It might work for somebody else but not you."

When he starts to tell you that kind of thing, don't buy it! Don't start worrying around about it and thinking, "Oh my, I'm afraid I'm not going to get healed. I sure don't feel healed. Why, I'm probably going to just get worse and worse...."

Remember this: It's the Word that does the work, not the one holding onto it. It'll work for anybody who'll put it to work. It'll work for you just like it worked for Jesus when He walked the earth.

He told Satan, *It is written!* No matter what the devil tries to tell you, refuse to let go of the Word. Tell him what is written concerning your situation. Let the Word fight its own fight. It'll whip the devil every time.

SCRIPTURE READING: Psalm 19:7-14

Open Their Eyes to the Light

"If our gospel be hid, it is hid to them that are lost:
In whom the god of this world hath blinded the minds of them
which believe not, lest the light of the glorious gospel of Christ,
who is the image of God, should shine unto them."

(2 Corinthians 4:3,4)

Since God doesn't save anyone against their will, does it really do any good to pray for people who consciously refuse to receive Jesus as Lord?

Yes. Yes! YES! IT DOES!

You see, in spite of the fact that most all unbelievers who have purposely refused to receive Jesus as Lord think they've made that decision of their own free will, the truth is, they haven't. The Word of God says they've been blinded by Satan. He's blocking their perception of the truth. So their decision hasn't been freely made at all.

That's important for you to grasp. Because through the prayer of intercession, you *can* interfere with the satanic forces and help take those blinders off! You can also change circumstances with your prayers and help create situations that will bring them in contact with the Lord. You're well within your spiritual rights when you do that.

I prayed with a friend of mine once who'd been praying for his lost brother for years. Jesus said in Matthew 12:29 to first bind the strong man and then enter his house and spoil his goods. So we said, "You spirit blinding the eyes of _____, you stop what you are doing to keep him out of the

kingdom of God. In Jesus' name, you stop NOW!"

Jesus also said in Matthew 9:38, "Pray ye therefore the Lord of the harvest that he will send forth labourers into his harvest." So we prayed, "Lord, send someone to _____ with the Word of God. You know who he will listen to. We claim _____ for the kingdom of God. We believe we receive his salvation and deliverance. In faith we praise You for it."

In almost no time at all his brother called him. "What have you been doing up there?" he asked. "In the past few days, everybody I've come across has started preaching to me!"

Our prayers had interfered with the forces Satan had been using to blind this man to Jesus and created the circumstances to bring him into the kingdom. Sure enough, within a few days, he was born again.

Use this same prayer for your loved ones and believe when you pray and you'll see the same results.

Don't sit by and let the devil take your friends and loved ones without a fight. Pray. Pray! PRAY! Come against the "god of this world." Take off the blinders and open their eyes to the glorious gospel of God.

SCRIPTURE READING: 2 Corinthians 4:1-7

Discover What Grace Can Do

"And with great power gave the apostles witness
of the resurrection of the Lord Jesus: and great *grace* was upon them all."

(Acts 4:33)

Most of us don't have any idea what *grace* really is. Oh, we know some basic facts about it. We know we were saved by it (Eph. 2:8). But we don't even begin to understand the real power it can release in our lives now, today!

If you want to get a picture of what grace can really do, look at what happened to the early Christians in Acts, chapter 4. They'd been threatened by the religious leaders of Jerusalem and commanded not to speak or teach anymore in Jesus' name. So, they were praying about the situation.

Roughly, what they said was this, "Now Lord, we've been threatened, but we aren't about to quit preaching and go hide out under some religious rug. Just turn the power up, give us boldness, and we'll go on."

Do you know what happened as a result of that prayer? Verse 33 tells us, "Great *grace* was upon them all."

Great grace. Grace so powerful that when those believers received it, the whole building shook. Grace so great it enabled the apostles to work "many signs and wonders...among the people" (Acts 5:12).

That one story alone should be enough to convince you that grace is not just some abstract spiritual state of mind. Grace is real. It's powerful. It provides the supernatural power to make things happen!

Now, do you want to know something really exciting? The Bible says that same grace that was available to that early church in Jerusalem is available to anybody who's ever sinned and fallen short of the glory of God.

Thank God, that means you and I qualify!

If the devil's been threatening you lately, follow the example of those early Christians. Get in prayer and say, "Lord, I don't care what the devil and his bunch say, I'm not going to back down. I'm going to keep on talking and living by faith—and I'm going to do it boldly. So just turn up the power!"

I guarantee you, if you're sincere about it, He'll do it; and you'll begin to discover what *grace* is really all about.

SCRIPTURE READING: Acts 4:8-33

A Miracle Inside You

"Not by might, nor by power,
but by my spirit, saith the Lord of hosts." **(Zechariah 4:6)**

I remember the first time I went with the Oral Roberts crusade team to a healing meeting. I was a student and a member of his aircraft crew. I had been a believer a little over four years and knew so little about the things of God, especially meetings like these. However, I was part of the team and eager to learn.

I followed the team inside this huge auditorium. It was filled with sick people. The place smelled, it was so full of disease. Just walking in there sent chills of fear up my spine.

I turned around and headed for the side door as fast as I could, talking to God under my breath. "Listen, I don't belong here," I told Him. "I'm getting on a Greyhound bus and heading home right now. They can get that airplane home without me."

Once I was outside the door, I started talking louder. Then suddenly, I froze. My feet wouldn't move. I knew it was God who'd stopped me because, inside, I was still on my way to the bus station. But outside, I was stuck to the sidewalk.

I looked up and hollered, "Turn me loose!" But I couldn't move.

Desperately, I prayed, "Please, let me go! I don't have anything for those people."

That's when God spoke back to me. Every cell in me heard it. He said, "I KNOW you don't have anything to give them. But I DO and that's why I baptized you in My Spirit."

My feet suddenly turned loose and I knew I had a choice. One was life and one was death. So I turned around and went back.

I was ready to run. But God stopped me. He knew HE was in me, and if I'd just stay and stir up what was in me, miracles would happen—and they did.

You have that same miracle-working God inside of you. And there are people all around you who need Him. So quit waiting to feel like you have the power to do it and get out there. Once you do, you'll discover that the power you've been waiting on has been right there inside you all the time...waiting on you.

SCRIPTURE READING: Exodus 3:1-14

A Healthy Dose of Love

"Love...is not touchy or fretful or resentful;
it takes no account of the evil done to it — pays no attention
to a suffered wrong." **(1 Corinthians 13:4,5, AMP)**

Walking in love is good for your health. Did you know that?

It's true! Medical science has proven it. Researchers have discovered that hostility produces stress that causes ulcers, tension headaches, and a host of other ills.

Now when you think of hostility, you may think of the type of anger you feel when something serious happens. But according to the experts, that kind of thing isn't what causes the worst problems. It's the little things: when the dry cleaners ruin your favorite outfit, for example. Or when the cafeteria lady puts gravy on your mashed potatoes after you've specifically told her not to. Sound familiar?

Just think how much stress you could avoid by being quick to forgive, by living your life according to 1 Corinthians 13 and not counting up the evils done to you. Imagine physical and emotional benefits of living like that!

If you've allowed yourself to be habitually bound by hostility, that may sound like an impossible dream, but it's not! Because as a born-again believer, you have the love of God inside of you.

If you'll yield to that love, it will set you free. Remember when Jesus called Lazarus forth from the grave? He was alive but still bound in the grave clothes. Jesus commanded the bindings to be loosed so that Lazarus could be free to walk.

Jesus wants that same kind of freedom for you. So get into agreement with Him. Say to those deadly habits that have you bound, "In the name of Jesus, loose me and let me go! I'm putting hostility, unforgiveness, and selfishness behind me. I'm going on with God. I'm going to live the life of love!"

Remember: It doesn't take a medical miracle to turn your life around. All it takes is a decision to yield to the force of love. Do it today!

SCRIPTURE READING: Proverbs 4:10-27

Put the Word First

"For skillful and godly Wisdom is the principal thing....
Prize Wisdom highly and exalt her, and she will exalt and promote
you; she will bring you to honor when you embrace her."

(Proverbs 4:7,8, AMP)

I want to tell you the only real secret to getting ahead in this world. It's simple. Put the Word of God first place in your daily life.

"Well," you may be saying, "I've heard that before. It's no secret." But when you understand what I mean, it could be a revelation to you.

You see, the Bible is not just a textbook, a storybook, or a history book. It's a handbook for living. It's the wisdom of Almighty God written down so that you can apply it to your everyday circumstances.

God says that Wisdom is the "principal thing." Principal means "first in importance." That means the Word of God needs to occupy the place of highest importance in all of your activities. I know from experience what an impact that can have on your life.

Twenty years ago I decided to read the gospels and the Book of Acts three times in 30 days. It seemed an impossible task at the time. With two small children and my house turned upside down from a recent move, I couldn't see how I could possibly spend that much time reading the Word and still get everything done. But I set myself to put other things aside and do it anyway.

Surprisingly enough, at the end of the first day I had accomplished more than I would have under normal circumstances. And by the end of that 30 days, I'd not only read the gospels and Acts three times, I'd kept all my housework done, my children taken care of, and refinished several pieces of furniture to boot! I was amazed.

You'll be amazed at what happens in your life too, if you give God's Word priority. But let me warn you, don't wait until you think you have the time. Satan will see to it that you never do.

Just do like I did and set other things aside. Invest your time in the Word first and that investment will soon be paying off in every area of your life.

SCRIPTURE READING: Proverbs 3:1-9

Expect a Harvest

"Give, and it shall be given unto you;
good measure, pressed down, and shaken together, and running over,
shall men give into your bosom. For with the same measure that ye mete
withal it shall be measured to you again." **(Luke 6:38)**

ive and it shall be given unto you. That statement came straight from the mouth of Jesus. Yet there are a great many believers who flatly refuse to believe it. In fact, they actually have the mistaken idea that it's wrong to expect to receive when they give.

The truth is—it's wrong *not* to!

What would you think about a farmer who planted seeds, then let his crop rot in the field? You'd think he was a fool, wouldn't you? And if he did it when others were starving, you'd think he was criminally irresponsible.

Well, it's just as irresponsible to give financial seeds and ignore the harvest God promised. Especially when that harvest could help send the gospel to people who are starving to hear it. It's just as wrong to ignore the key to

prosperity that Jesus Himself gave us as it is to let a wheat crop rot in the field.

God wants us to receive from the financial seeds that we plant. He wants us to be prepared to require no aid ourselves and to be "furnished in abundance for every good work and charitable donation" (2 Cor. 9:8, AMP). He wants us to have plenty—not so we can hoard it selfishly—but so we can give generously.

Next time you give, don't be afraid to expect a harvest! Release your faith for the financial rewards Jesus promised. Then, when they come, turn right around and plant them again. Keep the flow of giving and receiving going so that the Lord can bless the world through you!

SCRIPTURE READING: 2 Corinthians 9:6-15

See Yourself Strong

"And we were in our own sight as grasshoppers, and so we were in their sight." (Numbers 13:33)

How does the devil see you? Does he see you as a terrifying and mighty warrior of God...or does he see you as a wimp he can whip in a minute?

The answer to that question depends on you. I realized that one day as I was studying the children of Israel and their failure to enter the Promised Land. The key to their failure is found in these words: "And we were in our own sight as grasshoppers, and so we were in theirs."

The reason the Israelites were so terrified to fight the giants in Canaan wasn't because those giants were so big. It was because the Israelites saw *themselves* as so small! It was what they were in their *own* sight that defeated them.

The same thing is true for you as a believer. It's what you are in your own sight that will make the difference. If, in your own sight, you're a weak, powerless Christian, the devil will run over you three or four times a day or more if he's not busy. But when you begin to see yourself as God sees you, as a conquering son or daughter of the Almighty God equipped with the very power of God Himself, the devil will want to steer clear of you.

The devil would rather do anything than come against somebody who's bold and courageous because he's a coward himself. In fact, ever since Jesus came up out of that grave, Satan's heart has melted within him at the sound of that Name in the mouth of one who has faith in it.

If you're not strong in the Lord in your own sight, you need to change that. You need to get so full of God's Word and so full of the Holy Ghost that you walk around like a spiritual giant. Turn the tables on the devil and let him find out what it feels like to be a grasshopper for a change.

SCRIPTURE READING: Numbers 13:17-33

Don't Tell It Like It Is

"Death and life are in the power of the tongue:
and they that love it shall eat the fruit thereof." **(Proverbs 18:21)**

Words are serious business. And, as believers, we need to get serious about learning how to use them. We need to begin to put them to work for us like God Himself does. The Bible tells us that He uses words to "call those things which be not as though they were" (Rom. 4:17).

Most of us don't have the faintest idea how to do that. We've spent our lives "telling it like it is." We've constantly used our mouths to report on the sorry state of affairs around us. Thus, the very thought of calling "things which be not as though they were" seems a little crazy.

"You mean I'm supposed to say, 'I'm healed' when I'm feeling sick? I'm supposed to say, 'I'm prosperous' when I'm penniless?" we say. "That sounds like lying to me."

No, no. There's a vast difference between lying and speaking by faith. A lie is meant to deceive someone. It's designed to make someone believe something that's not true. But to speak by faith is simply to speak words that agree with the Word of God instead of the circumstances around you. It's speaking from your spirit instead of from your mind.

As the apostle Paul said in 2 Corinthians 4:13, "We have the same spirit of faith as he had who wrote, I have believed, and therefore have I spoken. We too believe, and therefore we speak" (AMP).

Now that's important. Read that verse again. "I have believed, and therefore have I spoken."

There are some folks who speak the words, but they don't have the faith to back it up, and as a result, they fall flat on their spiritual faces. They didn't actually "call things that be not as though they were." They called things that be not the way they *wished* they were.

Those are two very different things. The words may be the same. But just wishing and hoping won't get the job done. You've got to *"believe."*

Begin today bringing both your tongue and your heart in line with the Word. Stop "telling it like it is" and start speaking and believing the promises of God. Put the power of words to work for you.

SCRIPTURE READING: Proverbs 15

Don't Get in a Hurry

"And these words, which I command thee this day,
shall be in thine heart: And thou shalt...talk of them
when thou sittest in thine house, and when thou walkest by the
way, and when thou liest down, and when thou risest up.
...and they shall be as frontlets between thine eyes."
(Deuteronomy 6:6-8)

One of the reasons Gloria and I have seen the results we have in our lives and in our ministry is because when we realized what the Word of God would do, we literally immersed ourselves in it. We turned off the radio and television, we put down the newspaper, and spent nearly every waking moment of the time available either reading the Word, listening to tapes on the Word, or thinking about the Word.

All that time in the Word eventually had a powerful effect on us. It began to revolutionize everything about us. It began to turn failure into success.

All that didn't happen overnight, however. It took time. A great many believers don't realize that. They start out devoting themselves to the Word, but they make the mistake of expecting instant, miraculous results, and when they don't see them, they get disappointed and fall away.

Don't do that. Be patient. Give the Word time to do its work.

Jesus once said, "Man shall not live by bread alone, but by every word that proceedeth out of the mouth of God" (Matt. 4:4). The Word of God feeds the spirit man just as bread feeds the body. Food has to be built into your body. The vitamins and minerals it contains have a cumulative effect on it, don't they? In fact, almost anything that affects your body instantaneously is considered dangerous.

Much the same thing is true with the Word of God. It has a cumulative effect. Yes, at times God will act instantly and perform a miracle, but only to get things back on track. What He really intends is for you to feed on His Word to grow in strength and in faith and to bear fruit in due season.

So don't get in such an all-fired hurry. Stay in the Word. Be patient. The results *will* come!

SCRIPTURE READING: Deuteronomy 7:11-23

Take a Stand Against Strife

"The beginning of strife is as when water first trickles
[from a crack in a dam]; therefore stop contention before it becomes worse
and quarreling breaks out." **(Proverbs 17:14)**

Throughout the Scriptures, God warns us about the danger of strife. Yet, it's still one of the most common problems among believers. We let it get into our homes, our work places, our churches...everywhere!

Of course, we don't purposely let it in. We don't wake up in the morning and say, "I think I'm going to stir up some major strife today." We just inadvertently let it slip up on us one minor irritation at a time.

So, I urge you today to take a big stand against those little opportunities for strife. If you have a tendency to let things irritate you, decide to overcome that tendency. Arm yourself against them with the knowledge that this world isn't perfect, that there are people in it that aren't going to be nice to you. There are people who are going to stir you up and annoy you – on purpose or by accident.

Make up your mind that, by the power of God, you're not going to let them get your peace. That peace is so important to your well-being. It will keep your body healthy. It will keep your relationships healthy. It will put you in a place where God can guide your steps and save you from some very grave mistakes.

If you've spent a lifetime getting your feathers ruffled over every little thing, it may take a while for you to break that habit. You may have to work at it a moment at a time. But you can do it.

I know. I had to do that where worrying is concerned. I'd worried for so many years and had come from such a family of worriers that I did it almost without thinking. When I learned worrying went contrary to the Word of God, I had to give it up one minute at a time. With the help of the Holy Spirit, every time a worried thought would come to me, I would overcome it with the Word of God. And I did that until I broke that worrying habit for good.

You can do the same thing with strife. Ask the Holy Spirit to help you start to notice and overcome it one moment at a time. Then, every time you start to get upset about something, rebuke that strife in the name of Jesus and resist it. Say right out loud, "I am walking in the peace of God today."

You'll be surprised how much more wonderful living can be.

SCRIPTURE READING: Matthew 5:21-26,43-48

God's Medicine

"The words that I speak unto you,
they are spirit, and they are life." **(John 6:63)**

We've seen some tremendous medical breakthroughs in our generation. We've seen "miracle drugs" developed that can conquer many kinds of sickness and disease.

But, you know, in the 20-plus years I've been a believer, I've discovered another, much more effective, kind of medicine: the Word of God. There's never been a miracle drug that could equal it. God's medicine is the answer to every need. It is life. It is health. It is the power of God. And if you put it in your heart and act on it, *you will be healed*.

Sometimes people ask, "If God's medicine works every time, why are there so many believers who are still sick?" There are two reasons. Number one, because they don't take the time to plant the Word concerning healing deeply into their heart. And number two, because they don't *do* what that Word tells them to do.

Think of it like this: If a doctor prescribes medicine for you to swallow daily and you decide to rub it on your chest instead, that medicine isn't going to work for you. You have to follow the instructions and use it properly if you expect to get well, don't you? In the same way, if you read God's prescription for health and don't act on it, you won't reap any of its benefits.

Proverbs 4:22 says God's words are life and health to you. So don't wait until you get sick to start using them. Start now. Begin to put God's Word in your heart in abundance and it will be hard for you to get sick. That Word within you will constantly be keeping God's healing power at work in you.

And don't worry. There's no limit to the amount of God's medicine you can take. You can't get an overdose. The more you take, the stronger you get.

Start growing strong today.

SCRIPTURE READING: Proverbs 4:20-27

Vivé la Difference

"If one prevail against him, two shall withstand him;
and a threefold cord is not quickly broken." **(Ecclesiastes 4:12)**

There's power in unity. The devil knows that. That's why he's continually fighting it. He takes the differences between us, differences God put there to make us stronger, and tries to use them as a wedge to drive us apart.

Take men and women, for example. He's deceived us into fighting about which one is superior over the other. But I can settle that argument right now. Women are superior to men. If you don't believe that, you boys try having a baby. But then, men are superior to women. If you don't believe that, you women try having one without us.

It's the differences combined that make us strong!

People have even argued about whether God is male or female. But the Bible itself tells us that. He's both! That's right. In the Hebrew language, all words have gender. They're either male or female. But the Hebrew word "Jehovah" is both masculine and feminine. He's as much female as He is male and as much male as He is female.

Originally, mankind was that way too. When God first made "man," he was as much female as he was male. Then God separated the female part out and made "wo-man" or, "the man with the womb." After that, man and woman had to come together to be perfectly whole.

That's still true today. For example, when He puts together husband and wife teams, He often puts people together who have major personality differences. Where one is weak, the other is strong, and vice versa. So, when they become one, they're more powerful than they ever were apart.

There was a time when I didn't understand that. I got aggravated with God for calling me a wife who didn't care for so many things that I liked. But I finally realized God knew what He was doing. If He'd given me a woman who was as nuts about flying as I am, we would have spent the rest of our lives in the clouds. We wouldn't be preaching the Word. We'd be in some silly airshow flying upside down. "The Copeland Team!" or something.

Do you have people in your life who are irritatingly different from you? Don't let the devil use those differences to drive you apart. Thank God for them! Let Him teach you how to appreciate them. Let Him show you just how powerful you can be... together!

SCRIPTURE READING: Ecclesiastes 4:9-12

Be Willing!

"If ye be willing and obedient,
ye shall eat the good of the land." **(Isaiah 1:19)**

A healthy body. Enough money to pay all your bills and extra to invest in the work of the gospel. A godly marriage and happy, healthy children. Peace of mind. God has prepared a banquet full of blessings for you.

But those blessings are not just going to fall in your lap. You must be willing—as well as obedient—if you're going to eat the best from God's table.

So, be willing!

Don't be willing for Satan to put sickness on your body. Be willing, instead, to be well! In honor of Jesus' sacrifice at Calvary, refuse to accept anything less than divine health.

Don't be willing to live in lack, but be willing instead to live in divine prosperity and abundance. Refuse to allow Satan to stop the flow of God's financial blessings to you.

Be willing to receive God's best plan for your marriage and your children. Don't settle for the "norm" in the world. Live above it in a home full of love and harmony, a home that is what God meant it to be.

Don't allow Satan to substitute anxiety and ulcers for the peace and undisturbedness that Jesus bought for you. Be willing and obedient to cast all your cares on Him, for He cares for you.

Refuse to be robbed of the banquet of blessings that have belonged to you since you became a believer. Be willing to eat the good of the land!

SCRIPTURE READING: Deuteronomy 8:5-20

No More Dying to Do

"But we see Jesus, who was made a little lower
than the angels for the suffering of death, crowned with glory and honour;
that he by the grace of God should taste death for every man."

(Hebrews 2:9)

D eath. It's not a popular topic—even among believers. In fact, a great many are just plain scared of it. Oh yes, they *talk* about having eternal life. Yet when the devil tries to threaten their earthly survival with sickness or calamity, they panic.

Why? Because they haven't learned to look at death through God's eyes. Even though their spirit has been made immortal, they haven't renewed their minds to include that truth. If they had, when the devil tried to push their panic button, they'd just laugh and say, "You can't scare me, devil. I've done all the dying I'm ever going to do!"

That's true, you know. The Word of God says that you, as a born-again believer, are never going to see death (John 8:51). Jesus has been your substitute. He suffered death, so you wouldn't have to. And when He was raised, Hebrews 2:14,15 says, "He destroyed him that had the power of death, that is, the devil; And delivered

them who through fear of death were all their lifetime subject to bondage."

If you've made Jesus the Lord of your life, the only death you'll ever experience is behind you now. It occurred the instant you received Christ. At that moment, your old self—the one whose nature was to sin and rebel against God—died. Your body didn't die, but your spirit man—the *real* you—died to Satan and all of his works. You became "a new creature" (2 Cor. 5:17), immortal and absolutely incapable of death!

When you're finished with your work on the earth, you're not going to die. You'll simply shed your earthly shell and relocate to a far more glorious place.

Go to the Word and get God's perspective on death. Make a study of it. Once the reality of your immortality begins to dawn on you, the devil will never be able to threaten you with it again.

SCRIPTURE READING: Hebrews 2:9-15

Later is Here!

"Who then is a faithful and wise servant,
whom his lord hath made ruler over his household?" **(Matthew 24:45)**

The Word tells us that God shows Himself strong in behalf of those whose hearts are "perfect" toward Him (2 Chron.16:9). That word "perfect" doesn't mean that we have to do everything just right and live without making a mistake. Thank God, we don't have to do that. It means "devoted"—a heart consecrated, dedicated, loyal, and faithful to God.

The mistakes we make will not stop God from working in our lives. Only our lack of faithfulness can do that.

Who is faithful? The one who spends his time doing what God has called him to do. Or as Jesus put it, the one who takes up His cross and follows Him. The one who denies his fleshly desires and spends his life on the things God desires him to do.

Maybe God has been urging you to spend more time in His Word and in prayer or dealing with you about ministering more to the people around you. He may be calling you to pray for the sick or to teach the Word. But you're busy, so you glide on with good intentions and tell God you'll do it later. Well, later is here!

Decide today that you are going to be the faithful and wise servant. Find out what is stealing your time from the Lord. Serve His interests instead of your own.

Do you want to be a ruler in the household of God? Do you want Him to show Himself strong for you? Then take up Jesus' thoughts today. Take up His purposes and His plans. Now is the time to be faithful!

SCRIPTURE READING: Matthew 24:42-51

Be Unreasonably Committed

"Wisdom is the principal thing; therefore get wisdom:
and with all thy getting get understanding. Exalt her, and she
shall promote thee: she shall bring thee to honour, when thou dost
embrace her. She shall give to thine head an ornament of grace:
a crown of glory shall she deliver to thee." **(Proverbs 4:7-9)**

If you really want to get the wisdom of God, you'll have to do more than casually read the Scriptures a few minutes a day. You'll have to feed on them night and day. You'll have to get rid of the rubbish you've been feeding into your consciousness by reprogramming your mind with the Word of God.

"Oh, Brother Copeland," you may say, "that's unreasonable!"

Yes it is. But consider this: A music major in college practices for hours every day. Olympic skaters spend six to eight hours a day training for their routines. They do it because they're unreasonably committed to their goals.

The same is true for you. If you're going to achieve the kind of spiritual excellence you're hungry for, you're going to have to be unreasonably committed to the Word of God.

That may well mean that you'll have to carry a tape recorder around with you everywhere you go. It may mean that you'll have your razor in one hand and your tape recorder in the other or a tape recorder in one hand and a fork in the other.

Do whatever it takes to totally saturate yourself with the Word of God. I would speak to you no differently if I were your commanding officer about to send you into combat against the best-trained elite troops of a savage enemy.

You are God's frontline assault force. You have an enemy who is doing his dead level best to destroy you. In this crucial, all-out, no-holds-barred offensive, Satan will dispatch hell's choicest personnel to bring you down. If you're going to make it through in victory, you're going to have to put yourself in training.

Be unreasonably committed. Get wisdom.

SCRIPTURE READING: Proverbs 1:7-33

God's Discipline

"For whom the Lord loveth he chasteneth, and scourgeth
every son whom he receiveth. If ye endure chastening, God
dealeth with you as with sons; for what son is he whom
the father chasteneth not?" (Hebrews 12:6,7)

There's a terrible misunderstanding among believers today about God's method of disciplining His children. They'll point to some kind of disaster—a tornado or a car accident— and say, "I guess God sent that catastrophe to teach us something."

No, He didn't! A loving God doesn't send death and destruction on His children to instruct them. He doesn't unleash His bad dog to bite us on the leg, so we'll learn to wear our boots!

How does He chastise His own? With His Word.

Second Timothy 3:16,17 says, "Every Scripture is God-breathed—given by His inspiration—and profitable for instruction, for reproof and conviction of sin, for correction of error and discipline in obedience, and for training in righteousness, So that the man of God may be complete and proficient, well-fitted and thoroughly equipped for every good work" (AMP).

If you'll look in 2 Corinthians 7, you'll see an example of this. There the apostle Paul talks about a situation in the Corinthian church that needed correction. That church had gotten out of line and had to be disciplined.

How did Paul do it? Not by asking God to send an earthquake to shake them up! He did it by writing them a letter. He wrote them a word of reproof that hurt so badly they would have preferred being beaten with a stick. It cut deep into their spirits and brought them to repentance.

Your heavenly Father loves you and because He does, He *will* chasten you. But He'll do it with spiritual, not fleshly tools. He'll use the spirit-power in His Word to chasten unbelief and purify your spirit in such a way that you'll come out strong, not weak and condemned.

So quit bowing down to disasters and start subjecting yourself instead to the Word of God. Yield to the Word. Let it correct you and trim away the flesh and the lusts that lead you astray. Remember, the Sword of the Spirit is two-edged—one side is for Satan and the other side is for you. Let God use it to keep you in line!

SCRIPTURE READING: 2 Corinthians 7

God is Healing Our Land

"Shall their unbelief make the faith of God without effect? God forbid."
(Romans 3:3,4)

Faith-filled words. That's what changes things. They'll move mountains into the sea. They'll turn sickness into health. They'll turn a sinner into a saint.

They'll also take a sin-ridden nation and turn it into God's own country. That's right. If we believers then would back up the prayers we've been praying for this nation with words of faith instead of doubt and discouragement, we'd soon begin to see spiritual resurrection in the U.S.A.

God promised us that if we, His people, would humble ourselves and pray and seek His face and turn from our wicked ways, He would heal our land. And let me tell you, there are prayer warriors all over this country (I hope you're one of them) who are doing what that promise requires.

But, even so, you don't hear many people saying, "This is great! God is healing the land." You don't hear people speaking out by faith the promise of God. Instead, you hear them saying, "Oh my, oh my, did you hear what those terrorists are doing?" or some other destructive thing they've seen on TV.

Listen, we need to stop preaching what the terrorists are doing and start telling what God is doing! God said He is healing this land.

We must start speaking about this country by faith instead of going around spouting bad news all the time. Of course, that will sound odd to most people. Some of them may even think we've slipped a few cogs. But that's nothing new.

Let me tell you something: One handful of believers who are listening to, trusting in, and speaking out the Good News of God are more powerful than all the devils on earth. One handful of believers are more powerful than a whole army of unbelieving doomsayers. Their unbelief will not make the faith of God of no effect!

That's why over the last 20 years, Gloria and I have learned to turn a deaf ear to the bad news and just start praising and thanking God for His deliverance. Every word of praise we speak releases faith in our heart.

Get determined with Gloria and me right now. Take a firm stand with us that things are changing in this country. Settle it in your heart as you pray. Speak it out. Call it forth. God is healing the land!

SCRIPTURE READING: Nehemiah 6:1-16

Don't Think Like the World

"For the weapons of our warfare are not carnal, but mighty
through God to the pulling down of strong holds; Casting down
imaginations, and every high thing that exalteth itself against the
knowledge of God, and bringing into captivity every thought
to the obedience of Christ." **(2 Corinthians 10:4,5)**

If you think like the world thinks, eventually you will act like the world acts. Unrestrained thoughts produce unrestrained actions. So control your thoughts by bringing them into obedience to the Scriptures.

Program your mind with the Word of God. The Word is spirit and it is life. When your mind is totally saturated with the Word of God, your will becomes strong to exercise authority to overcome every ungodly thought and evil habit.

Don't let Satan deceive you into sacrificing the glory of God in your life for a few moments of self-indulgence and sin. Restrain your thought life. Meditate the Word instead of selfish, carnal thoughts. Keep your eyes on Jesus, the Author and Finisher of your faith.

SCRIPTURE READING: Psalm 119:11-18

Up in Smoke

"The tongue is a little member, and boasteth great things.
Behold, how great a matter a little fire kindleth! And the tongue
is a fire, a world of iniquity: so is the tongue among our members,
that it defileth the whole body, and setteth on fire the course
of nature; and it is set on fire of hell." **(James 3:5,6)**

Words. Use them right and they'll move mountains. Use them wrong and they can cause your entire life to go up in smoke.

"Now, Brother Copeland," you may say, "I find it hard to believe that major catastrophes can be caused by a few simple words. I just can't see the connection."

Look again at the phrase James used. "How great a matter a little fire kindleth!" Have you ever lit a few little pieces of kindling wood and set them in the fireplace beneath a stack of logs?

What happened?

Most likely, the fire began to spread first to one log then to another until finally you had a great big blaze going. After it was over, you couldn't go digging around in the ashes to find the kindling that started it all, could you? No! It would be burned. There would be no trace of it at all.

The tongue is like that. It first defiles the body, then sets on fire the whole course of nature with a blaze so great that it leaves no natural trace of its origin. The words that started it end up so deeply buried in the ashes that you'd never even know they were there.

So, don't ever underestimate the power of your words. I can assure you, Satan doesn't. He works constantly to get you to turn them in a negative direction. He'll fire darts of pain and sickness and discouragement at you just to get you to speak faithless words—words that will eventually send your life up in smoke.

Don't let him succeed. Instead, put out that fire by following the instructions in Ephesians 6:16. Do as the apostle Paul says and "above all, taking the shield of faith, wherewith ye shall be able to quench all the fiery darts of the wicked."

Speak words of faith and stop the fire before it starts *today!*

SCRIPTURE READING: James 3:1-10

Free From Debt!

"The borrower is servant to the lender." **(Proverbs 22:7)**

If you're up to your neck in debt today, I have good news for you. God wants to set you free from those debts and He has the power to do it.

I know. He did it for me.

I'll never forget it. I had $22,000 worth of bad debts at the time. I'd committed to God to pay them off and never to borrow another dime—but it looked to me like I'd never be able to do it.

We didn't see how, but we believed that "God is able." Day by day we looked to God for our deliverance from debt. Not asking Him every day, but thanking Him because we believed we received when we prayed. Eleven months later, we were out of debt. As we looked back, nothing spectacular had happened, but God worked in our finances continuously. As we were faithful, He was faithful.

God can do the same thing for you if you'll dare to believe His Word. If you'll make a commitment before Him to get out from under those debts and then obey Him every step of the way.

As you look at your situation right now, you may not be able to see how you could ever get out of debt, much less stay that way. Don't worry. I felt that way too, at first. I just didn't see how I'd ever be able to do much of anything without borrowing money.

But He showed me how—and He'll do the same thing for you.

There's no debt too big and no business too complicated for Him to handle. If you'll trust Him to manage yours, He will bring you out on top...and you'll never have to be a slave to debt again.

SCRIPTURE READING: Psalm 37:21-40

Protected by Love

"Love your enemies, bless them that curse you,
do good to them that hate you, and pray for them which despitefully
use you, and persecute you; That ye may be the children
of your Father which is in heaven." **(Matthew 5:44,45)**

Love your enemies...turn the other cheek...to most people that sounds like a pretty weak way to handle somebody who's causing them trouble. But, the truth is, it's the most powerful way there is. It's the way Jesus did it—and His way never fails.

Do you remember when Jesus went back to Nazareth and the religious folks were angry with Him and wanted to push Him off a cliff? What happened? He just walked right past them, and no one could lay a finger on Him. Another time they decided to stone Him, and He didn't retaliate that time either. He just walked off. No one could touch Him.

When Jesus walked through that crowd, He wasn't afraid. He knew they couldn't hurt Him because He was walking in the love of God.

When Jesus said to turn the other cheek, He didn't mean for you to stand there and have your brains beaten out. He meant for you to stand there in love and in faith believing that the protecting power of God that accompanies that love would keep you safe. He meant for a man to swing at you and not be able to hit you!

The story of Nicky Cruz as recorded in David Wilkerson's book, *The Cross and the Switchblade,* is a perfect example of that. Nicky was reputed to be the most ruthless gangleader of his time. Yet, when David Wilkerson stood in front of him, telling him about Jesus, Nicky was totally unable to hurt him. He thrust his knife at David several times. But every time he did, David just said, "Nicky, you can cut me into a thousand pieces and every piece will still say, 'I love you and God loves you.'" Because of love, Nicky couldn't get his knife close enough to David to hurt him. A supernatural force always stopped it short.

"But I don't have *that* kind of love!" Yes, you do.

Romans 5:5 tells us that the love of God is shed abroad in your heart by the Holy Spirit. All you have to do is make the decision to be motivated by that love rather than your own human feelings.

My friend, love never fails! You don't have to be afraid of failure anymore. In fact, you don't have to be afraid of anything. If you're walking in the love of God, you're living the most powerful kind of life there is.

SCRIPTURE READING: Matthew 5:38-48

Keep the Weeds Out

"So is the kingdom of God, as if a man
should cast seed into the ground." **(Mark 4:26)**

Jesus compared the kingdom of God with the planting of seed and reaping the harvest. It's a simple concept. One all of us understand. Why, then, aren't all of us producing bumper crops every season? Because we're sitting around waiting for God to do all the work.

He doesn't operate that way. He'll work *with* you, but He won't do it *all*. There are some essential things you must do by faith if you want to have a crop to reap at harvest time.

First, you must sow the seed of the Word in faith, expecting it to grow. You must find precious promises from God in His Word, plant them in your heart and in your life.

Next, you must water the seed. Water it every day with praise. Water it with the spiritual water of the Word. That Word contains life and those seed promises can't grow without it.

And finally, you have to keep the weeds out! When the weeds of un-forgiveness, doubt, fear, discourage-ment, (and all the other junk the devil tries to sow into your crop) try to en-ter in, get rid of them. They'll choke the Word.

That's going to take some diligence on your part. No one else will do it for you. You're going to have to weed your own crop yourself. So get tough about it. When a little weed pops up, kill it! Don't hang on to it for even a moment. Pull it up by its roots. Spray it with the Word. Don't be tempted to keep a wildflower when you can have the best—God's best.

Don't sit around waiting for God to produce your harvest. Start plant-ing. Start watching over your land (your heart and your mind) to keep it moist, watered with the Word, and free from weeds.

Commit to do your part and trust God to do His. You *will* have a bumper crop this season!

SCRIPTURE READING: Ephesians 4:22-32

Turn Up Your Hope

"May the God of your hope so fill you with all joy
and peace in believing — through the experience of your faith —
that by the power of the Holy Spirit you may abound and be overflowing
(bubbling over) with hope." **(Romans 15:13, AMP)**

You know, that's what I want to be...running over with hope! I want to dare to throw my whole life and everything I have into building a dream that comes from the heart of God. I want to get out there so far that without God's help, I can't get back.

Most people don't think that way though because they're afraid to fail. Fear of failure is dangerous. If you let it dominate you, it will cause you to do the one thing that inevitably guarantees failure and that's not attempting at all.

How do you counteract the fear of failure?

You turn up your hope. You get alone with God and listen to Him. You meditate on His promises until the picture is so clear on the inside of you that nothing can jar it out of you.

If you're lying on a sickbed and the doctor's told you you'll never walk again, instead of wallowing around in that bad report, you start dreaming. You start building a dream of climbing mountains and witnessing to people in the backwoods. Go to the Word that promises that those who wait upon the Lord shall run and walk and not faint nor be weary. Look at it until you see nothing else. Picture yourself walking for miles and running from one place to the next, telling everyone that Jesus has raised you up and made you whole.

That's what hope is all about. It's a divine dream. It's an inner image that's bigger than you are because it's built on the promises of God.

If you're a Christian, you ought to be a dreamer. Take the Word of God and build some dreams today.

SCRIPTURE READING: Psalm 33:18-22

Expect Results

"Ye have not, because ye ask not.
Ye ask, and receive not, because ye ask amiss." **(James 4:2,3)**

Are all your needs met today? If not, why not?

According to the Word of God, it's either because you're not praying about them at all or because when you do pray, you're praying wrong.

What does it mean to pray *wrong?* In many cases it simply means to pray *without* expecting results. Many believers do that, you know. They use prayer as a kind of spiritual wishbone. They just play around with it. "This probably won't do much good," they think, "but who knows? It won't hurt to give it a try."

If that's been your attitude, then change it! Start getting serious about prayer. Stop praying just because it's proper. Stop praying just because you always pray at this point in the church service. And start praying to get results.

Start praying in the name of Jesus, according to the Word of God, and expect to receive what you ask for every single time. Isn't that a little presumptuous? No, but it is *bold,* and you have a scriptural right to be bold.

According to the Word of God, you have a standing invitation from your heavenly Father to "come *boldly* unto the throne of grace, that [you] may *obtain*" (Heb. 4:16). That word *obtain* is a word of certainty. The dictionary says it means "to get possession of."

So, pray, expecting to get possession of what you need, not just once in a while, but every time! When prayers do go unanswered, don't just wander away saying, "I guess you never know what God's going to do." Tackle the problem with both hands! Go to God in prayer and in the Word and find out where you missed it and get the problem corrected.

When you go to God in accurate, Word-of-God-based, Spirit-inspired prayer, you *do* know what He's going to do. He's going to answer you. He's going to meet your need exactly as you asked Him. Start expecting Him to do it today.

SCRIPTURE READING: 1 John 5:4-15

Be Skillful

"The young lions do lack, and suffer hunger:
but they that seek the Lord shall not want any good thing." **(Psalm 34:10)**

Did you know that, according to the Word of God, there is no lack in the Body of Christ? Everything we could ever need, every problem we could ever face has been covered by the blood of Jesus. His exceeding great and precious promises have supplied it all.

Why then do we keep on suffering lack? Because we haven't, as Hebrews 5:13 says, become skillful in the Word of righteousness.

It takes *skill* to apply the Word of God. Most of us don't realize that. We just sling the Word around and try to use it any old way. We pray some ignorant prayer and then say, "Oh well, God knows what I mean" and expect it to be answered.

It's funny though. We'd never stand for that kind of carelessness in the natural realm. If our doctor came in and just threw a bottle of pills at us and said, "Here, take that," without even trying to find out what's wrong with us, we'd leave his office and never come back. Yet, we'll be shocked when that same careless attitude in the spiritual realm keeps our prayers from being effective.

We live in an "instant" society where everything is quick and easy. And too many of us are letting that instant mentality leak over into our walk with the Lord Jesus Christ. When someone needs healing, we bust through the hospital door, dab a little oil between their eyes and say, "Glory to God!" and out the door we go. Sometimes it doesn't take any longer than "In the name of Jesus be healed!" But sometimes there is something else that must be done.

The time has come for us to shake off that "instant" mentality and realize that there are situations where we're going to have to take some time and pray in the Holy Ghost. Times when we're going to have to sit there and listen for God's instructions.

If you've come up short in any area of life—whether it be healing or finances or anything else—determine to develop your Word skills where that area is concerned. Get out your Bible. Read all through the healing scriptures. Read all through the miracle scriptures. Read all through the promises of God. Read all through the blessings of Abraham.

Meditate on them. Ask God to speak to you through them and to enlighten you about the situation you're facing. Don't just sling the Word around. Dig into it. Fellowship with your Father over it. Let Him show you how to apply it skillfully, and eventually, you'll lack no good thing.

SCRIPTURE READING: Psalm 23

Don't Overlook the Blessings

"For our light affliction, which is but for a moment,
worketh for us a far more exceeding and eternal weight of glory."
(2 Corinthians 4:17)

It's easy to get your spiritual eyes fixed so firmly on the problems in your life, you overlook the blessings completely! As a result, you end up suffering through situations that should have you rejoicing.

Let me show you what I mean. Not long ago, this ministry was facing some terrific financial pressures. I stood in faith against them. I battled against them with the Word and in prayer.

What I didn't realize was this: During that time when the problems seemed so great—the blessings were even greater. This ministry was growing faster, ministering to more people, writing more letters, printing more publications, sending out more teaching tapes than ever before! It was a breakthrough time...a time for rejoicing. But I didn't know it because I was too busy thinking about the problems.

I was so tunnel-visioned, all I could see was the pressure, and I suffered through some hard times when I should have been shouting the victory.

But thank God, He woke me up before it was over. He woke me up to the blessings and reminded me that the problems are temporary, or subject to change, but God and His Word of victory are *never* subject to change!

If you've been suffering through some hard times lately, wake up to the blessings around you. You'll be much more effective in battling the problems if you're giving God the glory for the solutions He's already provided. Take your eyes off the trouble and look around you. You'll soon be shouting the victory!

SCRIPTURE READING: Psalm 13

Your Deadly Enemy

"I would not have you to be ignorant, brethren,
concerning them which are asleep, that ye sorrow not, even as
others which have no hope. For if we believe that Jesus
died and rose again...." **(1 Thessalonians 4:13)**

Many of us, even though we're believers, have seen grief and sorrow as such a natural part of life that we haven't even questioned them. In fact, if we're honest, we'd have to admit there are times when we actually want to feel sad and sorry for ourselves.

Why would we *choose* to feel sorrow? Because sorrow has an emotional kick to it. It offers a surge of feeling that, in the beginning stages, is almost intoxicating.

But grief and sorrow are dangerous things. I know because several years ago God showed me that they're not the innocent emotions we've thought they were. The force behind these emotions are actually spirit beings sent by the devil himself to kill, steal, and destroy.

They are a part of the devastating, satanic barrage Jesus took on Himself when He died on the cross (Is. 53). He bore grief and sorrow, so we wouldn't have to. If they come knocking on your door, remember they are not innocent emotions. They are deadly enemies that Jesus already carried away at Calvary.

Don't live as those who have no hope. You're a believer. You know that Jesus Christ died for you and rose again. That not only gives you hope where physical death is concerned, it gives you hope in every situation. Sorrow not!

SCRIPTURE READING: Isaiah 51:11-16

Discourage the Devil

"Blessed are ye, when men shall hate you,
and when they shall separate you from their company,
and shall reproach you, and cast out your name as evil, for the
Son of man's sake. Rejoice ye in that day, and leap for joy: for,
behold, your reward is great in heaven: for in the like manner
did their fathers unto the prophets." **(Luke 6:22,23)**

D o you want to know how to depress the devil? Just follow the instructions in that last verse. When persecution comes, when friends or family criticize you because you lay hands on the sick and believe in healing, and when co-workers call you a fanatic because you love Jesus and aren't afraid to say so, rejoice! Shout hallelujah and leap for joy!

I tell you that will discourage the devil to no end. He's expecting that persecution to hurt you. He's expecting it to damage your faith, to wipe you out, and to leave you in dismay.

I'm not saying you should enjoy the persecution itself. But you can learn to overlook the discomfort of those things by focusing your attention on the reward that's coming and the fact that Jesus said *you are blessed.*

The apostle Paul certainly knew how to do that. He was an expert on rejoicing in the midst of persecution. Satan was constantly stirring up trouble for him. But do you know what he said about all that persecution? He said it was not even worth considering compared to the glory that was about to be revealed.

If Paul could rejoice in the midst of beatings, stonings, shipwrecks, imprisonment, and almost every other kind of persecution, you can too!

Just do what he did. When he was told by the Holy Ghost that bonds and afflictions awaited him, he said, "But none of these things move me, neither count I my life dear unto myself, so that I might finish my course with joy, and the ministry, which I have received of the Lord Jesus, to testify the gospel of the grace of God" (Acts 20:24).

Don't get all caught up in what people think and what people say down here on earth. Get caught up in pleasing the Lord. Get caught up in finishing your course with joy. Get caught up in the glorious hope that's ahead. For that hope is enough to make anyone—under any circumstances—leap for joy!

SCRIPTURE READING: Acts 16:16-35

Tap Into the Truth

"When he, the Spirit of truth, is come, he will guide you into all truth:
for he shall not speak of himself; but whatsoever he shall hear, that shall
he speak: and he will shew you things to come." **(John 16:13)**

Jesus said the Holy Spirit would guide us into *all* truth. Not just enough truth to get by on. Not just an occasional truth to help us teach our Sunday school classes. All truth!

If you're a businessman, that means the Holy Spirit will show you how to increase your profits and reduce your expenses. If you're a mother, it means the Holy Spirit will show you how to settle arguments between your children. If you're a student, it means the Holy Spirit will show you how to excel in your classes.

In fact, if you know Jesus Christ and are baptized in the Holy Ghost, somehow inside you is the answer to every financial problem, every spiritual problem, and every physical problem that exists. You have answers for problems you don't even know about yet!

Back during World War II, for example, the United States ran into some serious trouble. Their ships were being sunk by the enemy faster than they could build new ones, a process which at that time took a year.

In an effort to solve their dilemma, a method was devised by which a ship could be built in a single day. The problem was, the process involved building the ship upside down and, when the ships were turned upright, the welds would pop and the ship would come apart.

The problem was presented to a deeply spiritual man who was a famous industrialist at the time. "I'll find out how to do it," he said. And, sure enough, after days of prayer and fasting, God showed him the welding formula that would hold the ship together.

If you're facing a problem today, don't drag around trying to handle it on your own. Take Jesus at His Word and start asking the Holy Spirit to give you the knowledge you need to solve it. Put the wisdom of the ages to work on your job, in your family, and in your world. Tap into the truths He's placed in you.

SCRIPTURE READING: John 14:6-17

Make Hell Tremble

"For this purpose the Son of God was manifested,
that he might destroy the works of the devil." **(1 John 3:8)**

I s the devil giving you fits today? Is he causing trouble for you at every turn?

If so, turn the table on him. Start making him miserable for a change. You have the power to do it, you know. You have the power residing in you to destroy his works, to heal, to deliver, to set the captives free. You have so much power in you that every time your alarm clock goes off, the devil should wail, "Oh no! That trouble-maker is up again!"

A few years ago, I got a letter from a little girl who had attended one of my healing services in Los Angeles. Although she was far too young to understand theology or anything like that, the Lord gave her a very simple and profound revelation as she watched people being healed.

She said that as she looked up at the platform, she couldn't see me at all. She just saw Jesus. And she also saw a devil. Do you know what the devil was doing? He was lying on the floor crying, "This can't be! This can't be! This can't be!"

Right now, at this very moment, the power of the Lord Jesus Christ is at work within you. And it's not just there to get you to heaven someday. It's there so you can give the devil a fit right here on earth. It's there so you can build the kingdom of God now—while there's still time.

Line up with God's Word and will for your life. Let the anointing of Jesus go forth from within you. All of hell will tremble. And you will never be quite the same again.

SCRIPTURE READING: 1 John 5:4-20

A Legend in Your Own Mind

"For I say, through the grace given unto me, to every man
that is among you, not to think of himself more highly than he ought
to think; but to think soberly, according as God hath dealt
to every man the measure of faith." **(Romans 12:3)**

Do you want to know one of the secrets of staying in the will of God, of keeping yourself from getting off track?

Don't overestimate yourself!

Proverbs 16:18 says, "Pride goeth before destruction, and an haughty spirit before a fall." How many times have we seen that borne out! How many times do we see believers get into trouble because they get an overblown idea of themselves. They begin to think they're so smart that they have it all figured out.

Then, the next thing you know, they're thinking they have to straighten everyone else out. Instead of just letting Jesus be Head of the Church, they feel like they have to step in and do the job.

Once that happens, it's just a matter of time before they're flat on their face in failure. Why? Because the Bible says God resists the proud! (1 Pet. 5:5).

Don't put yourself in a position where God has to resist you. Rate your own abilities soberly. Adopt an attitude of humility. Keep a watch on yourself, and when you catch yourself getting puffed up with your own greatness, repent and remember that every good thing you enjoy and every bit of success you've had has come by the grace of God and by His power.

Look back on your life and see how many times you could have lost what God had given you. See how many times, when you were floundering around making every mistake imaginable, His tender and precious mercy pulled you through.

Don't become a legend in your own mind. Instead, humble yourself beneath the mighty hand of God, and let God do the exalting—that prevents some very painful falls.

SCRIPTURE READING: 1 Peter 5:5-7; James 4:6-17

No Hard Hearts

"For the eyes of the Lord run to and fro throughout the whole earth, to shew himself strong in the behalf of them whose heart is perfect toward him." **(2 Chronicles 16:9)**

The Pharisees had a heart condition that grieved Jesus. Their hearts were hard and insensitive. If you'll look in Mark, chapter 3, you'll see what I'm talking about.

God was right there in their midst, and they, of all people, should have realized it. They knew the Scriptures backward and forward, and Jesus fit every messianic prophecy written there. But the insensitivity of their hearts literally blinded them to who He was.

The hearts of the Pharisees were also hardened to the needs of the people around them.

That very same thing is still happening today.

Just think again about what those Pharisees were doing. They were:

1. Criticizing the minister of God.
2. Protecting their religious traditions instead of obeying the Word of God.
3. Worrying about their own welfare rather than that of those around them.

Have you ever known any believers who fit that description? Sure you have! In fact, every one of us has done those things at some time in our lives.

Every one of us, to one degree or another, has fallen prey to the same mistake the Pharisees did. We've gotten so caught up in doing and saying all the "right" things that we've let the tender warmth of God's love inside us grow cold.

I know that's true because if it weren't, we'd be seeing tremendous moves of God among us. We'd be seeing revival on every corner.

That's what God longs to do. God longs to pour out His Spirit in supernatural power and abundance through His Church. But we've developed a heart condition that's holding Him back.

Today if you are desiring an outpouring of the Holy Spirit in your life and the manifestation of His power in your church, check the condition of your heart. If you find any hardness there, repent and ask God to change you. Ask Him to give you the kind of heart that will allow Him to show Himself strong on your behalf.

SCRIPTURE READING: Mark 3:1-6

Give More – Not Less

"There is that scattereth, and yet increaseth;
and there is that withholdeth more than is meet, but it tendeth to poverty."

(Proverbs 11:24)

When money gets tight, it's always a temptation to cut down on your giving. After all, it seems like the logical thing to do. Don't do it! You'll end up cutting off the flow of God's financial blessings just when you need them most.

I faced that kind of situation just a few years ago. This ministry had fallen behind financially—one million dollars to be exact. Gloria and I had been living by faith for 20 years at that time. We knew firsthand that God would meet our needs—"according to his riches in glory by Christ Jesus" (Phil. 4:19). We'd seen God prove that over and over again, not only in our personal lives but in the life of our ministry as well.

Yet this particular time, all the prayers and the faith that had brought us victory before just didn't seem to get the job done. In fact, as time went on, the situation grew worse instead of better.

By the end of the year our deficit had grown to be a million dollars.

Frustrated and weary, I finally went to God one day and laid the situation out before Him. "Lord," I said, "You see the condition of this ministry. I need a million dollars just to break even."

"Oh no, you don't!" the Lord replied.

I could hardly believe it. How could He possibly be telling me that I didn't need a million dollars? Hadn't He looked at the books? Hadn't He talked to my accountant? I was stumped. All I could figure was that I'd misunderstood something. So I went through it all again.

Again He said, "Oh no, you don't."

Despite my initial confusion, as I kept asking and listening, I began to understand what the Lord was telling me. He was saying that the red ink on the books wasn't the only thing wrong. There was a bigger problem behind it.

Then He showed me what I needed to do was to start giving ten percent of the ministry's income into ministering to the poor.

To the natural mind that looked like no solution at all. How do you solve a deficit by giving away what money you've got? But when I applied that solution, the million dollar deficit began to disappear.

Remember that next time the devil tries to put the squeeze on you. Break his hold on your finances by giving more instead of less. It won't be long until the prosperity of God is poured out on you!

SCRIPTURE READING: 1 Kings 17:1-16

The Key to Confidence

"Beloved, if our heart condemn us not, then have we confidence toward God. And whatsoever we ask, we receive of him, because we keep his commandments, and do those things that are pleasing in his sight." **(1 John 3:21,22)**

You can never "get away with" disobeying God.

Some people think you can. They think that if nobody finds out about it, it won't hurt anything. After all, God is merciful. He's not going to hold it against them, right? And if no one else knows...what's the difference?

What they don't realize is that their own heart will start giving them problems. Their own heart will start to condemn them. Everyone else may think they're great. They may be spouting faith talk all over the place, but when they come before God in prayer, they'll be filled with doubts and fears that keep their prayers from being answered.

That's one of the reasons why it's so important to live in obedience to the Lord. A life of obedience will give you a spiritual boldness you've never had before. It will give you a boldness in prayer, a boldness in faith. It will give you a confidence toward God, as the apostle John says, that those who are trying to get away with sin don't have.

I'm not saying that you have to be perfect. That you should never make a mistake. Just that you should walk in obedience to the light you have. Take the time to listen and be responsive to the Spirit of God. When He tells you to do something, do it.

As you do, that confidence will rise up within you. It won't be something you mentally drummed up or talked yourself into. It will just be there. Instead of being consumed with doubts and feelings that the Word of God isn't going to work for you, you'll find yourself filled with faith that it will. You'll begin to trust God and to flow with Him. You'll come to a place the Bible calls "rest in the Lord."

Remember this: Even though the eternal price for your sins has been paid, a life of disobedience will still cost you dearly. It will cost you the boldness that is rightfully yours in Jesus. It will rob you of faith and rock you with fear.

Don't let the condemnation of your heart cut your confidence short. Do the things that are pleasing in God's sight and walk tall in the kingdom of God.

SCRIPTURE READING: 1 John 3:21,22

Nothing to Lose

"Say ye to the righteous, that it shall be well with him:
for they shall eat the fruit of their doings. Woe unto the wicked! it shall be
ill with him: for the reward of his hands shall be given him." **(Isaiah 3:10,11)**

Have you ever been afraid to give yourself totally to the Lord because you think you might be deprived of some pleasure in this life? Chances are, you have. That's because Satan is working overtime to convince you that he can really make your life worth living. But don't believe him for a minute. The real truth is, yielding completely to the Lord won't cost you anything that's worth having. It will only cause you to live life to its fullest!

Jesus' life on earth was a perfect example of a totally yielded life. He was a walking example of the benefits godly living brings. Everywhere He went, Jesus made the deaf to hear, the blind to see, the lame to walk. He lived in perfect peace and absolute victory.

That all sounds pretty good to me. All He missed out on was the devil getting dominion over Him to kill, steal, and destroy. In fact, the devil couldn't do anything to Him until, by the Father's will, He laid down His life. Until that time Jesus walked in total victory over the enemy.

Do you think you would miss out on a lot if you lived that way? Of course not! You can walk in that same anointing and power and glory of God that Jesus did.

Do you have to give up your whole life to do it? Yes! You have to trade your life for the life of God. You have to trade your sickness for His healing, your poverty for His prosperity, your anxiety for His peace, your sin for His salvation.

So why hesitate? When it gets right down to it, you really have nothing to lose.

SCRIPTURE READING: Psalm 37:7-23

Can Strangers See Jesus in You?

"Now when they saw the boldness of Peter and John,
and perceived that they were unlearned and ignorant men,
they marvelled; and they took knowledge of them,
that they had been with Jesus." **(Acts 4:13)**

How would you like to be so full of the glory of God that it's unmistakable to those around you? How would you like for people to be able to know just by looking at you that you'd been with Jesus? It's entirely possible if you are born again and filled with the Holy Spirit. The same mighty power that changed you inwardly when you were saved can so revolutionize you outwardly that even strangers on the street will be able to see Jesus in you.

One of my favorite testimonies is the one Jerry Savelle tells of the time he was in a shopping mall with his wife Carolyn. He was sauntering from one store to another, casually passing time until Carolyn finished her shopping.

A woman walked up to Jerry and said, "Will you pray for me?" Since he didn't know the woman, he was puzzled. "Out of all the people in that mall, how was it that she'd picked *him* out?" he asked.

She said, "The Lord told me to come to this mall and someone would be here who could pray for me. I came here looking for that person. I noticed a beam of light. It would go into one store, wander around, then go to another store and wander around some more. I followed the light until I found where it was coming from—and it was coming from *you*!"

What was that light? The glory of God! It was shining from Jerry much like it shone from the face of Moses when he came down from Mount Sinai. And that radiant presence of God brought healing to that woman when Jerry prayed.

Just as the fact that Peter and John had been with Jesus was unmistakable, so was the fact that Jerry Savelle had been with Jesus when that lady walked up to him in the mall.

When you spend time with Jesus, it will be undeniable. His power and His glory will be reflected in you to the world. And His presence upon you will meet needs everywhere you go. Take time to be with Jesus today!

SCRIPTURE READING: Acts 4:1-20

Leave the Past Behind

"But this one thing I do, forgetting those things which are behind, and reaching forth unto those things which are before, I press toward the mark for the prize of the high calling of God in Christ Jesus." **(Philippians 3:13,14)**

Spiritual bumps and bruises. Inner aches and pains that just don't seem to go away. Most all of us know what it's like to suffer from them but too few of us know just what to do about them.

We limp along, hoping somehow those hidden wounds will magically stop hurting, thinking that maybe (with a little extra sleep or an extra helping of dessert) that nagging sense of depression will finally disappear.

But does it ever happen that way? No!

I know. I've been there.

But thank God, I'm not there anymore. You see, over the past few years, I've faced some fierce spiritual battles. And I've found out those battles can leave you bruised and beat up on the inside just as surely as a fistfight can leave you bruised and beat up on the outside.

Before I was born again, I learned just how physically devastating a real slug-it-out kind of brawl could be. Yet as bad as I felt, a few days rest would take care of me.

The healing of a bruised and beaten spirit, however, doesn't come that easily. In fact, the passing of time often actually worsens this condition.

The reason is this: Instead of putting painful failures behind us, we often dwell on them until those failures become more real to us than the promises of God. We focus on them until we become bogged down in depression, frozen in our tracks by the fear that if we go on, we'll only fail again.

But there is a way out. If depression has put you into a spiritual nosedive, all you have to do to break out of it is to get your eyes off the past and onto your future—a future that's been guaranteed by Christ Jesus through the exceedingly great and precious promises in His Word.

Chances are, that won't come easily to you at first. Your mind has probably had years of practice in focusing on the past. Like an old horse that habitually heads for the barn, your thoughts will probably start galloping that direction every time you give them any slack.

So, don't give them that slack. Keep the reigns tight. Purposely meditate on the Word of God. Replace thoughts of the past with scriptural promises about your future and be diligent about it. Then, instead of being a wounded soldier, you'll become the conquering warrior God made you to be.

SCRIPTURE READING: Philippians 3:12-21

Don't Let Your Faith Slip

"Therefore we ought to give the more earnest heed
to the things which we have heard, lest at any time we
should let them slip." **(Hebrews 2:1)**

Something very serious has been happening to the Body of Christ. We've been letting the things which we have heard, the message of faith and righteousness, slip.

I'm not just talking about those believers who've been so surrounded by religion that they've never heard about the power that's theirs in Christ Jesus. I'm talking about those like you and me, those who have heard the Word and have known the thrill of living by faith. We've let that faith slip!

In my own life, for example, there have been times when I'd pray for healing. I'd say all the right words, "Thank God, I believe I receive..." and all that. But inside I'd be thinking, "I wonder why God isn't healing me?"

You see, even though I'd said that I believed I was healed, I hadn't really. I'd staggered at the promise of God, believing what my body told me instead of the Word of God.

I don't care how long you've been a believer or how long you've been practicing the principles of faith. You can easily slip into unbelief about the promises of God. And, once you do, it will cost you dearly.

"But if slipping into unbelief is so easy," you may say, "how can we avoid it?"

Hebrews 4:11 tells us: "Let us labour therefore to enter into that rest, lest any man fall after the same example of unbelief."

We must labor! Not by working with our hands and feet or struggling to get God to do something, but by spending time in God's Word—hanging on to the promises of God by faith day after day. We must labor by hearkening to the Word and refusing to let it slip.

Don't get casual about the Word. Don't make the mistake of thinking, "Oh I *know* all that faith stuff. I know how to receive my healing." If you do, you'll slack off and one of these days the devil will catch you unprepared and steal you blind.

Instead, dig more deeply in the Word than ever. Labor! Be diligent to keep your faith from slipping—and you won't have to fall!

SCRIPTURE READING: Hebrews 10:23-39

Feast on the Word

"Man shall not live by bread alone, but by every word
that proceedeth out of the mouth of God." **(Matthew 4:4)**

The Word of God is to your spirit as bread is to your body. When your body feeds on physical food, it produces a physical power called strength. When your spirit feeds on the spiritual food of the Word, it produces spiritual power called faith. And just as you can't eat one meal and then feed on the memory of it for several weeks, you can't just remember what the Word says and stay strong in faith. You have to read it. Even if you've read it a hundred times, you need to read it again.

Try this: Close your eyes and see yourself slicing a lemon. Now stick that lemon slice between your teeth and when I say, "Three," bite down on it so hard that the juice squirts into your mouth. One. Two. Three. Bite!

Chances are, you have such a vivid memory of what it's like to bite on a lemon that your mouth is watering right now. But let me ask you this, "Have you received any nourishment from that memory?" No.

Remembering the Word of God isn't enough. You must continually feed on what it says. Get it out and read it. Go to church and hear it preached.

One day, you'll read a familiar verse...a verse you've read thousands of times before...and suddenly God will give you the greatest revelation you've ever had. A completely fresh revelation from that old familiar verse! And it's likely to be exactly what you needed to know about your current situation.

Yes, you can feed on the Word that is on deposit in your spirit. But remember this: You can't get continued results if you don't spend time in prayer and in the Word of God allowing the Spirit to nourish you daily.

Don't try to live on the memory of your last spiritual meal. Replenish the force of faith within you. Feast on the Word of God today.

SCRIPTURE READING: John 6:48-58

Be Separate

"Wherefore come out from among them, and be ye separate, saith the Lord, and touch not the unclean thing; and I will receive you." **(2 Corinthians 6:17)**

We're surrounded by a world which is ruled for the most part by Satan. How can we avoid getting caught up in it? How can we stand apart?

You'll find the answer in John 17:17. There Jesus was speaking to the Father about all those who would believe on Him. "Sanctify them through thy truth," He says. "Thy word is truth." Sanctify means "to separate unto." So Jesus is saying, "Separate them by the Word." The Word separates!

When you initially believed the Word of God, you were born again. You were separated spiritually from the kingdom of darkness and separated unto the kingdom of Light. Now that's where a lot of people stop. They let the Word of God do its initial separating work and then go right on living like everybody else. Spiritually, they're still separated from death. But physically and mentally, they're up to their necks in it. They're poor. They're sick. They're worried. They're confused. They're upset. In other words, they're just like everyone else in the world.

But if you'll give the Word of God first place in your life, it will continue to separate you from the poverty and the anxiety and the sickness and the hatred and the darkness of your old habitat.

There's something else that the Word of God will do for you too. It will not only separate you from the things of this world, it will separate you unto the things of God.

You can't simply separate yourself from any old destructive habit without separating yourself unto something else. You can't turn away from the things of the world unless you turn to something stronger. I'm telling you, you can scream and squall and kick the altar bench and everything else trying to get rid of the sin in your life. You can cry, "Dear God, take this sin away from me." But all the begging in the world won't separate you from your sin. It's the Word that does it!

Make a decision to give the Word first place in your life. Make it a quality decision, a decision from which there is no retreat. Lock into the Word and let the Word do its work. Let it separate you from the things of the world and unto the things of God.

SCRIPTURE READING: 2 Corinthians 6:14-18

We're Winning

"Only rebel not ye against the Lord, neither fear ye
the people of the land; for they are bread for us: their defence is departed
from them, and the Lord is with us: fear them not." **(Numbers 14:9)**

Thousands of years ago, God told the children of Israel to go up and occupy the land that He had given them. He told them to take it, by force and without fear, from the ungodly ones who were dwelling there.

He's still saying that today. God is still trying to get us, as His people, to take the good land He's given us. He's still trying to get us to use the power He's given us to run the wicked one out.

You see, this earth doesn't belong to the devil. It belongs to God (Ps. 24:1). The devil's just moved in and taken control of things because we believers haven't stopped him.

That *is* our job, you know. Jesus took Satan's legal rights away from him on resurrection morning. Then Jesus put us in charge of enforcing Satan's defeat. The Scripture says that Jesus is going to sit at the right hand of the Father until His enemies are made His footstool (Heb. 10:12,13). Do you know what that means? It means Jesus is waiting on *us* to kick the devil and his crew out of the affairs of this earth.

He's waiting on us to carry out the victory He won at Calvary and occupy this land.

But just like Israel had to rise up physically to take the land of Canaan, you and I have to rise up in the Spirit if we're going to establish the dominion of God in the earth. We're going to have to get moving. We can't do it sitting down!

Listen, you may not know it, but we're at war. We're in a spiritual battle—and we're winning. In fact, if you realized what was already established in the spirit world, you'd laugh at the devil every time he showed his face.

So today if the devil has control of an area of your life or your church or your community, rise up in the Spirit through faith and prayer and the Word and start taking that territory back. Don't be afraid. His defense is departed from him. He has no weapon that can stand against you.

The Lord is with you. Rise up in the name of Jesus and take back the land!

SCRIPTURE READING: Exodus 14:10-31

Step Into the Light

"Thy word is a lamp unto my feet, and a light unto my path."
(Psalm 119:105)

As long as you live by the Word of God, you never have to be in the dark again. You never have to remain in confusion about which path to take. You never have to grope blindly along, struggling to find your own way.

Isn't that great? Isn't it exciting to know that the Word of God will give you all the light you need every day of your life if you'll allow it to?

Build your faith in that Word and renew your commitment to it as you make this confession today:

"Father, in the name of Jesus, I commit myself to walk in Your Word. I recognize that Your Word is integrity itself—steadfast, sure, eternal—and I trust my life to its provisions.

"You have sent Your Word forth into my heart. I let it dwell in me richly in all wisdom. It does not depart out of my mouth; I meditate in it day and night so that I may diligently act on it.

Your Word is an incorruptible seed, abiding in my spirit, and it's growing mightily in me now, producing Your nature, Your life.

"I thank You, Father, that Your Word is my counsel, my shield, my buckler, my powerful weapon in battle. It is a lamp unto my feet and a light unto my path. It makes my way straight before me, and I never stumble or fall for my steps are ordered by Your Word.

"I recognize the strategies and deceits of Satan and I put a stop to them by speaking Your Word out of my mouth in faith.

"I am confident, Father, that You are at work in me both to will and to do Your good pleasure. I exalt Your Word. I hold it in high esteem and give it first place in my life. I boldly and confidently say that my heart is fixed and established on the solid foundation—the living Word of God. Amen!"

SCRIPTURE READING: Psalm 119:89-105

You Don't Have to Fall

"Brethren, give diligence to make your calling and election sure:
for if ye do these things, ye shall never fall." **(2 Peter 1:10)**

You shall never fall. When you think about it, that's a startling statement, isn't it? Most of us have been tripped up by the devil so many times we don't like to think about it.

But the Word of God says it doesn't have to be that way. He says there's something that can keep us on our feet. What is it? *Diligence.*

If you haven't already, you need to realize how important diligence is. You need to face the fact that you simply can't live a life of victory without it.

You can't stand strong on the Word of God and not pick your Bible up during the week. Sunday morning alone isn't going to get the job done. Yet most believers try to get by on that. That's precisely why we have thousands of churches all over the world filled with born-again people who don't have enough faith to blow their hats off. No diligence.

I remember several years ago when I ministered to a lady who was healed of cancer. She'd gotten into the Word, taken a stand of faith, and had been delivered. But several years later she called me and said, "Brother Copeland, I wish you'd pray for me. This cancer has come back on me again."

Right away I recalled the scripture the Lord had given us to stand on those years before: "No weapon formed against you shall prosper." So I said, "Get your Bible and let's go back to Isaiah 54:17."

In the background I could hear her whispering to someone else in the room, "Where's my Bible?" When I heard that, I almost cried out. I knew she wasn't going to make it. Why? No diligence.

Listen, this is a daily thing. The devil's out there 24 hours a day devising ways to make us fall. Jesus is on the throne 24 hours a day giving us power to resist him, and we need to be exercising our faith *all* the time.

If you're going to stand in the days ahead, you're going to need a lot more than Sunday school faith. You're going to need some full-grown, mountain-moving faith, and there's only one way to get that: By giving yourself to the Word more diligently than you ever have before.

So do it. Give diligence to make your calling and election sure; and no matter how slippery the situation gets, you won't have to fall!

SCRIPTURE READING: 2 Peter 1:3-10

Don't Serve the Problem

"Let the wicked forsake his way, and the unrighteous
man his thoughts: and let him return unto the Lord, and he will
have mercy upon him." (Isaiah 55:7)

You can't win a victory as long as the problem is the biggest thing in your life!

The Lord woke me up to that fact a few years ago. At that time I was facing some difficulties in my ministry that seemed so big to me, I thought about them from morning till night. Even though I was standing against them, I was thinking more about those problems than about the scripture promises I was standing on.

Then I saw something in Matthew 6:24,25.

"Ye cannot serve God and mammon. Therefore I say unto you, Take no thought for your life."

I'd read that scripture hundreds of times, but that day I saw something I'd never noticed before. I saw that immediately after Jesus said, "No man can serve two masters," He said, "Take no thought." Suddenly it hit me: *We serve our thoughts!*

That's why the fifty-fifth chapter of Isaiah says for us to forsake our thoughts, and by the Word, take God's thoughts. That's why 2 Corinthians 10:5 says to cast out thoughts that challenge the Word and bring into captivity *every* thought to the obedience of Christ.

Do you want deliverance from your problems today?

Then quit serving them! Quit allowing them to consume your thought life. And don't wait until circumstances change to do it. Instead, realize that circumstances won't *ever* change until you switch from wrong to right thinking.

I know that's not easy to do, especially in the midst of heavy darkness and trial. But you *can* do it if you'll do these three things:

First, remember you aren't alone. You have the Word (God's thoughts). You have the Holy Spirit to strengthen you and you have the mind of Christ.

Second, get around people who are full of faith. Instead of rehearsing your problem, let them do the talking. Make yourself listen. Join in with their faith and resist darkness.

Third, praise God. Do whatever it takes to make yourself praise. When you begin to praise, God's presence will turn back those worried thoughts and make them fall!

Your problems are *not* the biggest thing in your life. Jesus is. Serve Him with your thoughts and He will set you free!

SCRIPTURE READING: Isaiah 55

Receive Your Miracle

"For with the heart man believeth unto righteousness;
and with the mouth confession is made unto salvation." **(Romans 10:10)**

D o you need a miracle? Then believe it, confess it, and receive it!

"Oh Gloria, I just don't know if I can do that."

Yes, you can! You've already done it once. When you made Jesus the Lord of your life, you believed, confessed, and received the greatest miracle in the universe, the miracle of a reborn spirit! Every other miracle you receive will come in exactly the same way.

You start by simply believing what God's Word says concerning your area of need, by letting that Word change your heart and mind.

A lot of people try to skip that step. They try to believe for a miracle without spending enough time in the Word to change their heart and mind. They just want to confess it with their mouth and have it instantly appear. But that won't happen. It's what we *believe in our heart* and say with our mouth that we receive.

If you don't have enough faith yet to believe for the miracle you need, then get it. "Faith cometh by hearing, and hearing by the word of God" (Rom. 10:17). So start filling the ears of your heart with the Word until faith for your miracle is born.

That's what the woman did who had the issue of blood. She believed in her heart that Jesus would heal her. Then she spoke her faith out loud. Then she acted on that faith—and she received her miracle.

It wasn't Jesus' decision. He didn't suddenly say, "You know, I think I'll work a miracle for that little lady today." No. *She* made it happen. She took her faith and drew on the power of God. That's why Jesus said, "Daughter, your faith has made you whole" (Matt. 9:22).

You have that same opportunity. God's power is always present everywhere. Your faith will bring it into your life, body, or circumstances. Do it. Reach out to Jesus. Believe, confess, and receive your miracle today.

SCRIPTURE READING: Matthew 9:18-31

Courage Comes From Faith

"Be strong and of a good courage; be not afraid,
neither be thou dismayed: for the Lord thy God is with thee
whithersoever thou goest." **(Joshua 1:9)**

Courage comes from trusting God. It can't be mentally drummed up. It comes from believing what God says regardless of what the circumstances look like. Courage comes from faith!

Where does discouragement come from? From fear and unbelief. It comes when you listen to the devil's lies about what God is *not* going to do for you.

As the people of God, you and I must shake off discouragement and rise up with courage! We must quit looking at our own abilities and failures and limitations and start looking to God. We must rise up in the name of Jesus and the power of His Spirit and establish the kingdom of heaven upon earth.

If you've been discouraged lately, stop listening to Satan's lies. Stop receiving evil reports. Whenever someone tells you God is not going to deliver you, you tell them, "He's already delivered me in the name of Jesus."

Once you begin to realize who you are and what you've been given by the power of God, you'll quit letting the devil run all over you. God didn't suggest that you be strong and courageous. That is His command!

SCRIPTURE READING: Joshua 1:1-9

Let It Flow

"Whosoever drinketh of the water that I shall give him
shall never thirst; but the water that I shall give him shall be in him a well
of water springing up into everlasting life." **(John 4:14)**

L ove. Joy. Peace. Patience. Gentleness. Goodness. Faith. Meekness. Temperance. Powerful forces the Bible calls the fruit of the Spirit. They're the character traits of God Himself and when the Holy Spirit came to dwell in you, He brought them with Him, so they could become your character traits too.

They're designed to bubble up inside you, to gush forth like a powerful stream constantly protecting and cleansing you from the inside out.

Have you ever noticed that you can't put any trash in the mouth of a flowing fountain? When it's shooting that water up, the force of its own outflow protects it and keeps it clear of any impurities from the outside. Well, the spiritual fountain within you works the same way. When you're allowing the forces of love and joy and peace and gentleness and all the others to flow out, the devil can't get any of his junk in.

How do you keep the Spirit flowing? You pump your heart so full of the Word of God that the forces of eternal life start bubbling out. Just a little at first...and then stronger and higher.

Choose to keep those forces streaming out of the fountain of your heart. Refuse to let selfishness and sin stop the flow. You have a fountain filled with unbeatable LIFE forces inside you and it's ready to come forth. Let it flow!

SCRIPTURE READING: Jeremiah 17:7-13

Receive His Mercy

"O give thanks unto the Lord;
for he is good: for his mercy endureth for ever." **(Psalm 136:1)**

God's mercy endureth forever! His willingness to act on man's behalf is still operating in the earth. His mercy never runs out. Neither has it abated nor weakened.

"Praise the Lord! His mercy endureth forever!" Mighty and powerful things happened when Israel said these words. They are words of praise and adoration to God.

When Solomon finished building the house of the Lord, the trumpeters and singers lifted their voices as one, and with trumpets, cymbals, and instruments of music, they praised the Lord saying, "For He is good: for His mercy endureth forever."

Jehoshaphat appointed singers unto the Lord to go before the army and say, "Praise the Lord! For His mercy endureth forever."

It has been thousands of years since the Lord said His mercy extended to a thousand generations, and His mercy continues to reach you day after day. HE is still plenteous in mercy unto them that call upon Him. With your spirit, dare to stretch your faith to take in the boundless mercy of God. And say with your mouth, "The Lord He is good and His mercy endureth forever. His mercy surrounds *me* even today!"

SCRIPTURE READING: 2 Chronicles 5:1-14

Watch and Pray

"Watch and pray, that ye enter not into temptation:
the spirit indeed is willing, but the flesh is weak." **(Matthew 26:41)**

Have you ever been frustrated with the weaknesses of your flesh? Have you ever resolved never more to yield to a particular sin, yet when the temptation came, you fell right back into it?

It's happened to all of us. Even the disciple Peter. He swore he would never deny Jesus...but he did it anyway, time and time and time again.

There *is*, however, something we can do to keep from falling prey to temptations like that. We can "watch and pray." That's what Jesus told Peter and the other disciples to do in the Garden of Gethsemane. He knew they were about to be tempted, and He knew that the weakness of their flesh would overcome them if they didn't strengthen their spirits through prayer.

That's true for you and me too. That's why in Jude 20 and 21, God tells us much the same thing that Jesus told the disciples that night. He says, "But you, beloved, build yourselves up [founded] on your most holy faith... praying in the Holy Spirit: Guard and keep yourselves in the love of God" (AMP). God knows even better than we do that our flesh has been trained to flow with the world's stream. He knows that even though our born-again spirits are reaching for God, our untrained flesh will always have a tendency to fall into sin.

So, He's given us the ability to pray in other tongues, to strengthen our spirit and build it up until it takes ascendancy over our flesh. As we pray in the Spirit, Romans 8:26 tells us, the "(Holy) Spirit comes to our aid and bears us up in our weakness; for we do not know what prayer to offer nor how to offer it worthily as we ought, but the Spirit Himself goes to meet our supplication and pleads in our behalf" (AMP).

Is it any wonder the apostle Paul said, "I thank my God, I speak with tongues more than ye all!" (1 Cor. 14:18). It is one of the most powerful tools God has given us.

So don't neglect to use it. Follow the instruction in Ephesians 6:18 and pray "always with all prayer and supplication in the Spirit...watching thereunto with all perseverance."

Don't make the mistake that Peter made. When temptation comes to your door, don't let it catch you sleeping. Be prepared. Make sure your spirit is strong enough to rise above it.

SCRIPTURE READING: Matthew 26:30-44

Let Your Life Begin Again

"Behold, now is the day of salvation." **(2 Corinthians 6:2)**

Did you know that Jesus has un-locked the prison doors of guilt that have kept you captive? It doesn't matter who you are or what you've been. I don't care if you've been a prostitute, a murderer, a thief, a dope dealer, or a churchgoing guy who's never made Jesus Christ Lord of your life. The Bible says that today is the day of salvation.

A new life is only a prayer away.

Gloria and I discovered that for ourselves more than 25 years ago. Actually, it was Gloria who took the first step. She found out that the Bible said that not even a sparrow falls without God's knowledge. "Well," she thought, "if God knows and cares when the sparrows fall, He must know what terrible shape my life is in right now. And if He cares, maybe He can do something with it."

Gloria didn't know anything about the Bible. She didn't even know for sure that God would let her start over. But when she told Him she wanted Him to take over her life, something supernatural happened on the inside of her. She was born again.

"But what about my past?" you may say. "I feel so guilty about it!"

When you've been born again and made a new creature in Christ—that past doesn't belong to you anymore. And it would be ridiculous to walk around feeling guilty about someone else's past, wouldn't it?

What would you think if I took a little baby on my lap, a pretty little thing just a few months old, and said, "Oh, isn't she precious? But just think about her past."

You'd think I was crazy! "What past?" you'd say. "She doesn't have any past!"

Well, it's the same way with you once you've been born again. You don't have any past. Your life begins again the day you make Jesus Lord of your life. Then, when Satan comes around trying to remind you of what a worm you were before, just tell him he's knocking on the wrong door.

You've been kicked around long enough. There's no need to wait any longer. The prison door is open. Walk through to Jesus and let your life begin again today.

SCRIPTURE READING: Matthew 10:29-33

Put Your Imagination to Work

"And God is able to make all grace
abound toward you; that ye, always having all sufficiency in all things, may
abound to every good work." **(2 Corinthians 9:8)**

If you have a desire to give, yet financial failures keep holding you back, you may be surprised to learn that what you need is *not* more money. What you need is a spiritual breakthrough. You need to take the Word of God and shatter the images of poverty and lack within you. You need to replace them with a vision of the sufficiency of God. Then more things, including money, will come.

How? By spending time thinking on the prosperity promises He's provided for you in His Word. By meditating on them. By believing you receive those promises actually being fulfilled in your life.

Begin to see yourself, for example, being a generous giver to people in need. In your mind, see yourself as a giver instead of the one who is always in need. Each time you do, the promise of God will become more real to you and your faith will grow.

"Oh my, Brother Copeland, surely you're not saying I should use my *imagination!*"

Yes, that's precisely what I'm saying. What do you think God gave it to you for? Coupled with the Word of God, your imagination is a tremendous thing. However, never forget, without the Word, your imagination will become worldly and bind you *instead of feeding your faith.*

Let me warn you though, sometimes creating such new images of hope are tough—especially when there are old images of doubt blocking the way. If you've been broke, for instance, all or most all of your life, it may take you a while for you to see yourself prospering in God. But you can do it if you stay in the Word.

Just keep meditating the Word of God. Eventually you'll be transformed by the renewing of your mind. When that happens, financial failures will never be able to stop you again.

SCRIPTURE READING: 2 Corinthians 8:1-14

Keep Paddling Upstream

"Set a watch, O Lord, before my mouth;
keep the door of my lips." **(Psalm 141:3)**

Do you really believe that you need to watch over your mouth? Most believers don't. You can tell that just by listening to their conversations. They profess, for example, to be trusting God concerning their health. But you're likely to hear them say something like this: "I'm just sure I'm going to get the flu. I get it every year. I'll be sicker than a dog too, you'll see...."

Do people like that have what they say?

Oh yes! Check with them a few weeks later and they'll be quick to tell you that they got just as sick as they said they'd be. But, odds are, if you try to tell them there's any connection between the words they spoke and the illness they suffered, they'll look at you as if you were out of your mind.

Of course, if they'd dig into the Word of God and find out what it has to say about the subject, they'd realize that the words they speak have a tremendous impact on their lives. They'd see that it quite literally determines their future. If you're a born-again believer, you've already experienced the most powerful examples of that. You believed with your heart and confessed with your mouth the Lord Jesus and you changed the eternal course of your life. You *know* firsthand just how powerful your words can be.

Yet, even so, if you're like me, you still find that speaking faith-filled words consistently is tough to do. I've been at it myself for more than 22 years now and, despite all the time I've spent on it and all the experiences I've had, it's still something I have to watch all the time.

You see, the world around you is in negative flow. Like a rushing river, it's always pulling at you, trying to get you to flow with it. Living by faith and speaking words of faith is like trying to paddle upstream. You can do it—but it's a great deal of work. And there's never a time you can afford to take a vacation from it. All you have to do is relax a little bit and you'll just start drifting right back down the river.

Make the decision right now to set a watch over your lips. Determine to consistently fill your mouth with the Word of God. "Attend to my words; incline thine ear unto my sayings" (Prov. 4:20). Let God's Word be your watch and everything you say will take you a little further upstream!

SCRIPTURE READING: Romans 10:8-17

Possess God's Rest

"There remaineth therefore a rest to the people of God....
Let us labour therefore to enter into that rest, lest any man fall
after the same example of unbelief." **(Hebrews 4:9,11)**

God's rest. Considering the hectic, busy lives you and I live that sounds like a pretty good thing to have, doesn't it? But exactly what is that rest? And how do we enter it?

The third and fourth chapters of Hebrews compares God's rest with the children of Israel taking possession of the Promised Land. That land was to be a place where their every need would be met, a place of freedom from their warring enemies, a place no one would ever drive them from again. All they had to do was go in and possess it. But something kept them from it: unbelief and disobedience.

As believers, we, too, have the opportunity to enter a Promised Land of abundance and peace. A land where we can rest from our struggles and enjoy the victory of God. To enter it we must do what the children of Israel failed to do. We must simply trust God and obey His voice.

How do you come to that place of trust and obedience? By getting to know your Father. By spending time fellowshipping with Him in prayer and in the Word. That is the labor that will bring you into His rest!

I'll never forget when I first discovered that. I had been learning the principles of faith, striving hard to do them. It seemed back then that keeping doubt and unbelief out of my heart was difficult. Then, one day, I began to labor to know the Father instead of just knowing *about* Him.

When I did that, He began to reveal Himself to me. He gave me glimpses of His heart, His nature, and His love. As He revealed to me how much He wanted to do for His children, it changed my striving into peace, my doubt into trust, my fear into bold obedience. It enabled me to enter His rest.

Get to know your Father. Work at it. Make it your "labor." He has a Promised Land of rest that is waiting for you!

SCRIPTURE READING: Hebrews 4:1-11

A Living Example of Love

"And hope maketh not ashamed; because
the love of God is shed abroad in our hearts by the Holy Ghost
which is given unto us." **(Romans 5:5)**

Don't ever worry about not having enough love inside you. The Word says God's love *is* shed abroad in your heart by the Holy Ghost. God's love *is* in you. What you need to do is make a decision and let it flow.

Pray this prayer today.

"In Jesus' name, I make a fresh and strong commitment today to live the life of love, to let the tenderness of God flow through me and heal the wounded hearts of those I meet.

"Father, teach me to love even when things go wrong. To be patient and kind when the children are underfoot. To overlook the spiteful words of an angry spouse. To rejoice when someone at the office gets the raise that I thought I needed. Teach me to talk in love, to lay gossip quietly aside and to take up words of grace instead.

"Lord, Your Word says that Your love is already inside me...that it has been shed abroad in my heart. So today, I resolve to remove every obstacle that would keep that love from flowing freely into the lives of others. I put resentments behind me, and I forgive all those who've done me wrong.

"In the days ahead, cause me to increase and excel and overflow with Your love. Cause me to be what this world needs most of all...a living example of love. Amen."

SCRIPTURE READING: 1 John 4:7-17

Meditate on the Word

"And [God] brought [Abram] forth abroad, and said,
Look now toward heaven, and tell the stars, if thou be able to number them:
and he said unto him, So shall thy seed be. And he believed in the Lord;
and he counted it to him for righteousness." **(Genesis 15:5,6)**

Do you ever have trouble believing the Word of God? Not just agreeing with it mentally, but really believing that what it says will work for you?

I do. There are times when the promises in the Word stagger my mind. There have been times when I've felt so defeated and the circumstances around me looked so bad that it was tough for me to believe I was "more than a conqueror" even though I knew God said I was.

What do you do when your mind staggers like that at the promise of God? You meditate on that promise.

Scriptural meditation simply means thinking about and reflecting on the Word of God. It means pondering a particular scripture and mentally applying it to your own circumstances again and again until that scripture permanently marks your consciousness.

That kind of meditation can affect your life in a way that almost nothing else can. It can, quite literally, alter your mind. That's what happened to Abram.

When God first told him that he was going to father a nation, he was an old man. His wife, Sara, was also old too. What's more, she had been barren all her life. How could an aging, childless couple have even one child—much less a nation full of them? Abram couldn't even imagine such a thing. It contradicted his entire mind-set.

But God knew the mental struggle Abram would have, so He didn't just make him a verbal promise and leave it at that, He gave Abram a picture of that promise to meditate on. He took him out into the starry night, turned his eyes to the sky and said, "So shall thy seed be."

Can't you just see Abram staring out at the stars, trying to count them? Filling the eyes of his heart with the promise of God?

That's what meditation is all about. Taking time to envision the promise of God until it becomes a reality inside you. It's tremendously powerful, and by focusing on the scriptural promises God has given you, you can put it to work in your life just as Abram put it to work in his.

Don't just read the Word. Meditate on it today.

SCRIPTURE READING: Romans 4:13-25

A Supernatural Cycle of Blessing

"Cast thy bread upon the waters:
for thou shalt find it after many days." **(Ecclesiastes 11:1)**

One of the most exciting things I ever discovered about God's law of sowing and reaping was the fact that financial harvests are *not* seasonal. If you plant year round, you can be receiving year round.

Don't misunderstand. I'm not saying your harvest will come instantly. It usually won't. You may have to wait for it for several months. What I'm saying is, if you'll keep planting consistently, you'll receive just as consistently. If you'll continually cast your bread on the water, eventually it will come in on every wave!

Of course, some people never get to enjoy that kind of constant blessing. That's because, instead of giving, they keep waiting to receive. They stand on the beach saying, "I wonder where my prosperity is? As soon as it comes in, I'll start giving."

God's economy doesn't work that way. He said, "Give and it will be given to you again. The way you measure it, it shall be measured back to you" (Luke 6:38). *You* have to make the first move. You have to send a ship out before your ship can come in.

Think about that next time you're tempted to complain about the things life brings your way. Remember that whatever you've been casting out there is always what you find on down the road. If you've been giving doubt, unbelief, and fear, that's what has been coming to you. If you've been giving nothing, then nothing is what you get.

You're holding the seeds of your own future in your hand right now. Step out in faith and use them to put the supernatural cycle of blessing in motion. Start now planting one good seed after another. Eventually you'll enjoy a good harvest every single day!

SCRIPTURE READING: Luke 6:31-38

Heart to Heart

"For who has known or understood
the mind (the counsels and purposes) of the Lord
so as to guide and instruct [Him] and give Him knowledge?
But we have the mind of Christ, the Messiah, and
do hold the thoughts (feelings and purposes)
of His heart." **(1 Corinthians 2:16, AMP)**

Isn't it exciting to realize that you can hold the thoughts and feelings and purposes of God's very own heart in your heart? Isn't it thrilling to know the Creator of heaven and earth wants to be one spirit with you and transmit His thoughts to your mind?

First Corinthians 6:17 says that when you were joined to the Lord you became one spirit with Him. He came into union with you so that He can talk to you heart to heart. God wants you in this harmony with Him so that His thoughts can become your actions. He wants you to walk so closely with Him that you never lack power to overcome the evil of this world. He wants you to be so in tune with His Spirit that you are able to feel His heart of compassion toward those around you who are hurting or bowed down with sickness and pain. He wants to be one with you, so He can reach out through your hands and fulfill His purposes in the earth.

Make a fresh commitment today to walk in union with your God. Give your attention to His Spirit in your inner man. Determine to yield to His voice and not to the voices of the world or the flesh!

Allow the mind of Christ to flow through you!

SCRIPTURE READING: 1 Corinthians 2

Don't Underestimate Your Prayers

"I exhort therefore, that, first of all,
supplications, prayers, intercessions, and giving of thanks,
be made for all men; For kings, and for all that are in authority;
that we may lead a quiet and peaceable life in all
godliness and honesty." **(1 Timothy 2:1,2)**

That verse is clear, isn't it? The instruction is plain. Yet even in these tumultuous days when our nation is so desperately in need of God's guidance, most of God's people don't do what that verse commands.

Why not?

I believe it's because most of us are overwhelmed by the problems we see around us. "How could my prayers make a dent in the national debt?" we think. "How could my faith affect foreign policy?"

In other words, we fail to pray because we fail to realize just how powerfully our prayers can affect this country.

It's time we caught hold of that. It's time we realized that if we'd just be obedient to 1 Timothy 2:1,2, there's no council of any kind on earth, no king, no president, no congress, no anything that could overthrow God's purpose for His people.

God has called us to intercede. He has commanded us to pray for those in authority. He has given us His Word, His power, His name, His authority, and His faith. We have all the tools necessary to pray effectively for our government and its leaders.

I urge you to intercede. It is your responsibility as a believer to get involved in the affairs of your country. God wants this great land of ours, and the only way He's going to get it is through His ambassadors, you and me.

Pray for this nation. Every day. And never again underestimate the world-changing power of those prayers.

SCRIPTURE READING: Daniel 2:1-30

Evidence of a Miracle

"Now faith is the substance of things
hoped for, the evidence of things not seen." **(Hebrews 11:1)**

Don't ever short-circuit a miracle by trying to *see* it in progress! So many believers do that. They'll lay hands on someone and pray for healing or deliverance and then, when they don't see any immediate, outward change take place, they'll withdraw their faith and assume nothing happened.

The Lord taught me an unforgettable lesson about that once when I was in Jamaica. I was preaching to a group of about 150 people in a church that was lighted only by a single kerosene lantern. It was so dark I couldn't see anyone's face. All I could see was my Bible and the feet of the man right in front of me.

Suddenly I realized that I'd always depended on the facial expressions of the people I was preaching to to determine how my sermon was being received. Knowing what I did about faith, I knew that was dangerous. So I made a quality decision at that moment never to preach another sermon except by faith. I would not be swayed by the expressions of people.

Before that series of meetings was over, I saw just how important that decision could be. The Jamaicans, who tend to show very little expression anyway, sat through every sermon without any outward reaction at all.

One lady was completely healed of blindness during one of those meetings. She never let on that anything had taken place. She was almost rigid when she found me outside and said simply, "Brother Copeland, I was blind, but now I can see. Thank you." That was all! A miracle had taken place, and by watching, you wouldn't have been able to tell anything had happened at all.

Next time you're tempted to evaluate what God is doing by the looks of things, don't do it. Remember instead that it is faith, not appearances, that makes miracles happen. It's the only real evidence that you need!

SCRIPTURE READING: Hebrews 11:1-13

A Firm Foundation

"These things I command you, that ye love one another."
(John 15:17)

In Luke 6:47,48, Jesus said:

"Whosoever cometh to me, and heareth my sayings, and doeth them, I will shew you to whom he is like: He is like a man which built an house, and digged deep, and laid the foundation on a rock: and when the flood arose, the stream beat vehemently upon that house, and could not shake it: for it was founded upon a rock."

That's probably a familiar scripture to you. But today I want you to do something new with it. I want you to put it together with what Jesus said in John 15:17:

These things I command you,
that ye love one another.

Love. That one word sums up all Jesus said for us to do. If you'll build your life on it, even the most violent storms of this world will be unable to shake you. It will make you solid in every area of your life.

If you'll build your family on love, you can win back those the devil has stolen from you. You can win them to Jesus with the love of God.

If you'll build your business on love, you'll prosper beyond your wildest dreams. I had a friend who did that. He went into a television and radio business in his church. He wanted to buy a station from a Jewish man and he offered such a good price for it that the owner was stunned. "Why would you offer me such a wonderful price?" asked the Jewish owner. "Because the Word of God says that if I will bless you, God will bless me. So I'm going to see to it that you get the better part of this deal," answered my friend.

Before it was all over, that Jewish station owner had made Jesus Lord of His life. He and my friend ended up prospering and preaching the gospel of Jesus Christ together on the radio.

When love rules, prosperity can flow!

Commit to living the life of love today. Commit to building your house upon the rock. Then when the storms of life begin to blow—at home, at work, or in any situation—you can enjoy the solid security of knowing that love never fails.

SCRIPTURE READING: 1 Corinthians 13:8-13

Give God a Way In

"And I will rebuke the devourer for your sakes,
and he shall not destroy the fruits of your ground;
neither shall your vine cast her fruit before the time in the field,
saith the Lord of hosts. And all nations shall call you blessed:
for ye shall be a delightsome land." **(Malachi 3:11,12)**

God is vitally interested in your finances. He wants to multiply and protect them. But He won't be able to—unless you open the door for Him to do it.

How? Through tithing.

When you tithe, you give God the legal right to intervene in your financial affairs, to bless you richly, and to defend you against the destruction the devil brings. When you tithe, you lay a foundation for success and abundance. You establish deposits with God you can draw on when you need them.

But don't wait until your back is against the wall to start. Begin now. Start developing your faith when things are going well by meditating on the blessing God's Word promises you as a tither. Learn to act on that Word now, and when Satan tries to put you in a financial corner, he'll fail. His power over you financially will have already been broken. Because you've established yourself on the covenant of God, Satan will have no chance against you. God will rebuke him for your sake.

If you haven't yet opened the door and given God a way into your finances, don't wait any longer. Do it today. Then, when the pressures of tomorrow come, you'll be prepared and protected by the special privileges that are guaranteed to those who tithe.

SCRIPTURE READING: Hebrews 7:1-9

Get Out From Under

"Ye are of God, little children, and have overcome them:
because greater is he that is in you, than he that is in the world."

(1 John 4:4)

Under the circumstances... Have you ever caught yourself using that phrase?

"I suppose I'm doing pretty well under the circumstances."

If you've ever said something like that, I want you to kick those words out of your vocabulary right now. Because you, as a victorious child of God, don't have any business living your life "under" your circumstances. You don't have any business letting problems and situations rule over you.

Two thousand years ago, Jesus—the One who is in you—ransacked Satan's kingdom. Through His death at Calvary, He legally entered the regions of the damned and stripped Satan of everything. He took away all his armor. He took the keys to death and hell. He bound that strong man, looted his kingdom, and Colossians says He spoiled principalities and powers and made a show of them openly, triumphing over them.

Then Jesus turned around and gave that victory to you. YOU are of God. Remember that! You have overcome through Jesus because He lives in you. You never have to live "under" the circumstances again!

SCRIPTURE READING: Colossians 1:9-15

See Yourself Risen With Jesus

"Constantly keep in mind Jesus Christ,
the Messiah, [as] risen from the dead." **(2 Timothy 2:8, AMP)**

This is the key to holding onto the blessings of God. When pressure comes, when troubles and trials are bearing down on you, remember Jesus Christ, risen from the dead!

Remember that when Jesus arose, you arose. When He came out of hell and defeated the enemy, you came out of hell and defeated the enemy. His victory is your victory because you're in Him.

In the hard places, remember that. When the devil tells you you're not going to get your answer this time, remember that. When he tells you there's no way out, you remember Christ, the Anointed One, the Victorious Conqueror, risen from the dead and seated at the right hand of the Father!

If there's an image Satan hates more than any other, it must be that image of Jesus, rising from the dead, stripping him forever of his authority, and openly displaying his defeat to all of heaven and hell. That's the picture you need to keep in the forefront of your mind. Think about it until it's etched into your heart so deeply that nothing Satan says or does can get it out of you.

That's when the gifts of God will be established in your life. That's when the devil won't be able to talk you out of your inheritance with trials and tribulations. *Keep in mind Jesus Christ, risen from the dead!*

SCRIPTURE READING: Hebrews 12:1-13

When Somebody Does You Wrong

"Behold, I give unto you power to tread on serpents
and scorpions, and over all the power of the enemy: and nothing
shall by any means hurt you." **(Luke 10:19)**

Somebody's done you wrong! Sooner or later it happens to all of us. Somewhere along the way, we all get hurt or cheated or lied to or abused.

It's as predictable as it is painful. Yet when it happens most of us find ourselves strangely unprepared. In our outrage, we often cry out to God against the one who wronged us. We ask for justice, or even vengeance, and end up making things tougher on everyone involved—including ourselves.

If that's been true of you, it's time you found out how you can put the power of God to work for you the next time somebody does you wrong.

Step one: Identify the enemy! Right here's where the majority of us make our biggest blunder. We mistakenly identify our enemy as the person who hurts us. Don't waste your energy ranting and raving or plotting and scheming against *people* who cause you pain. They're simply under the devil's influence. Aim your spiritual ammunition at the right target. It's the devil who's behind it all. Go after him!

Step two: Fire! Once you've gotten your spiritual guns pointed in the right direction, fire! Hit the devil fast and furiously with the Word of God.

Use the name of Jesus and power that's been given you as a believer and bind the devil from doing you any further harm in that area. Then move on to the next and most important part of this spiritual battle.

Step three: Pray the prayer of intercession. In Matthew 5:44,45, Jesus gives us these instructions: "Love your enemies, bless them that curse you, do good to them that hate you, and pray for them which despitefully use you, and persecute you; That ye may be the children of your Father which is in heaven."

Crying out for the vengeance of God to strike like a lightning bolt when somebody does us wrong isn't acting like our Father. Remember God has great, great mercy. Not just for me and you, but for everyone!

The devil will probably think twice before he bothers you again. Next time someone causes you pain, put the power of God to work for you. Identify the real enemy. Hit him hard with the authority you've been given as a believer. Then pray the prayer of intercession.

SCRIPTURE READING: Matthew 6:6-15

Hell Can't Put Out the Light

"In Him was Life and the Life was the Light of men.
And the Light shines on in the darkness, for the darkness
has never overpowered it." **(John 1:4,5, AMP)**

Whenever things around you get dark and you feel the devil is about to overpower you, remember this: You have the Light of the world in you, and try as they may, all the forces of hell can't put it out!

Even when you're at your weakest, even when you feel like the light within you is small, the devil's darkness is no match for you.

Let me show you what I mean. Imagine for a moment that you're in a large auditorium that has no windows or doors to let in outside light. The place is so black you can't see anything, not even your hand in front of your face. There's nothing around you but complete darkness!

Now, imagine one little lightning bug flying around that auditorium. Every eye in there would turn toward it. As small as that little light is in comparison to the great darkness around it, you would still be able to see it. That massive blackness wouldn't be able to do a thing to shut off that bug. Everywhere he flew, the darkness would just have to yield. It would always be dispelled by his light.

When the circumstances around you begin to get black and you're tempted to despair, think about that lightning bug. Meditate on the fact that Jesus Christ, the Light of the world, is in you. When the revelation of that hits you, you'll never again let the darkness back you into a corner. You'll start chasing it down—overcoming it with your light!

SCRIPTURE READING: Ephesians 5:8-16

No Consolation Prize

"But let patience have her perfect work,
that ye may be perfect and entire, wanting nothing." **(James 1:4)**

I talk a lot about faith. But there's another force that goes along with it that's just as important. It's patience, the ability to stand fast on the Word of God even when your victory seems slow in coming.

Patience is not automatic. It won't go to work unless you let it go to work. So many people don't understand that. They somehow think faith and patience will go to work for them without their help. They just let the devil tear their lives apart and then they say silly things like, "Well, I guess God sent that trial to strengthen my faith."

Don't you ever get caught saying that!

In the first place, James says, "Let no man say when he is tempted, I am tempted of God" (James 1:13). And in the second place, that trial isn't going to make your faith stronger. In fact, it'll destroy it if you'll let it.

If I were to give you a set of weights, would that set of weights make you any stronger? No. As a matter of fact, if you dropped one of them on your foot, you could end up painfully weaker. It's what you do with them that counts, right?

Well, the same thing is true when you run into some kind of trying circumstance the devil's brought your way. If you just lay down and let it run over you, it will damage you. But if you'll let patience have her perfect work, if you'll remain consistently constant, trusting in and relying confidently on the Word of God, you'll end up perfect and entire, wanting nothing.

"Wanting nothing." That phrase alone should convince you that patience is no consolation prize. It's a first-rate power that will put the promises of God within your reach. It's a force that will make a winner out of you.

SCRIPTURE READING: Genesis 26:15-22

Leaving the Low Life Behind

"For whosoever will save his life shall lose it:
and whosoever will lose his life for my sake shall find it." **(Matthew 16:25)**

The high life...or the low life? God's kind of life...or the world's kind of life? You can't have them both. It's one or the other. You have to choose.

You may try to put off that choice. You may try to hang on to the low life while reaching out for the high life at the same time, so you can see if it's something you really want before you give up everything the world has to offer. But, believe me, *you're not that tall!*

You'll never be able to sample the high life for yourself until you're willing to let go, until you're willing to take God at His Word and trust Him to take care of you.

What will happen to you when you do that? You'll start living the kind of life God describes in the first chapter of Psalms. You'll be like "a tree planted by the rivers of water, that bringeth forth fruit in season; your leaf also shall not wither; and whatsoever you do shall prosper."

In West Texas talk that means your roots will go down so deep that no drought can dry you up and no storm can blow you down. No matter what happens in the world around you, you'll prosper.

The stronger the wind blows, the more you'll bend in the breeze. Depression and inflation won't be able to break you. When the rains stop coming and everyone else is withering away, you'll just keep on thriving and bearing the fruit of the Spirit because you're drawing up nourishment from the riverbed!

That's what the high life is like and there's nothing that the world has to offer that can even compare. I know that from experience. Once you dare to let go and trust God...so will you.

SCRIPTURE READING: Matthew 16:13-26

Tradition – A Killer!

"Thus have ye made the commandment
of God of none effect by your tradition." **(Matthew 15:6)**

Cancer. Heart disease. Multiple sclerosis. When we think of killer diseases, those are the names that come to mind. But the truth is, there's a far more deadly killer on the loose in the Church today. And it's destroyed more lives than any of us can imagine. It's called *tradition*. Traditions rob believers of their healing. They steal the power from the promises of God. Here are three you should beware of:

1. The tradition that says it's not always God's will to heal you.

It *is* God's will to heal you! It says so in His Word. If you don't believe that it is, then you can't pray in faith believing you'll receive. You're like the farmer who sits on his porch and says, "I believe in crops, but I'm not going to plant any seed this year. I'll just believe, and if it's God's will, my crop will come up." That farmer will never see his crop. Faith is the seed of healing – if you don't plant it, it won't grow. A prayer that includes the words, "If it be thy will" won't produce a healing harvest. You must know without a doubt that healing is always God's will for you.

2. Another tradition we hear is that healing has passed away. That there are no miracles today. But the Word of God proves that's not true. In Exodus 15:26, God says, "I am the Lord that healeth thee." He also tells us that He does not change (Mal. 3:6). He has never changed since the beginning of time. For healing to pass away, God would have to pass away...and He is not about to do *that!*

3. The third dangerous tradition is this one: "God gets glory from Christians being sick." That tradition totally violates the Word of God. The Bible says that people gave glory to God when they saw the lame walk and the blind see. God receives glory from your healing – not your pain!

The world is looking for a way out of sickness and disease, not a way into it. Let's break down those traditions and deliver a hurting world from the most dangerous killer of all.

SCRIPTURE READING: Mark 2:1-12

Choose Friends Wisely

"I wrote you in my [previous] letter not to associate
(closely and habitually) with unchaste (impure) people."

(1 Corinthians 5:9, AMP)

The company you keep has such an influence on your spiritual life. Fellowshipping with godly people will help speed you on to victory, while fellowshipping with those who are ungodly will drag you down to defeat.

That's why the Bible has some things to say about your friends. That's why it tells you to separate yourself from the world. Because evil companions will corrupt you.

Now, I'm not talking about ministry. Jesus Himself ministered to sinners. You have to mix with them to preach to them and pray for them. What I'm talking about here are the people you choose for friends.

If you want to walk in the things of the Lord, don't choose friends who walk in the things of the devil, people who talk and act ungodly, who don't give God any place in their lives. They'll pull you down. As you rub shoulders with them, you'll expose yourself to temptation. You'll get so familiar with sin it will start to appear less repulsive to you. Sooner or later, you'll fall into it.

So choose your friends wisely. Fellowship with those who call on the name of the Lord out of a pure heart (2 Tim. 2:22). Expose yourself to their love and peace. Let their faith rub off on you!

SCRIPTURE READING: 1 Corinthians 5:9-13

Take the First Step

"The steps of a [good] man are directed
and established of the Lord, when He delights in his way [and
He busies Himself with his every step]." **(Psalm 37:23, AMP)**

God's will is to lead you on a day-by-day basis. He's given His Spirit to guide you every day.

Most believers don't know that. They expect God to reveal His complete will for their lives in one big revelation. Don't make that mistake. Don't just sit around waiting for God to show you whether or not He wants you to go to Africa for the rest of your life.

Let Him begin to lead you in little things first, to tell you what you need to do about this situation or that one. He'll show you what you need to change. And, as He does, you'll change one thing at a time.

The truth is, you probably already know one thing God wants you to do.

You might not know why He wants you to do it. You may not know where it's leading, but you've heard His voice in your heart.

If you want to keep on hearing Him, you'll have to set aside your own ambitions and desires. Spend time in prayer and in the Word. Tune your ear to the voice of His Spirit.

Learn to trust Him. Remember that He's smarter than you are and be willing to do what He says whether you can understand it with your mind or not. Obey even His smallest instructions. If you do, He'll eventually change your whole life…one little step at a time.

SCRIPTURE READING: Genesis 12:1-8

Not of This World

"Whatever is born of God is victorious over the world; and this is the victory that conquers the world, even our faith." **(1 John 5:4, AMP)**

Years ago the devil started a rumor. He told a few Christians that as long as they lived in the world, they had to suffer as the world did. He told them they had to share the diseases and the defeat, the poverty and the failure of those around them.

It was a crafty lie—and it worked. Believers accepted it and began to spread it among themselves. You may have even heard it yourself. If so, I want to help you put that rumor to rest today. I want to help you get the facts straight once and for all.

You see, despite what you may have heard, health, prosperity, and victorious living aren't concepts some comfort-hungry believer selfishly dreamed up. They are *God's* ideas.

You may say, "That sounds good, Gloria, but we've got to be realistic. We live in a world that's full of problems. And as long as we live in this world, it seems to me we're going to have our share."

Yes, that's true. Even Jesus said, "In the world you have tribulation and trials and distress and frustration." But notice, He didn't stop there! He went on to say, "But be of good cheer— take courage, be confident, certain, undaunted—for I have overcome the world.— I have deprived it of power to harm, have conquered it [for you]" (John 16:33, AMP).

Most believers don't have any trouble believing the first part of that verse. They know all too well how many tribulations, trials, distresses, and frustrations surround them. But they're less certain about the last part. They haven't yet experienced for themselves exactly what Jesus meant when He said He had deprived those things of power to harm them.

Why not?

Because they're still living as though they're part of the world.

But, listen. Jesus said you and I are to be "sanctified," or separated from the evils of this world. How? Through the Word of God! (John 17:17).

The Word of God will separate you from the world. His Word will set His dream for victory into motion in your life. If you'll receive it and believe it, speak it and act on it, that Word will set you apart from those around you. It will take you from trouble to triumph again and again.

SCRIPTURE READING: John 17:1-17

Abide in Jesus

"If a man abide not in me,
he is cast forth as a branch, and is withered." **(John 15:6)**

If I were to ask you to make a list of a hundred things you need to do to please the Lord today, you could do it, couldn't you? In fact, you probably have so many spiritual "do's" and "don'ts" cluttering up your mind that you'd hardly know where to start.

But you can relax. I'm not going to suggest you make a list of them. Instead, I'm going to help you simplify things by giving you only one: "Abide in Jesus."

The one thing you're truly responsible for is your union with Him. If you keep your union and fellowship with Him intact, everything else will be taken care of.

"But Gloria, I'm facing some big problems right now. My life's turned upside down. I'm so rushed I don't know whether I'm coming or going. I don't have time to fellowship with the Lord today."

That's when you need to do it the most! You need to maintain your union with the Lord particularly when the storms of life come. I know that's often not easy to do. Whether the storm is a sickness in your body or financial problems or family strife, the temptation will be to settle your attention and your mind on that problem. You won't even want to think about anything else.

That's what the devil planned on. That's the reason he sent that storm in the first place. To distract you from fellowshipping with God. To draw your attention away from your union with Him.

Don't fall into the devil's trap. Instead, keep your thoughts and affections trained on the Lord. As you do that, the force of faith will begin to flow out of you. And that flow will repel every form of darkness. It will bring you in triumph through every storm.

Fellowship with Jesus today.

SCRIPTURE READING: Philippians 3:1-11

You Hold the Key

"I will give unto thee the keys of the kingdom of heaven:
and whatsoever thou shalt bind on earth shall be bound in heaven:
and whatsoever thou shalt loose on earth shall be loosed in heaven."

(Matthew 16:19)

The Greek text of that scripture would literally read, "I give you the keys of the kingdom. Whatever you declare locked on earth is locked in heaven and whatever you declare unlocked on earth is unlocked in the heavenlies."

The heaven Jesus was talking about there isn't the heaven where God resides. He was talking about the battle zone, about the heaven where Satan's forces are operating.

He was telling us that God has given us power to bind the wicked spirits in heavenly places and to loose the angelic powers of God to work in our behalf.

Philippians 2:9,10 says, "We have been given a name which is above every name, and at the name of Jesus every knee shall bow!" Where? In heaven, in earth, and under the earth. That covers it all!

As believers, we have total authority over the powers of Satan. We can take authority over the evil spirits that are trying to destroy this nation. We can take authority over them in the name of Jesus and pull down their strongholds.

It is time we began to realize how important we are to world affairs. Since the day Jesus gave us the Great Commission, the life or death of the world has been in the hands of the Church. We are the ones who have the mighty name of Jesus and the awesome strength of the gospel to bring life and abundance to every creature. We are the ones whose prayers can change every office of authority in this land.

It's up to you and me to begin to intercede right now and use the power God has given us. We may come from different lands with different backgrounds, but we all have one thing in common—Jesus Christ is our Lord. And that alone is enough to alter the spiritual complexion of this earth.

SCRIPTURE READING: Acts 4:1-14

Pure Spiritual Power

"But the fruit of the Spirit is love, joy, peace, longsuffering, gentleness, goodness, faith, meekness, temperance: against such there is no law." **(Galatians 5:22,23)**

So many believers think of the fruit of the Spirit as little more than a passive list of pleasant qualities that can help improve their personalities. But they're far greater than that! They're pure spiritual power.

Love is so powerful, the scripture says, that it never fails. Patience is so powerful it cannot be stopped. No matter what the circumstances, it will not quit. Temperance is so powerful it can master all the unruly desires of your flesh.

The fruits of the Spirit are not weak; they're strong. So strong all the demons of hell can't stop them. So strong that if you'll let them flow out of you, they'll correct the problems in your life. They'll keep you steadfast when all the people around you are falling down. They'll keep you on your feet when governments fail and when the storms of life come.

We are living in dangerous days. There's only one way you can make it through in victory. You must begin to release those powerful fruits of the Spirit God has placed inside you. Believe me, if you're born again, they *are* there. Learn to yield to them and as 2 Peter 1:10 promised, you shall never fall!

SCRIPTURE READING: 2 Peter 1:1-10

Put Your Spirit in Charge

"So too the (Holy) Spirit comes to our aid
and bears us up in our weakness; for we do not know what prayer to offer...
but the Spirit Himself...pleads in our behalf with unspeakable yearnings
and groanings too deep for utterance." **(Romans 8:26, AMP)**

As long as you live on this earth, you're going to be saddled with a weakness. What is it? The flesh and blood body you live in. It's a body that's subject to death. A body that's subject to the physical world around you.

Your reborn spirit doesn't want to sin. It wants to be completely obedient to God. But the weakness of the flesh causes you to fall prey to the temptations around you.

Does that mean you're doomed to a life of failure till Jesus comes and that flesh body is glorified?

No! It means you need to build your spirit up, to strengthen it, until it dominates your flesh. We are told to crucify the flesh. Your spirit man must dominate your body. Praying in the Spirit by the Holy Spirit applies spirit to flesh. It causes your spirit to rise up and take charge. Just like using barbells strengthens your arms, praying in other tongues strengthens your spirit. You see, your spirit is more powerful than your flesh, and as you give it outflow, the flesh will simply have to yield to it. Most believers don't understand that. They'll be overwhelmed by some sin, and instead of conquering it by the things of God such as praying in the Spirit, they'll simply keep struggling to overcome in natural ways. So they end up failing again and again.

If you're caught in that cycle, take heart! God hasn't commanded you to be more spiritual than you can be. He knows your weakness and He's given you a way to overcome it. He's given you the ability to pray in tongues—and with your understanding to wield the sword of the Spirit which is the Word of God. And no matter how badly you're failing in everything else, you can do these things!

Be warned though, Satan will try to talk you out of it. He knows that once you learn how to bring the flesh in line, he'll have no foothold left in your life. You'll shut the door on him and he won't be able to get in.

Renew your commitment to praying in the Spirit today. Make a quality decision to follow the command God gives in Jude 20 and "build yourself up on your most holy faith—make progress, rise like an edifice higher and higher—praying in the Holy Spirit!"

SCRIPTURE READING: Romans 8:14-32

Perseverance Gets Results

"I tell you, although he will not get up
and supply him anything because he is his friend, yet because
of his shameless persistence and insistence, he will get up
and give him as much as he needs." **(Luke 11:8, AMP)**

If, as God tells us in 1 Timothy 2:4, it's His will for *all* men to be saved, why aren't we seeing more of the masses of lost people born again every day? Have you ever wondered that?

I have...and as I've sought the Lord about it, I've come to realize that, for the most part, it's because those of us who are already saved don't pray persistently for those who aren't. Instead of persevering—staying before the Father, praying for them to receive the bread of salvation—like the man in Luke 11:8 did for his friend, when we don't see immediate results, we simply give up and go home.

What we don't realize is this: Perseverance is the key to success in intercession!

Why? It's certainly not because you have to change God's mind. He never changes. His mind's made up. He wants all men saved. The reason you have to persevere in intercession is to put pressure on the demonic forces that are trying to keep God's will from being accomplished. Those forces must be broken down through prayer so that strongholds are destroyed and spiritual blinders are removed from the spiritual eyes of the people you're praying for.

You see, God will not go against the will of any person. But He will move through your intercession to reveal Himself to them. Through your persistent prayers, He will bring them to the knowledge of their need for Him. Then they'll reach out for Him and spiritual rebirth can take place!

If you're sitting around waiting on God to save Aunt Mary or Uncle Jim or your best friend...stop sitting around! Get busy interceding for them. Persevere in prayer. Pray the prayer in Ephesians 1:16-23 for them, refusing to give up until they're safely inside God's kingdom.

Jesus has already laid down His life so that they can be saved. The question is, will you?

SCRIPTURE READING: Luke 11:1-10

Go for Revelation Knowledge

"Grace and peace be multiplied unto you
through the knowledge of God, and of Jesus our Lord." **(2 Peter 1:2)**

If you were to look up the Greek word that's translated "knowledge" in that scripture, you'd find out that it means more than just a mental understanding of something, more than the kind of knowledge that can be gained through your senses. It means exact knowledge. Knowledge that's been revealed directly to your heart by the Spirit of God. I call it *revelation knowledge.*

The lack of that kind of knowledge has caused more faith failures than anything else I know of. That's because most Christians believe the Word with their minds, but they haven't meditated on it enough for it to "light up" in their hearts. If they had, that Word would absolutely revolutionize their lives. Nothing in heaven or earth would be able to shake them loose from it.

I know a widow who got hold of that kind of revelation one afternoon. She'd been meditating in the scriptures that say if you're a widow, God Almighty has taken His place as your provider and leader of your household.

She'd been feeling a little sorry for herself up until then. But when she received the revelation that God was actually head of her household now, she started talking to Him like she would a husband.

"I'm telling You, Lord, the plumbing in this house is pitiful. Will You please get it fixed?" she said. From that moment on, she never had any more trouble with her plumbing.

If you need something from God, determine right now that you're going to do what that widow did. Determine that you're going to meditate the Word until you get a revelation like that. Keep that Word before you until you receive a revelation of Jesus as your healer or your deliverer or your financier—whatever you need Him to be. Don't settle for a shallow mental understanding of Him. Get a deep revelation and His grace *will* be multiplied to you!

SCRIPTURE READING: Psalm 1

God's Country

"The things which are impossible with men
are possible with God." **(Luke 18:27)**

Right now you and I are standing face-to-face with situations in our nation that need to be changed. Some of those situations look totally impossible. But they're not. Because this country belongs to God.

He's the One who brought the United States of America into existence. He had a special purpose for it. He needed a country where the gospel could be preached freely and not suppressed.

It was God Himself who stirred the heart and mind of Christopher Columbus and planted within him the dream of charting a new course to the West. Columbus said so in his own journals: "It was the Lord who put into my mind—I could feel His hand upon me—the fact that I could sail from here to the Indies, [he wrote]. All who heard of my project rejected it with laughter, ridiculing me. There's no question that the inspiration was from the Holy Spirit because He comforted me with rays of marvelous inspiration from the Holy Scriptures."

Who brought Christopher Columbus to America? God brought him. This is God's nation. He raised it up, and it's not going to be taken away from Him.

The next time you're tempted to look at situations in this country as impossible, remember who it belongs to. Then you can discover America just like Christopher Columbus did—by faith.

SCRIPTURE READING: Psalm 106

Let God Be Glorified

"And Jesus went forth...moved
with compassion...and he healed their sick.
And great multitudes came unto him, having with them
those that were lame, blind, dumb, maimed, and many others,
and cast them down at Jesus' feet; and he healed them: Insomuch that
the multitude wondered, when they saw the dumb to speak, the maimed
to be whole, the lame to walk, and the blind to see: and they
glorified the God of Israel." **(Matthew 14:14, 15:30,31)**

Religious tradition says that God gets glory when we bear up nobly under the agony of sickness and disease. But that's not what the Bible says. It says God gets glory when the blind see and the lame walk and the maimed are made whole!

In India or Africa where people haven't been taught those kinds of religious traditions, when somebody stands up and announces, "I come to you as a messenger from the most high God," people believe what he has to say. When they hear that Jesus, the King of Kings, shed His blood for them; when they hear that He's sent His messenger to tell them that He'll deliver them from sin and sickness and death today, they get excited. They don't argue with the Word of God. So you know what happens?

People begin to get healed. People start throwing away their crutches and flinging off their bandages!

When we learn to hear the Word of God like that, the same thing will happen to us. God is no respecter of persons. His Word works for everyone. It's how we receive it that makes the difference!

SCRIPTURE READING: Acts 17:1-11

Start Speaking Faith Now

"Out of the abundance of the heart the mouth speaketh.
A good man out of the good treasure of the heart bringeth forth
good things: and an evil man out of the evil treasure
bringeth forth evil things." **(Matthew 12:34,35)**

Words won't work without faith any more than faith will work without words! It takes them both to put the law of faith in motion.

Many believers don't realize that. They'll continually speak words of doubt and unbelief, then they'll jump up one day and say a couple of faith words and expect mountains to move — and to their dismay, they don't.

Why not?

Because as Matthew 12:34,35 says, it's the words that come from the heart that produce results. The person who just throws in a couple of faith words now and then isn't speaking them from the abundance of his heart, so they're not effective.

Does that mean you shouldn't start speaking words of faith until you're sure you have the faith to back them?

No! Speaking words of faith is good spiritual exercise. If you want to receive healing by faith, for example, fasten your mind and your mouth on the Word of God where your health is concerned. Instead of talking about how miserable you feel, quote Isaiah 53:5. Say, "Jesus was wounded for my transgressions. He was bruised for my iniquities. The chastisement of my peace was upon Him; and with His stripes, praise God, I was healed!"

If you'll continue to meditate on those words and continue to say them, the truth in them will begin to sink in. They'll take root in your heart and begin to grow. And eventually you really will be speaking from the abundance of your heart.

When that happens, it won't matter what the circumstances look like. You'll *know* you have what you've been believing for and the devil himself won't be able to talk you out of it. You'll cross the line from hope to faith, and you'll start seeing those mountains *move!*

SCRIPTURE READING: Matthew 12:33-37

Under Pressure? Plant!

"Be not deceived; God is not mocked:
for whatsoever a man soweth, that shall he also reap." **(Galatians 6:7)**

If you feel like you're under pressure these days, you're not alone. Satan is putting more pressure on more people right now than ever before. He's pressuring us mentally, financially, emotionally, and every other way he can. The pressure has gotten so great everywhere that governments don't know what to do. Businesses don't know what to do. Families don't know. Churches don't know.

But, praise God, *Jesus* does! He says we can give our way right out from under any pressure the devil brings to bear.

Giving is always Jesus' way out. Whenever there's a need, He plants seed! In fact, in Mark 4, He compares the entire kingdom of God to a seed. Just think about the importance of seeds for a moment. Every living thing on this earth came from a seed. You came from a seed. Then you were born again from the seed of God's Word. Jesus Himself was The Seed planted by God. God sowed Him in sacrifice. He came forth and grew up into many brethren.

So, when Satan puts you under pressure, go to Jesus and let Him tell you how and where to plant. If you'll do it, that seed will grow up until it breaks the powers of darkness and lack. It will release you from the pressure the devil's been putting on you.

I've seen it happen. When Jerry Savelle first began to work for my ministry, he didn't have but one suit of clothes and one shirt with a pair of slacks to his name. He wore one, then the other, night after night to every service we held. He didn't have the money to even think about buying another suit. I'm telling you, he was under pressure where clothes were concerned!

Then he found out about the principle of seed-faith and harvest. So, he went downtown in the city where we were in a meeting and found a fellow on the street who needed clothes and gave him some. Immediately people started giving Jerry clothes. It started in that meeting and they've been doing it ever since. Today, there are many preachers in Africa wearing Jerry Savelle suits! (Even if the sleeves and pant legs *are* way too short!) He's still sowing and reaping the greatest clothes harvest I've ever seen.

If the devil's pressuring you, don't panic...plant! Plant your time. Plant your money. Plant the clothes off your back. When your harvest comes in, you can laugh and say, "Hey, Devil, who's feeling the pressure now?"

SCRIPTURE READING: Mark 4:1-20

Strike It Rich

"And if ye be Christ's, then are ye Abraham's seed, and heirs according to the promise." **(Galatians 3:29)**

One of the problems that hung around me for years was poverty. But I remember the day I decided I wasn't going to be poor anymore. I was reading in the Word where it says that the blessing of Abraham has come upon the Gentiles by Jesus Christ (Gal. 3:14). Then I got down to the twenty-ninth verse where it says, "If ye be Christ's, then are ye Abraham's seed, and HEIRS ACCORDING TO THE PROMISE." Suddenly the truth hit me. I got so excited I could hardly stand myself.

I turned back over to Deuteronomy 28 and – line by line – I read those promised blessings. "Blessed in the city, blessed in the country. Blessed going out, blessed coming in. Blessed in your barns, blessed in your fields, blessed in all the works of your hands." Man, I had struck it rich!

I'd been going to school in Tulsa, Oklahoma, and I was living in a dumpy little house nobody would want to live in. But when I read those promises in the Word, I saw the light. I realized God already had redeemed me from the curse of poverty.

Well, that afternoon in my back bedroom, I took my Bible in my hand and I said: "I want to announce to Almighty God in heaven and to Jesus Christ of Nazareth, to all the angels of heaven, to all the demons of hell, and to anybody else that cares anything about hearing it, that from this day forward my needs are *met* according to God's riches in glory by Christ Jesus."

I told Him, "I'm standing on Your Word, and I'm looking to You to take care of me. I'll never ask a man for a dollar."

That was many years ago and I never have. You know why? Because that decision connected me to the power of God. It'll do the same for you.

SCRIPTURE READING: Deuteronomy 28:1-13

Plant a Seed and Watch It Grow!

"And he said, Whereunto
shall we liken the kingdom of God?
or with what comparison shall we compare it?
It is like a grain of mustard seed, which, when it is sown in the earth,
is less than all the seeds that be in the earth: But when it is sown,
it groweth up, and becometh greater than all herbs, and shooteth out
great branches; so that the fowls of the air may lodge
under the shadow of it." **(Mark 4:30-32)**

Jesus compares the workings of the kingdom of God to planting seeds in the earth. "When the seed is sown," He said, "it grows up...."

Notice He didn't say that it would occasionally grow up. Or it grows up if it's God's will. He said, "It grows up and becomes greater." Period.

God's economy isn't like ours. It isn't up one day and down the other. It's always the same and it always works perfectly. If you have good earth, good seed, and good water, you're going to have growth. It's inevitable.

So, if you're facing a need, don't panic...plant a seed!

That seed may take the form of money or time or some other resources you have to give. But, no matter what form it takes, make sure you put life in it by giving it in faith and surrounding it with praise and worship. Say, "Lord, as I bring You my goods, I bring myself. I give myself to You—spirit, soul, and body."

Pray over that seed. Fill it with faith, worship, and the Word. Then plant it. You can rest assured—*it will grow up and become greater!*

SCRIPTURE READING: Genesis 1:11-31

Exercise Your Rights

"He was wounded for our transgressions,
he was bruised for our iniquities: the chastisement of our peace
was upon him; and with his stripes we are healed." **(Isaiah 53:5)**

Jesus came to earth and gave Himself as a sacrifice for sin in order to buy back for you everything that Adam lost. He came to destroy all the works of the devil...sickness and disease included. Once you receive Him as Lord of your life, all the rights and privileges God originally intended you to have (the right to things like fellowship with God, health, and prosperity) are restored.

But *you* are the one who has to exercise those rights!

You see, the devil is an outlaw and even though Jesus has taken away his authority in the earth, even though he has no legal right to kill or steal from the children of God, he'll do it anyway...as long as you'll let him get away with it.

You must enforce his defeat by speaking the Word of God in faith. Act on His Word now. Demand that sickness and disease leave you in the name of Jesus. Then refuse to back off that demand. Resist the devil with all you've got. He might fight you for a while, but sooner or later, he *will* have to flee from you!

SCRIPTURE READING: Matthew 8:1-17

His Still Small Voice

"But the anointing which ye have received
of [God] abideth in you, and ye need not that any man teach you:
but as the same anointing teacheth you of all things,
and is truth." **(1 John 2:27)**

Have you ever noticed that you are sometimes aware of certain things even before you know what the Word says about them? That's because the Holy Spirit is inside you teaching you the truth. He speaks into your spirit. Then your spirit relays His promptings to your mind. Suddenly, you'll have a new thought. "I need to forgive that person," you'll think, or "I need to stop saying those unkind things."

As you become more aware of the Spirit of God in your everyday affairs, you'll be quicker to hear and obey those promptings. You'll actually get in the *habit* of allowing the Spirit of Truth to reveal the will of God to you. And, believe me, that's *one* habit God wants you to have!

One of the first things that the Spirit said to me when I began to listen to His promptings was "spend more time in prayer." As I obeyed, I began to be impressed to spend at least one hour a day in prayer. After I'd begun to do that, He revealed it to me in His Word (Matt. 26:40).

Since then, I have talked with people from all over the world who are hearing the same thing. Believers everywhere are hearing the Spirit of God direct them to more prayer.

God hasn't given the Holy Spirit to just a few special Christians. He's given Him to all of us. And if we'll just learn to be sensitive to His voice, He'll guide us into all truth!

Think about how different your life would be if you knew the truth of God about every situation! Doesn't that just make you want to listen to your spirit? Doesn't it make you want to be on the keen edge of what God is saying?

Start tuning your ear to His still small voice within you. Honor Him and welcome His guidance into your everyday affairs. Listen for His promptings and be quick to obey. He's ready to speak to you.

SCRIPTURE READING: John 15:1-15

Don't Be Disturbed

"The Lord bringeth the counsel of the heathen to nought:
he maketh the devices of the people of none effect." **(Psalm 33:10)**

You may be facing trouble today that's being caused by people who have willfully plotted to do you harm. They may be trying to steal your business, your home, your children, or even to destroy your marriage. If so, I have a word of encouragement for you. According to Psalm 33:10, God will bring the plans of those people to nought. He will make their devices of none effect. The counsel of the heathen is brought to nought, but the counsel of the Lord stands forever!

Remember this: When you make God your stronghold in the time of trouble, no one can overcome you. No matter how powerful they are in the natural, the odds are in your favor because you trust in the Lord. They may think they've got an edge over you, but God is on your side and that gives you the advantage!

Rest assured, you *are* eventually going to triumph over this trouble. In the meantime, if you'll set your affections on the Lord, the thoughts of His heart continually will be coming into your heart. "The mouth of the righteous speaketh wisdom, and his tongue talketh of judgment. The law of his God is in his heart; none of his steps shall slide" (Ps. 37:30,31). God's counsel will give you stability when all the world around you is shaking. Evil tidings will not be able to steal your peace. The thoughts of God will immediately rise up and rebuke the evil tidings from taking root in your heart.

Don't let the temporary successes of the troublemaker disturb you. Instead, "mark the perfect man, and behold the upright: for the end of that man is peace" (verse 37).

SCRIPTURE READING: Psalm 33:1-10

Change the Image

"For we are saved by hope: but hope that is seen is not hope:
for what a man seeth, why doth he yet hope for? But if we hope for that
we see not, then do we with patience wait for it." **(Romans 8:24,25)**

According to Romans, hope is actually looking at something that you can't see. How do you do that? You do it by looking at the promises of God in the Word until with your inner eyes—the eyes of your spirit—a picture is formed.

For example, one of the hardest things I ever had to do was face the fact that the inner image I had of myself physically was fat. It didn't matter how hard I tried to change, it wouldn't go away. I was always on a diet. I must have lost (and regained) hundreds of pounds over the years.

I finally had to admit that as long as my inner image of myself was fat, my outer self was going to match it. Remember, it's faith that changes things, and without the inner image of hope, faith cannot work.

So I decided to fast for seven days. I searched my Bible for every scripture I could find on food and eating and I found many.

I meditated on every one of those scriptures and prayed in the Spirit for seven full days. What was I doing? I was laying hold on a different inner image.

This is not something you can do overnight. It takes time. Especially if the inner image you're changing has been there for years.

But you *can* do it. Go to the Word of God today and begin to change the images inside you. Change them from images of despair to images of hope. Get a blueprint in your heart and your faith will build on it!

SCRIPTURE READING: Romans 4:16-21

Real Intercession

"And he saw that there was no man,
and wondered that there was no intercessor." (Isaiah 59:16)

When somebody hurts us, our natural human reaction is to strike back...to ask God to clobber them. But that's not God's way.

I realized that one time when some relatives of mine got robbed. I was praying about the situation and puzzling over it. "Lord," I began to ask, "why did You let that happen? Why didn't You just knock that thief over the head when he tried to do that?"

Suddenly, God enabled me to back up from that situation and look at it with spiritual, instead of just purely natural eyes.

When I did that, I knew the answer to my question almost as quickly as I had asked it. It was because of His mercy. God has great, great mercy. Not just for me and my family but for theirs too.

Think about that next time someone does you wrong. Instead of asking God to knock that person in the head, like I did, consider the fact that—as ornery as he may be—he may well have a grandmother somewhere who's praying for him to be saved. Stop and remember that God loved him enough to die for him, that He's longing to pardon—not punish him.

Then you can begin to pray *for* him instead of against him, uniting yourself with his grandmother (or anybody else who happens to be praying for him). You can go to the Lord for mercy for him and you can go up *against* the devil on his behalf. That's real intercession and it throws the forces of darkness into total confusion. They have absolutely no defense against it.

The Lord is looking for people who are bold enough, committed enough to do that. Dare to be one of them. When you're tempted to clobber somebody, dare to change his life instead.

SCRIPTURE READING: Luke 6:27-36

Take Correction

"Reprove not a scorner, lest he hate you;
reprove a wise man, and he will love you. Give instruction
to a wise man, and he will be yet wiser; teach a righteous man...
and he will increase in learning." **(Proverbs 9:8,9, AMP)**

There is one thing you can do that will accelerate your spiritual growth more than almost any other thing: learn to take correction—from the Spirit of God and from His people.

So few believers seem to be able to do that. When their preacher gets in the pulpit and preaches about something they already know, about some aspect of life they've already submitted to the Lord, they think he's great. They like him because he makes them feel good. But the moment he stands up and begins to preach about something they're doing wrong, they take offense.

God says that's foolish. He says, in Proverbs 1:7, only fools strike out at, or despise, correction.

So don't be like that. When your pastor or anyone else in the Body of Christ has a word of correction for you, receive it gratefully. Appreciate those who share the wisdom of God with you. When someone points out somewhere that you've missed it, instead of reacting against them, examine yourself and say, "Is that right? Does that agree with the Word? Do I need to make a change there?"

If the answer to those questions is yes, then make the changes you need to make to get your life in line.

I know that's not easy. None of us likes to be corrected. But if you'll make up your mind you're going to receive that correction anyway, that you're going to remain teachable, you'll be able to go on and grow in spiritual things much more quickly.

One man said, "If you think you've already arrived, you aren't going anywhere." Remember that next time someone corrects you. Love that person and thank him for speeding along your spiritual progress. If you'll do that, you'll come out ahead every time.

SCRIPTURE READING: Proverbs 3:11-24

How's Your Spiritual Maintenance?

"The cares and anxieties of the world,
and distractions of the age, and the pleasure
and delight and false glamour and deceitfulness of riches,
and the craving and passionate desire for other things
creep in and choke and suffocate the Word, and it
becomes fruitless." **(Mark 4:19, AMP)**

Did you know that the seemingly innocent things in your everyday life can suffocate your spiritual life if you allow it?

A friend of mine said the Lord told her in prayer one day that this nation had become a nation of maintenance men. "You have so many things to maintain," He told her. "You maintain your house. You maintain your car, your yard, your machines, your hair...."

It's true. You can become a maintainer of so many natural things that you don't have any time left to maintain your own spirit!

When you find yourself in that situation, it's time to simplify your life. I've had to learn that myself. Now when I'm considering something I think I need, I don't just count the cost in dollars and cents. I think about how much time it will take to maintain it. I check to see if I can spiritually afford it.

Second Timothy 2:4 says, "Don't get entangled in the affairs of this life." One thing I've learned over the last 20 years: Nothing is as important as spending time in prayer and in the Word with the Father. Absolutely nothing in my life is as vital as that.

SCRIPTURE READING: Mark 4:18-24

Stand Up and Be Counted

"I exhort therefore, that, first of all,
supplications, prayers, intercessions, and giving of thanks,
be made for all men; For kings, and for all that are in authority;
that we may lead a quiet and peaceable life in all
godliness and honesty." **(1 Timothy 2:1,2)**

We are commanded to pray for our country and our leaders. But having prayed, God expects us to *act*. The elections in the United States are vital to the future of this nation. Our country is in the midst of a spiritual outpouring, and it's vitally important that the right people be elected. We must see to it.

Don't wait until election time is upon us before you start seeking God for whom to vote. Begin to pray now so that the news media and other voices from every corner cannot influence you and cannot draw you in a direction away from the Spirit of God. Pray so that you won't be influenced by natural reactions and natural responses to cleverly designed commercials and ideas.

Start praying now about the coming elections. Whether they are small local elections or major national elections, make them a part of every prayer you pray. Then thank the Spirit of God for His wisdom concerning for whom to vote. Thank Him for giving you His wisdom about what to say and when to say it to others. Thank Him for giving you wisdom to declare the name of Jesus and declare that this shall be a God-indwelt, God-ordained, God-overseen administration.

So register. Pray. Vote. Then stand up and be counted by the power of the living God.

SCRIPTURE READING: 1 Timothy 2:1-8

Be Courageous

"Be thou strong and very courageous,
that thou mayest observe to do according to all the law,
which Moses my servant commanded thee: turn not from it
to the right hand or to the left, that thou mayest prosper
whithersoever thou goest." **(Joshua 1:7)**

Living a life of faith takes courage. Most people don't realize it, but it does! It takes courage to stand up in the face of sickness and declare you're healed by the stripes of Jesus. It takes courage to believe for prosperity and put your last dime in the offering plate when poverty is staring you in the face. There are going to be some days when you'd rather pull the covers over your head and hide than take another faith stand against the devil. But you can't. Because the battle of faith isn't fought once and then forgotten. If you want to keep living in victory, you have to fight it again and again.

There's no way around it. Of course, some of God's people still try to find one. The Israelites, for example. They thought their battles should be over when they crossed the Red Sea. So when they heard reports of giants living in the Promised Land, they decided they couldn't face the fight. Their courage failed them. So they took a 40-year detour through the wilderness.

But you know what? They still couldn't avoid that fight. When the time came for the next generation to enter the Promised Land, the giants were still there!

This time, however, they found the courage to face them. Where did they find it? In the Word of God.

Their leader, Joshua, had obeyed the instruction of the Lord and kept that Word on his mind and in his heart day and night. He'd meditated on it and let it constantly remind him that God was on their side.

If you're going to fight the good fight of faith to the finish, you'll have to do just like Joshua did. You'll have to continually draw courage from the Word of God. So make up your mind to do it. Get into that Word and let it change you from a coward to an overcomer. Then march into battle and slay the giants in your land.

SCRIPTURE READING: Joshua 1

Why Did God Create *You?*

"What we have seen and [ourselves] heard
we are also telling you, so that you too may realize and enjoy
fellowship as partners and partakers with us. And [this] fellowship
that we have (which is a distinguishing mark of Christians)
is with the Father and with His Son Jesus Christ,
the Messiah." **(1 John 1:3, AMP)**

Man is something really special. He is made in the image of God. He is made to have fellowship with God.

Some people get the idea that God made man, so He'd have someone to dominate. But God is not a dominator. God is love and love needs to have someone to give to. That's why God made man. He made him, so He could give him His love.

God could have given His love to the angels, and He did that. But giving to angels didn't provide total fulfillment. Why? Because angels aren't made in His image.

You're the same way. Let's say, for example, you have a puppy as a pet. You can fellowship with that little pet just so much, but then there comes a time when you need somebody to talk to. There comes a time when you need to have communication on your own level.

The reason you're like that is because you're created in the image of God. That's how He is. He has a desire to fellowship with someone like Himself.

Dare to believe you're something really special today—a one-of-a-kind creation made by God in His very own image. Dare to receive His love and dare to love Him back!

SCRIPTURE READING: Genesis 1:26-31

A Word About Angels

"For he shall give his angels charge over thee,
to keep thee in all thy ways." **(Psalm 91:11)**

It's time to set the record straight. Angels are not kid stuff. They're not little fat babies with long blonde hair and bows and arrows in their hands. Angels are big, strong warriors. They are real. They are powerful. And, if you are a believer, they are a vital part of your life.

We see examples of what angels can do all through the Bible. For instance, when the children of Israel were fleeing from Egypt with Pharaoh's army hot on their heels, the Bible tells us that suddenly the wheels on the Egyptians' chariots got fouled up. They just quit rolling!

Who do you think caused that? The angels, of course!

They haven't retired since then either. Angels are at work today just as they've always been.

A few years ago in one of Israel's major wars, the enemy had their guns trained on Israeli cities. Those guns were the finest military equipment money could buy. They had a range of at least 20 miles and were equipped with electronic gun sights for accuracy.

But something very odd happened. Every time they fired those guns at the Israelis, they either overshot or fell far short of their targets. We know there was nothing wrong with the guns because later the Israelis captured them and fired them back at the enemy with perfect success.

What happened? Angels, that's what!

My friend, that isn't just a fairy tale. That's a real-life example of the involvement of angels in the lives of God's people today. And, if you're a child of God, then you have a right to expect God's angels to do the same kinds of things for you.

So, start expecting! Say, "Thank You, heavenly Father for giving Your angels charge over me to keep me in all my ways." Once you've spoken that word of faith, stand fast. Don't fear. Don't waver. Just be patient and keep believing, and you will surely see the salvation of the Lord.

SCRIPTURE READING: Acts 12:1-17

Time to Get Serious

"O God, thou art my God; early will I seek thee....
I [will] remember thee upon my bed, and meditate on thee
in the night watches." **(Psalm 63:1,6)**

If you're going to live in divine health, there are going to be times when you'll have to be downright extreme about the Word of God. Times when you may be facing a sickness so severe that you need more than just a few moments in the Word and a quick prayer to receive your healing.

I want to tell you, in very practical terms, what I would do in a situation like that.

The moment I woke up in the morning, before I did anything else, I'd take Communion. I'd say, "Lord, I dedicate my body all day today to the service of my Lord Jesus Christ. I take Jesus' pure blood shed for me."

Then I'd put the devil in his place. I'd say, "I rebuke you, Satan. You're not going to put any sickness and disease on me today. Regardless of the symptoms, regardless of what my body thinks about it, by the power of Jesus through His Spirit, I have overcome this sickness because He that is within me is greater than he that is in the world."

Then, all day long, I'd thank God for my healing. I'd choose some teaching tapes that would fill my mind and my spirit with the anointed Word of God, and I'd listen to them throughout the day. In the afternoon, I'd praise God and receive Communion again to remind myself that the blood of Jesus is in my veins, that I'm part of God's family.

You don't have to wait until the second Sunday of each month or whatever to receive Communion. Jesus just said, "As often as you do this, do it in remembrance of Me." And if you're facing a serious attack of the devil, you need to remember Him all day and all night. You need to consider Jesus until thoughts of Him push the thoughts of that sickness right out of your mind.

That night before bed I'd receive Communion again, then I'd praise myself to sleep. If I woke up in the night, I'd reach over and get my Bible and read all the healing scriptures and make the devil sorry he woke me.

When the devil launches a serious attack against your body, don't mess around. Get serious about the Word. Put yourself under its constant care and it will take good care of you.

SCRIPTURE READING: Hebrews 4:9-16

Unity of Faith

"And he gave some, apostles; and some, prophets;
and some, evangelists; and some, pastors and teachers;
For the perfecting of the saints, for the work of the ministry,
for the edifying of the body of Christ: Till we *all* come in
the unity of the faith, and of the knowledge of the Son of God,
unto a perfect man, unto the measure of the stature
of the fulness of Christ." **(Ephesians 4:11-13)**

*ill we **all** come in the unity of the faith.* What this scripture means is simply this: If we're ever going to become truly powerful in the kingdom of God, if we're ever going to be any great threat to the devil, we're going to have to grow up—together.

It won't be enough for just a few of us to grow up on our own and say, "Too bad" about everybody else. It doesn't work that way. We're a part of each other. The Bible calls us one body...the Body of Christ.

Let me give you an example. When I began teaching God's revelation on the laws of prosperity, I started getting incredible flack. Preachers started calling me and chewing me out because I wouldn't borrow money and things like that. Finally God said to me one day in prayer, "Don't teach on the laws of prosperity any more until I tell you to."

"Why not?" I asked.

"There's strife in the camp," He told me. "Other preachers are mad at you and in strife over it."

I didn't realize then that the level where we stopped would affect us all. I didn't realize that even I wouldn't be able to go on and operate in the additional laws of prosperity until the rest of the Body would go with me.

We're not islands unto ourselves. I can't do anything without affecting you. You can't do anything without affecting me. We're joined together by God but held together by one another (Eph. 4:16). We can only grow up...together!

Learn to walk in love. Refuse to fall prey to division and isolation. Feed on the Word daily and encourage your brothers and sisters by feeding it to them too, so we can all grow up to be "a perfect [or mature] man, unto the measure of the stature of the fulness of Christ."

SCRIPTURE READING: 1 Corinthians 12:13-28

A Little Every Day

"Unto what is the kingdom of God like?
and whereunto shall I resemble it? It is like a grain
of mustard seed, which a man took, and cast into his garden; and it grew,
and waxed a great tree; and the fowls of the air lodged
in the branches of it." **(Luke 13:18,19)**

If you're going to grow in the kingdom of God, you're going to do it just like a seed that's been planted in the ground. How does a seed grow? All at once? No, it grows constantly—24 hours a day—a little all the time until it accomplishes what it was created to do.

Most of us don't operate that way spiritually. We study and pray very hard for a few days and then quit. Then, when some disaster comes, we make a mad attempt to pray and stand on the Word, all the while realizing that, for some reason, we're just not as strong as we ought to be.

There's no such thing as an overnight success in the kingdom of God! Real strength, real growth comes as you consistently and constantly keep the Word before your eyes, in your ears, and in the midst of your heart. Not just when you want to or when you feel like it, but constantly, like the seed, a little all the time.

A man came up to me once and said, "Man, your ministry just took off overnight, didn't it?"

"If it did," I answered, "it was certainly the longest night I ever spent in my life!"

From his perspective my success did seem to spring up quickly. That's because he didn't see me during all those hours and weeks and months and years I spent in the Word of God. He didn't see the daily process that lay behind that success. He just saw the results.

Make up your mind to begin that daily process of constant growth today. Determine to start putting the Word in your heart consistently. Every day a line here, a line there—a tape here, a tape there.

Begin to act as though that Word is true every hour of the day regardless of what comes or how you feel. Keep adding to your faith, meditating on it, confessing it, seven days a week.

Eventually, your faith will be bigger than you ever dreamed it could be.

SCRIPTURE READING: Luke 13:18-21

Rekindle the Fire

"Draw nigh to God, and he will draw nigh to you." **(James 4:8)**

Remember when you first got into the Word and were so excited about the things of God? Remember when you could hardly wait to read the next chapter in the Bible or listen to the latest teaching tape? There was only one word to describe you—HOT! Your reborn spirit was on fire for God.

When Ken and I first heard the message of faith, we were like that. We were so on fire that nothing else in the world interested us. We had learned that we could trust God's Word just like we could trust the word of a close friend, and we were hungry to find out everything He had promised us in His Word.

Back then, it seemed all I did was read God's Word. I read faith books. I listened to tapes. I was dedicated. My total interest was the Word of God.

But slowly that changed. At first I didn't even realize it was happening. Then the Holy Spirit went to work on me and showed me that I had grown lukewarm. I had let the fire die down. I still read the Word, but I had lost my enthusiasm.

Maybe you've had this same experience. If so, I want to tell you how to get the fire back. It worked for me and it will work for you.

God's Word says to draw near to Him and He will draw near to you. In order to do that you will have to first drop the things that are stealing your time from reading the Word. Delight yourself in His Word. Become diligent again. If you will give your attention to the things of God, soon your desire for God will increase. Your desire will follow your attention. The more you attend to something, the more your desire is drawn to give attention to that thing.

I can show you that this is a natural principle. If you play golf, you'll go for months at a time without even thinking about it. Then one day you'll make time in your schedule to go to the course and play a round or two. The next day you may want to play again. Your desire gets stronger and stronger the more you play.

This same thing will happen in the spirit realm. Your soul's desire will follow whatever you spend your time doing. Start building yourself up by praying in the Spirit. Believe and act on everything God says to you. Before long that flicker that's been wavering in your spirit will grow again into an all-consuming FIRE!

SCRIPTURE READING: Revelation 3:13-22

God's Will is Liberty

"Now the Lord is that Spirit:
and where the Spirit of the Lord is, there is liberty." **(2 Corinthians 3:17)**

L iberty. If you could put the will of God into one word, that would be the word. God wants people to be free. Free from sin and sickness, poverty, oppression, and every other curse.

That freedom is what Jesus came to provide. He said, "The Spirit of the Lord is upon me, because he hath anointed me to preach the gospel to the poor...to heal the brokenhearted, to preach deliverance to the captives, and recovering of sight to the blind, to set at liberty them that are bruised" (Luke 4:18). That's what He trained His disciples to do. And if you're a born-again believer, that's what He wants you to do too!

Some people say, "Well, I don't know about that. That may not be God's will for today."

But listen, the Bible says God never changes. He hasn't changed His will for the earth. He doesn't do one thing a while and then go do another thing for a while. Jesus' life was a perfect picture of God's will 2,000 years ago—and it still is! That's why He left instructions for us to go and do the works that He did. That's why He sent the Holy Spirit to empower us to do them.

Jesus still wants to do the will of the Father here on earth—but He does it through us. He has to work with us until we're willing to lay down our traditions and let Him do *His* thing. That's what the early Church did. They started out with a bang because they did as Jesus taught them. Everywhere they went people became free.

Let's pray for the Church of today to begin to deliver the liberty of God to the world. It's time to quit questioning the will of God and start carrying it out instead. He said the works that He did we would do also and even greater works (John 14:12). It's time for us to take up where Jesus left off and set the captives free!

SCRIPTURE READING: Isaiah 61:1-11

Move Closer Every Day

"I am the vine, ye are the branches:
He that abideth in me, and I in him, the same
bringeth forth much fruit: for without me ye
can do nothing." **(John 15:5)**

Abiding in Jesus isn't something that comes automatically to any believer. It's a life-style that involves discipline and effort.

We have to choose to give ourselves to our union with Him, to give Him first place where our attention is concerned. If we want to grow spiritually, if we want to walk in power and in fellowship with the Lord, we'll have to spend the time it takes to know Him.

That's not something we can do for a while and then forget about either. We must continue in it every day. For the moment we stop moving closer to Jesus, we always start drifting away.

You see, here in this natural world you're surrounded by ungodliness. You live in a body that is totally natural. Unless you purposely counter that with daily prayer and time in the Word, your body and your mind will simply give in to the pressures around you and go the way of the world.

Right now, make a decision to give yourself to the things of God. Focus your attention on the Lord. Surround yourself with His Word. Listen to preaching and teaching tapes while you're getting dressed, driving to work, preparing dinner, working on your car, exercising, cleaning house, and when you go to bed. Listen to the Word of God anytime, anywhere!

Abide in Him today.

SCRIPTURE READING: John 15:1-11

Let Your New Man Out

"I beseech you therefore, brethren,
by the mercies of God, that ye present your bodies
a living sacrifice, holy, acceptable unto God,
which is your reasonable service." **(Romans 12:1)**

When you made Jesus Christ Lord of your life, you became what the Bible calls a "new creature." Inside, you're not the same person you were before. You have the nature of God born into you. But it's not enough for you just to have that new nature on the inside. You have to let it take over the outside as well.

Don't expect that to happen automatically. You have to make a decision to bring your body into obedience to the new man within you. You must determine to do what Romans 6:12 says and "let not sin...reign in your mortal body."

I know that sounds tough, but remember, you're not in this alone. You have a Helper inside you to enable you to carry out that decision. His name is the Holy Spirit. He's there to strengthen you. He gives you the power to put sin out of your life and under your feet.

Make that decisive dedication of your body today—and let that new man that's on the inside of you begin to come out!

SCRIPTURE READING: Romans 6:12-23

Spiritual Armor for Spiritual War

"For we wrestle not against flesh and blood,
but against principalities, against powers, against
the rulers of the darkness of this world, against spiritual
wickedness in high places." **(Ephesians 6:12)**

Unfortunately most of us don't know the first thing about fighting the kind of war this scripture refers to. For, as Ephesians 6:10-12 says, it's not a battle of flesh and blood, but of the spirit.

Most believers are so earthly minded (or carnally minded) that they never even realize where the enemy's attacks are actually coming from. They blame circumstances and people, and they waste their energy fighting natural conditions instead of supernatural causes.

We need to wake up to the warfare that's going on in the heavenly realm!

We can get a glimpse of it in the Book of Daniel, chapter 10, verses 12-20. There, we find that Daniel had been fasting and praying for 21 days, awaiting a word from the Lord. Then an angel appeared to him 21 days later with the answer. What took him so long? He was fighting the enemy in the heavens.

That confuses some people. They say, "Devils fighting in heaven? I thought *God* reigned in heaven!" What they don't understand is that the Bible teaches there are three different areas called heaven:

1. The heaven where God resides.
2. The stellar heavens (what we call "outer space").
3. The heavens around this earth (the atmosphere surrounding this planet).

This last heaven is where spiritual war takes place. (That's why Ephesians 2:2 calls Satan the prince of the power of the air.) "The air" is where wicked spirits operate. From there, they attempt to rule the nations to which they've been assigned.

—And rule them they will unless the prayers of God's people keep them from it.

God has an army marching in this land. If we band together, we can prevent the wickedness in high places from ruling our nation. The time has come for us, as believers, to pray. So, put on your full armor and take your place in the ranks of the faithful in intercession for our country and the nations of the world!

SCRIPTURE READING: Daniel 10:1-14

No Burden

"For the [true] love of God is this,
that we do His commands — keep His ordinances
and are mindful of His precepts and teaching. And these orders
of His are not irksome — burdensome, oppressive,
or grievous." **(1 John 5:3, AMP)**

Do you know why the Word of God and the orders God gives to you in your spirit are not burdensome or oppressive? Because everything He tells you is for your good and for your victory!

God knows what it takes to live in victory in this present evil world. In fact, He's the *only* one who knows. The people of this world cannot tell you how to live victoriously. They don't know how. But God does! He can make things work, even in the middle of darkness, and if we'll follow His instructions, commands, and precepts from His Word, we can too!

Let me give you an example. One commandment that God gave to us is to love one another and forgive one another as He has forgiven us. This command is not grievous because it's the key to our freedom. If you can walk in the love that's been shed abroad in your heart, you'll have joy every day. But if you don't walk in this commandment of love, somebody will get your joy before lunch! God knows that. So, He made a command of love and forgiveness because love works! Without love, there won't be any joy, and the joy of the Lord is our strength.

Don't resent God's teachings. Don't consider His ways a burden to your life-style. Rejoice over them. Take them gladly by the hand and let them lead you all the way to victory!

SCRIPTURE READING: 1 John 5:1-5

Dare to Decide

"Be it according to thy word." **(Exodus 8:10)**

I used to worry about making decisions for God. I used to be afraid to step out on faith and declare I was going to do something new that He'd shown me to do. I'd think, "What if I fail?" I was so scared of failing, I'd muddle around in indecision for weeks. Then one day I found out it wasn't my power that was going to carry it out anyway. *But it took my decision to move God in on the scene.* Once I decided what I was going to do and set it down firm, God backed me!

What I learned is a truth from the Word of God that, if you'll pay attention to it, will revolutionize your life. It's truth that carries an awesome responsibility with it, but it's a fabulous thing to realize.

Here it is: The right, the privilege, and the power to DECIDE has been left by God in the hands of men.

You have the right, for example, to decide where you're going to spend eternity. You have a right to make that decision, and God will back your decision.

God can do everything for you but decide. He's provided the power. He's provided His name. He's provided the blood of Jesus. He's provided the kingdom of God. He's even made us partakers of it (Col. 1:12).

But He's not going to stuff that inheritance down our throats. Somewhere down the line we each have to make the decision to receive it.

Now the beautiful part is this: When you make that decision, God will back you to the hilt with His power. Once you make a decision to be born again, there's no devil in hell big enough to stop you. All you have to do is decide.

Decide now. Declare your decision. Let it be done unto you according to your words.

Is God leading you in some new direction? Is He leading you to step out in faith for healing or prosperity or to take a whole new step of ministry? Don't let fear hold you back.

SCRIPTURE READING: Romans 4:13-21

Compassion in Action

"But when he saw the multitudes, he was moved
with compassion on them, because they fainted, and were scattered abroad,
as sheep having no shepherd." **(Matthew 9:36)**

Compassion. That's the one thing people need more than anything else in this world. They need someone to reach out to them with the compassion of God.

Compassion is a deep yearning that responds to the needs of people. It's much deeper than sympathy. Sympathy can just sit around feeling sorry for people. Compassion has to *do* something for them.

Compassion is what motivates God, and Jesus' life on earth was a picture of that compassion in action. His whole ministry was driven by it. It was compassion that caused Him to multiply the loaves and fishes, heal the sick, cast out demons, and raise the dead. It was compassion that compelled Him to go to the cross. And it's that same compassion that He now longs to pour out through you.

That's a staggering thought, isn't it?

It's staggering to realize that we believers are the only body Jesus has on this earth now. His healing must flow through our hands and our faith. His compassion must move us to provide for the hungry. It must compel us to cast out demons and set the captives free.

"But, Brother Copeland, I don't have that kind of compassion!"

Yes, you do. If you have the Spirit of God dwelling inside you, you do— because He *is* that kind of love! You simply need to activate it.

How? Just like Jesus did when He walked the earth. Through prayer and fellowship with the Father. Look through the Gospels and notice how much time Jesus spent alone with the Lord. That time activated the compassion of God within Him. It caused Him to feel what God feels about the suffering of mankind. It stirred Him so much that whenever He encountered a need, He met it by the power of God.

Follow His example. Spend time in fellowship with your Father. Meditate on His compassion until it rises up strong on the inside of you. Stir it up until the desire to see others set free becomes paramount in your thinking.

Jesus has sent you to reach out and touch a love-starved world with His compassion.

If you don't do it, who will?

SCRIPTURE READING: Mark 6:32-46

Bless the Lord

*"By him therefore let us offer the sacrifice
of praise to God continually, that is, the fruit of our lips
giving thanks to his name." (Hebrews 13:15)*

Great things happen when you continually confess the mercy of God. Faith rises up on the inside of you. The reality that God loves you begins to sing through your spirit.

What's more, it brings honor to your Father when you believe His Word and magnify His love and mercy. You honor Him when you speak of His goodness and loving-kindness, when you talk about Him as your Father of love who does only good. It blesses Him when you praise Him as the great God of the universe who is eager to bless and who even gave His own Son because He so loved the world.

David was a man after God's own heart. He knew how to praise his God.

Until you have the Word dwelling in you richly so that you can speak psalms and praises out of your own spirit, use the praises of David to magnify God. Speak them or sing them out loud to the Father.

Put His words continually on your lips. You will soon begin to experience the thrill and the joy of realizing that God is indeed "rich in mercy" because of His great love with which He loved us. Your faith will rise to new heights and your Father will be blessed! And you will be blessed.

SCRIPTURE READING: Psalm 89:1-18

Run to God

"If we confess our sins, he is faithful and just to forgive us our sins, and to cleanse us from all unrighteousness." **(1 John 1:9)**

It's wonderful to know you've been set free from the law of sin and death. It's glorious to know you never again have to submit to the slavery of sin. But what do you do when, in spite of those wonderful, glorious truths, you *still* miss the mark? What do you do when you stumble and fall into sin?

Run to your Father and repent!

That sounds simple. But oddly enough we often do just the opposite. Instead of running to God, we let fear and guilt drive us further and further from Him. We start thinking things like, "Well, I've missed it now. I might as well forget the rest of it and live like the devil."

Don't make that mistake. Don't let Satan talk you into sinning in one area of your life just because you missed it in another. When you get off track with God, just confess it and get right back on.

"But, Brother Copeland, I feel so guilty when I tell God what I've done that it's hard for me to make myself do it."

I know. I used to feel that way too. Then, one day, God said to me, "Kenneth, when you confessed that sin wasn't when I found out about it. I knew about it all the time! When you confessed it is when you got rid of it, when you were cleansed of its effects in your life."

When you make a mistake, when you miss the mark, remember, you have an advocate with the Father, Jesus Christ the Righteous (1 John 2:1). Run to Him! He knows what you are going through. You don't need to be afraid. He didn't tear you apart for the sins you committed before you made Him Lord of your life, did He? Then how much more merciful and loving do you think He'll be now that you're His own? Now that you're reaching out for Him and have a heart for Him?

Don't run from God. Run to Him. Receive His forgiveness. Receive His cleansing. No matter how badly you've sinned, He's eager to forgive and to cleanse you of all unrighteousness.

SCRIPTURE READING: 2 Samuel 11:1-5, 2 Samuel 12:1-13

Avoid Big Failures

"This I say therefore, and testify in the Lord,
that ye henceforth walk not as other Gentiles walk,
in the vanity of their mind, having the understanding darkened,
being alienated from the life of God through the ignorance
that is in them, because of the blindness of their heart:
Who being past feeling have given themselves over
unto lasciviousness." **(Ephesians 4:17-19)**

There's a subtle strategy Satan uses to take control of our lives. The Bible calls it "lasciviousness" and it means "to have no restraint."

Lasciviousness has been preached as being extreme immorality, but it doesn't start out that way. It begins with just a few seemingly innocent thoughts. Then those thoughts grow and grow until they begin to produce serious sin.

One afternoon as a nine-year-old boy, for example, I just yielded to the desire to curse. I knew better, but I did it anyway. I had a relative who was so good at West Texas cussin' that I thought he invented it. I was intrigued and I wanted to try it.

When I let go of all restraint and began to say those curse words, something evil moved in on my thinking that seriously affected me for some 20 years. A law was set in motion. As a result, my flesh gradually became boss over my entire being.

Don't let Satan use the strategy of lasciviousness on you. Make up your mind and heart today to obey God in the little things. Avoid big failures by walking in His Spirit one small step at a time. Major victories will eventually be yours.

SCRIPTURE READING: Ephesians 4:22-31

The Deciding Witness

"In the mouth of two or three witnesses
every word may be established." **(Matthew 18:16)**

You've been there many times, standing in the valley of decision. Perched precariously between victory and defeat. On one side of you is the word of the world authored by Satan that says, for example, "You're not going to get healed." On the other side of you, the Word of God is saying, "My Word is Yea and Amen" and "By His stripes, ye were healed." Who will determine how it all turns out? *You* will. You're the establishing witness.

I remember a fellow once who wanted me to pray for him. I said, "Now the Word says you're healed." He interrupted me and said, "Yeah, I know it says that, but I've got this terrible pain here...."

I looked him in the eye and said again, "The Word says, 'By His stripes, you were healed.'"

"I know it," he answered, "but I've got this terrible...."

I shook my head. "Listen, the Word says you're healed!"

He turned beet red. "I KNOW IT SAYS THAT, BUT I'VE GOT THIS...."

Finally, he stopped and stared at me. He didn't realize it, but he'd allowed his physical symptoms to become his evidence. It was what he believed. No matter what the Word said, he believed the thing he could see and feel.

But when he got quiet, I said to him, "Look, you're wanting me to agree with you and you're mad because I won't. But if I agree with you, you're going to die. Now if you'll agree with me and the Bible, we can get you healed."

Suddenly he saw it. His eyes lit up. "Oh, praise God! I see what you mean. I agree with the Word of God!"

I put my hands on his head and God healed him instantly.

You see, when he finally decided to get in agreement with God, he could have received it in his bedroom or driving down the road or anywhere else. He could have received any time he decided to become the establishing witness.

You pray and establish your witness. That's your part. If you'll do it, God will back you—and when He backs you, everything else either has to get in line or get out of the way.

You're the deciding witness. What do you say?

SCRIPTURE READING: Matthew 18:15-20

Subject to Change

"While we look not at the things which are seen,
but at the things which are not seen: for the things
which are seen are temporal; but the things which
are not seen are eternal." **(2 Corinthians 4:18)**

Don't center your attention on what you can see in this natural, physical sense realm. Everything you see is temporal and subject to change. So, put your faith in the unseen eternal realm. The things which are eternal are not subject to change.

God's Word is eternal and it contains 7,000 promises to cover any circumstance you'll ever face. And, no matter what happens in this shifting, changing world you live in, those promises will forever be the same.

No matter how bad your body feels, the Word will always say, "By His stripes you were healed" (1 Pet. 2:24). No matter how bad your bank book looks, the Word will always say, "My God shall supply all your need according to his riches in glory by Christ Jesus" (Phil. 4:19).

Don't settle for the meager existence the world says you can have. Lay hold of what the Word says you can have. Center your attention on the eternal truths of God and look not to the things which are seen. After all, they're subject to change!

SCRIPTURE READING: 2 Corinthians 4:8-18

Revolutionary Love

"Love bears up under anything and everything that comes,
is ever ready to believe the best of every person, its hopes are fadeless
under all circumstances and it endures everything [without weakening].
Love never fails — never fades out or becomes obsolete
or comes to an end." **(1 Corinthians 13:7,8, AMP)**

Love never fails. Nothing works without it, and there can be no failure with it. When you live by love, you cannot fail.

It takes faith to believe that love's way will not fail. The natural mind cannot understand that because the natural man and his world are ruled by selfishness.

But when you practice love by faith and refuse to seek your own, you put the Father into action on your behalf. As long as you stay in love, God the Father seeks your own. He sees to it that you succeed. Walking in love is to your great advantage!

Agape love is a new kind of power. It makes you master of every situation.

No weapon that is formed against you will prosper. No one even has the power to hurt your feelings because you are not ruled by feelings but by God's love. You are loving as He loves.

This love is revolutionary. If we fully understood the great return from living God's love, we'd probably be competing with each other, each of us trying to love the other more. And without a doubt, everyone would emerge from that competition a winner! For love is truly the only sure secret to our success.

SCRIPTURE READING: Romans 12:9-21

Leave Foolishness Behind

"Evil pursueth sinners: but to the righteous
good shall be repayed." **(Proverbs 13:21)**

Satan has had us in a poverty mentality so long that it's tough for us to grasp just how intensely God really does desire to prosper us — even though He's demonstrated that desire again and again.

Take Abraham, for example. God made him an *extremely* wealthy man. Genesis 13:2 says he was rich in cattle, in silver, and in gold.

Then, of course, there was Solomon. The Bible says he surpassed all the kings of the earth in riches and wisdom.

God's servant Job possessed such great wealth that he was called the greatest of all the men of the East. That was before Satan put him through the wringer. Afterward, God blessed him with more than twice what Satan had stolen.

The problem is, just the thought of the kind of wealth God gave to those men scares most believers today. They're afraid it would destroy them.

God has said that "the prosperity of fools shall destroy them" (Prov. 1:32).

But that doesn't mean you should avoid being prosperous. It means you should avoid being a fool!

I challenge you, this week, to go to the Book of Proverbs and find out for yourself what God says about the characteristics of a fool. Let the Holy Spirit search your heart. If you see ways in which you've been a fool, repent and make a firm decision not to be caught in that trap again.

Let the Word of God inspire you to leave foolishness behind and stir within you the faith to reach out and receive what you, as a redeemed child of the living God, have a divine right to — not the curse of poverty, but the blessing of prosperity!

SCRIPTURE READING: Genesis 15:1-6

Seed of Faith

"For verily I say unto you, If ye have faith
as a grain of mustard seed, ye shall say unto this mountain,
Remove hence to yonder place; and it shall remove; and nothing
shall be impossible unto you." **(Matthew 17:20)**

Someone once said that the reason I can live like I do is because I have "special faith." But, you know, that's just not true. I don't have "special faith." God has given me the same measure of faith He's given to you and every other believer. The only reason my faith looks like it works better is because I *use* it!

If you've been living in the shadow of a mountain, waiting for God to give you some kind of special faith, make a change today. Step out and put the measure of faith you have to work moving the spiritual, physical, mental, or financial obstacles Satan has brought against you.

Romans 12:3 says God has dealt to *every* man the measure of faith. Believe Him! Step out in faith about that faith! Say, "Heavenly Father, I thank You that through faith in Jesus Christ, You have shared Your nature and Your Spirit with me. I am grateful for the measure of faith imparted to me as a believer.

"I make the decision today to walk in that faith. To put it to work on the situations around me. I commit myself to operate in mountain-moving faith, for I know that it is impossible to please You without it (Heb. 11:6).

"As I plant this faith and water it with Your Word (Rom. 10:17), I expect it to grow and overcome the mountains in my life and in the lives of those I intercede for.

"Thank You, Father, that as I do this, nothing shall be impossible to me! In Jesus' name. Amen."

SCRIPTURE READING: Luke 8:41-56

Your First and Highest Calling

"God is faithful, by whom ye were called unto the fellowship of his Son Jesus Christ our Lord." **(1 Corinthians 1:9)**

D o you know what God wants you to do more than anything else today? He wants you to fellowship with Him.

He wants you to walk with Him and talk with Him. To discuss the things of life with Him. He wants you to draw near to Him and partake of His very nature.

So many of us get so caught up in striving to please God in the things we do that we forget our first and highest calling is just to *be* in fellowship with Him.

That's right. God longs for us just to want to be with Him.

Have you ever considered how much it would mean for you to just come to God and say, "Father, I didn't really come today to get anything. I've prayed about my needs already and Your Word says they're met according to Your riches in glory by Christ Jesus. So I just came to be with You. If You have anything You'd like to tell me, I'm ready to listen...and I want you to know that whatever I see in Your Word, I'll do it. I'll put it into effect in my life."

Why don't you tell that to God today? He's waiting to have fellowship with you.

SCRIPTURE READING: 1 John 1:1-7

Live Free From Fear

"He that dwelleth in the secret place of the most High
shall abide under the shadow of the Almighty. I will say of the Lord,
He is my refuge and my fortress: my God; in him will I trust.
Surely he shall deliver thee from the snare of the fowler,
and from the noisome pestilence." **(Psalm 91:1-3)**

I s it possible to live free from fear in this dangerous and unpredictable world? Yes, it most definitely is! Because protection is a solid promise of God.

But it's not a promise that's offered to just anyone; it is promised to those who abide in the Lord. To abide means "to dwell, to remain, and to continue." To abide in the shadow of the Almighty is to live in continual union with Him, keeping His Word and obeying His voice. Those who abide in the Lord can live without dread of what the devil will do.

Let me make this clear though— God's promise of protection doesn't guarantee that the devil will leave you alone! It means that God will give you a way of escape every time the devil rears his ugly face at you.

If you are afraid of the dangers around you, spend more time in the Word and in prayer until your trust in God overcomes your fear. Draw closer to the Lord until you are abiding in the shadow of the Almighty and—no matter how dangerous this world becomes—He shall surely deliver you.

SCRIPTURE READING: Psalm 91:1-16

Prepare for Persecution

"Yea, and all that will live godly
in Christ Jesus shall suffer persecution." **(2 Timothy 3:12)**

D id you catch that? He said all who live godly lives are going to suffer persecution. Not just the super-saints, not just the believers behind the Iron Curtain, not just the missionaries in hostile lands—but ALL.

If you're going to live for God, you're going to run into persecution somewhere along the line. The devil's going to make sure of it!

Now I'm not saying that to frighten you or to depress you. I'm saying it because I want you to be prepared.

When you're wise to the strategies of the devil, it's harder for him to use them successfully on you to confuse you and get you off track.

Second Corinthians 10:4 says, "For the weapons of our warfare are not carnal, but mighty through God to the pulling down of strongholds." So stay armed and ready for Satan's attack. Then, whenever and however it comes, it won't bring your life to a halt or even slow you down.

That's especially important right now because we're living in the last days. The devil's time is drawing short. He is desperate. He is going to do everything he can to stop the Church. But Jesus said the gates of hell would not prevail against His Church!

Remember the more we grow to be like Jesus and the more God's glory is revealed through our lives, the bigger threat we are to Satan's kingdom. Jesus said, "Rejoice and be glad at such a time, and exult and leap for joy, for behold, your reward is rich and great and strong and intense and abundant in heaven" (Luke 6:23, AMP).

So, when persecution comes your way, and you know it will, rejoice and be glad. Take the Jesus cure and begin to leap and jump and praise God! There is no way persecution will hurt you if you do that. I've tried it and it works.

SCRIPTURE READING: Acts 6:1-15

Tune in to the Spirit of Grace

"For the grace of God that bringeth salvation hath appeared to all men, TEACHING US that, denying ungodliness and worldly lusts, we should live soberly, righteously, and godly, in this present world." **(Titus 2:11)**

Grace teaches us! The "Spirit of grace" instructs us from the inside. Let the Holy Spirit of God counsel you and teach you how to live in this present world.

If you listen to the voice of the world, you will be worldly minded, or carnally minded, which is death. But, if you tune in to the voice of the Spirit of Grace, you can become spiritually minded; and, according to the Word, that is life and peace. So, when the Spirit of God speaks to you through that still small voice inside your heart, listen and obey Him. His way works! Trust Him and remember that He's got your well-being in mind.

Maybe He's asking you to eliminate some activity that's consuming too much of your time and attention. Or maybe He's prompting you to get up a little earlier and spend more time in the Word and in prayer. Whatever it is He is telling you to do, if you'll do it, you'll be stronger in the grace of God, and consequently, in the blessing of God.

Don't hesitate another moment. DO IT! If you want a change, make a change.

SCRIPTURE READING: 1 Corinthians 1:3-8

From Religion to Reality

"For [God] hath made [Jesus] to be sin for us,
who knew no sin; that we might be made the righteousness
of God in him." **(2 Corinthians 5:21)**

When you were born again, you weren't half-reborn, you weren't made half-righteous or a quarter righteous. You were made *the righteousness of God in Christ!* You were made a "joint-heir with Him." According to Strong's Concordance that word "joint-heir" refers to "a personal equality based on an equality of possession."

Jesus went to the cross to give you what He already possessed. He rose again so that you could be recreated in His image. You are the victory of Almighty God! You are more than a conqueror in Christ Jesus. You are everything to the Father that Jesus is. John 17:23 actually says that God loves you as much as He loves Jesus.

Once you dare to accept that fact, your life will be forever changed. You'll no longer be satisfied to just sit around whining and wishing things were different. You'll want to step up to the position of authority that Jesus has given you, to take your rightful place beside Him and learn to operate the way He does.

As His people, we are everything to God that Jesus is.

If you'll receive that message. If you'll dare to believe it. If you'll dare to put it into action. It will radically alter your life. It will take you from religion to reality!

SCRIPTURE READING: John 17:16-26

That Glorious Name

"And I will do—I Myself will grant—whatever you may ask
in My name [presenting all I AM] so that the Father may be glorified
and extolled in [through] the Son." **(John 14:13, AMP)**

*I*n Jesus' Name. It's more than a phrase we tack on to the end of our prayers. All that God is and does is represented in the name of Jesus. *The Amplified Bible* says when you ask in His name, you present your requests to the Father on the credit of *all* that Jesus is. So you can boldly expect to have those requests granted—not because you're worthy, but because He is!

What's more, the name of Jesus carries authority over all other names. In Philippians 2:5-11, the apostle Paul tells us, "God also hath highly exalted him [Jesus], and given him a name which is above every name: That at the name of Jesus every knee should bow, of things in heaven, and things in earth, and things under the earth."

In spite of all the Word of God has to say about the power of the name of Jesus, most believers don't seem to put much stock in it. They'll pray in the name of Jesus, then turn right around and say, "I sure hope God answers that prayer." They don't realize that if they only had the faith to believe it, Jesus' name alone carries enough clout to *guarantee* their prayers will be answered.

They even let religious slang rob them of the power of using that Name. I've heard many a well-meaning believer end his prayer with the phrase, "For Jesus' sake." But Jesus didn't say to pray *for His sake*. He said to pray *in His name*.

I used to make that mistake myself. One night I was praying because I was suffering from a stomachache. "Oh, for Jesus' sake," I prayed, "heal my stomach."

After I'd said that a few times, the Lord spoke up on the inside of me. "Wait a minute," He said, "whose stomach is hurting here, Mine or yours?"

"Mine!" I answered.

Then He very plainly said, "In that case, pray for *your* stomach's sake, in *My* name!"

Jesus' name. Dig into the Word and find out just how much power and authority it really carries. Then use that power every time you pray. Stop "hoping" God will answer and start expecting Him to cause every circumstance in your life to bow its knee in honor of that glorious Name!

SCRIPTURE READING: John 16:13-24

The Heart of the King

"The king's heart is in the hand of the Lord,
as the rivers of water: he turneth it whithersoever he will."

(Proverbs 21:1)

Think about that for a moment! God has reserved the right to override the will of a nation's leader, if need be, to see that His people are governed according to His will.

What's more, God will hear the prayer of any government leader. Even if he's the worst reprobate in the whole world. He heard the prayer of old King Nebuchadnezzar. Believe me, that means He'll listen to any leader!

You see, Nebuchadnezzar was king of Babylon. He was an ungodly ruler of an ungodly nation. However, he'd taken captives from the land of Judah. He had some of God's people under his authority. So, God began to deal with him.

Again and again, God warned him, "Nebuchadnezzar, you're going to lose your mind if you don't straighten up." And, sure enough, he went just as crazy as could be.

He stayed that way for years too. Then one day he cried out to God and God heard him.

Despite his status as a heathen king of a heathen nation, God intervened repeatedly in Nebuchadnezzar's life and heard him when he finally cried out for help. Why? Because he had God's people under his control!

That same principle still holds true today. If we'll open the way through prayer, God will deal with *our* leaders!

If we will humble ourselves in unity and pray, God can change the injustice and corruption that exist in our country or any country for that matter. He'll change the hearts of everyone from the White House on down to make sure His children are governed justly.

Make it a point to pray for our leaders *today!*

SCRIPTURE READING: Daniel 4:1-37

Put Patience to Work

"Cast not away therefore your confidence,
which hath great recompence of reward. For ye have need
of patience, that, after ye have done the will of God,
ye might receive the promise." **(Hebrews 10:35,36)**

Most of us have a distorted idea about patience. We think of it as something designed to help us suffer failure gracefully, but according to these scriptures, it will actually put us on the path to success!

Patience (or being consistently constant) is the power twin of faith. They work together to see to it that the promises of God are fulfilled in your life.

Say, for example, you need a job. You can go to the Word and see clearly that God promises to provide your needs. You can see He takes pleasure in the prosperity of His servants. Once you see that, faith takes hold and you shout, "Hallelujah, I've got the job I need."

But what happens to that faith tomorrow morning when you go to three interviews and get turned down all three times? Then what? That's when patience has to take over! That's when you have to make a decision to stay constant, to act as if nothing's changed.

The truth is, if you based your confidence on the Word of God, nothing has changed. It says exactly the same thing it said yesterday.

So, if you'll put patience to work, you know what you're going to say after those three unsuccessful job interviews? You're going to say, "Hallelujah, I've got the job I need!" just like you did before.

You see, faith opens the door to God's promise for you; and patience keeps it open until that promise is fulfilled.

Do you have your faith sights set on a promise of God today, a promise you've been waiting on for some time? Don't let the delay discourage you. Put patience to work. The Word guarantees you *will* receive your reward.

SCRIPTURE READING: Hebrews 6:10-15

Living the Love Life

"Greater love hath no man than this,
that a man lay down his life for his friends." (John 15:13)

We often think of "laying down your life" for someone else in terms of dying. That's what Jesus did. He loved us so much He laid down His life by dying in our place so that we could live.

But now, He's asked us to lay down our lives in a different way. He's asked us to show our love, not by dying for others, but by *living* for them.

Exactly what does that mean?

Sometimes it means giving our lives by spending time in prayer for someone. Other times it means giving of ourselves with love and understanding. Many times it means laying down our own selfish desires in order to meet the needs of another.

Romans 15:1 puts it this way, "We then that are strong ought to bear the infirmities of the weak, and not to please ourselves."

When you lay down your life, you live to please God instead of yourself. You let your life be guided by His love. If love leads you to the person next door, you follow. When love calls you to intercede for someone in need, you yield.

Commit yourself today to lay down your own life—and take up the love life. Say:

"Father, in Jesus' name, I see from Your Word that You were willing to give of Yourself, in the person of Your Son, for all men. I understand that because Jesus is Lord of my life, I, too, am called to give myself to others. I choose to accept that calling today.

"I'll give of my time. I'll give of Your love in me. I'll be strong and lift up those who are weak. I'm willing to be available to be used of You so that those around me might experience the abundant life You have provided.

"You have loved me, Lord, with the greatest love there is. I count it a privilege now to share that love with others. I thank You for it in Jesus' name. Amen."

SCRIPTURE READING: Galatians 5:22-26, Galatians 6:1-3

From Tradition to Truth

"Bless the Lord, O my soul, and forget not all his benefits:
Who forgiveth all thine iniquities; who healeth all thy diseases;
Who redeemeth thy life from destruction; who crowneth thee with
lovingkindness and tender mercies; Who satisfieth thy mouth
with good things; so that thy youth is renewed
like the eagle's." **(Psalm 103:2-5)**

Is there actually a divine purpose behind the bad things that happen in your life? Could it be that the sicknesses and calamities you experience are somehow a part of God's plan for you?

Before you can ever begin to experience the healing, delivering power of God, you've got to know the answer to those questions. You have to settle them once and for all. If you even suspect that God is the source of your misfortunes, you won't be able to believe Him for deliverance from them. Your faith will be crippled because you'll think that by escaping those things, you'll be opposing His will.

In order to receive all the benefits God desires to give you, you must be absolutely sure that He is a good God. You must be certain that His will for you is health, not sickness; prosperity, not poverty; happiness, not sorrow— 100 percent of the time! Psalm 103 alone is enough to prove that's true. But if it's not enough to convince you, there are many others too. One of the best known is Psalm 136:1 that says, "O give thanks unto the Lord; for he is good: for his mercy endureth for ever."

If religious traditions have robbed you of the goodness of God, if it's taught you He brings trouble into your life so He can teach you something, start today washing those traditions away with the truth. Get out your Bible and let God Himself tell you through His own Word that He is the God that heals you (Exod. 15:26). Dig into the Scriptures and discover for yourself that He is a God of mercy (Ps. 86:5), loving-kindness (Jer. 9:24), and compassion (Ps. 145:8).

Put your doubts to rest and open your heart to receive the truth about your heavenly Father. It's the only thing that can truly set you free.

SCRIPTURE READING: Psalm 89:1-28

Don't Let Division Stunt Your Growth

"And I, brethren, could not speak unto you
as unto spiritual, but as unto carnal, even as unto babes in Christ.
I have fed you with milk, and not with meat: for hitherto ye were not able
to bear it, neither yet now are ye able. For ye are yet carnal:
for whereas there is among you envying, and strife,
and divisions...." **(1 Corinthians 3:1-3)**

Envying, strife, and divisions had reduced the early Corinthian Christians back to the natural, or carnal, state that they were in before they were born again. It had so stunted their spiritual growth that they couldn't understand the things the apostle Paul wanted to teach them.

Satan has sent the same spirit of division among us today. He knows that a house divided against itself will fall. He also knows if we all come together in the unity of our faith, we'll arrive at the full stature of Christ Jesus (Eph. 4:13). So he has assigned a spirit of division to operate in our personal lives, our church lives, our social lives, and our family lives. His goal is the same as it was in Corinth: To bring envying, strife, division, and to stunt our spiritual growth.

But we don't have to yield to that spirit. Instead Paul says, "[by] speaking the truth in love, [we] may grow up into him in all things, which is the head, even Christ."

Compare "speaking the truth in love" to "envyings, strife, and divisions." Diametrical opposites, aren't they? You can't do both of them at the same time. As you speak the truth in love, you grow up. As you envy, fuss, and separate from one another, you go back to babyhood.

Don't let Satan stop your spiritual growth by giving in to the spirit of division but speak the truth in love and "grow up into Him in *all* things!"

SCRIPTURE READING: James 4:1-11

Gloria *G l o r i a*

Prescription for Life

"If any one intends to come after Me,
let him deny himself — forget, ignore, disown, lose sight
of himself and his own interests — and take up his cross, and...
follow with Me. For whoever wants to save his [higher...] life,
will lose [it]...and whoever gives up his life for My sake
and the Gospel's, will save [it]." **(Mark 8:34,35, AMP)**

When Jesus said those words, He wasn't just giving us a prescription for getting to heaven. He was telling us how to live a superior life right here on earth.

You see, there's a high life that we can live right here, right now. But to get in on it, we have to lay down the way of life that most of us are accustomed to. We may have to let go of the very things we've been trying so hard to latch onto. We have to set our hearts instead on doing what God wants us to do.

That's what Jesus did. He didn't live His life for Himself. He lived it completely for God. He did only what the Father told Him to do—*and He lived in total victory.*

It's time to realize that getting born again is not something we do just to miss hell. Our purpose is to please God. To lay down our lives in order to fulfill His desires. To be His special possessions in the earth and to do whatever He tells us to do. Our top priority is to give ourselves to Him and to live in communication with Him. To spend enough time with Him that we can hear His voice and respond in obedience.

Only when we do that will we be genuinely fulfilled. Only when we do that will we be able to live the high life we've been longing for.

SCRIPTURE READING: Acts 20:7-24

Covenant Prosperity

"But thou shalt remember the Lord thy God:
for it is he that giveth thee power to get wealth, that he may
establish his covenant." **(Deuteronomy 8:18)**

What is God's reason for prospering His people? Is it so we can watch bigger TV's? So we can buy finer houses and more luxurious cars?

Establishing God's covenant on the earth and giving to those in need: Those are God's purposes for prosperity!

I've had some people tell me, "Well, Brother Copeland, Jesus' ministry was poor and He got along just fine." That's ridiculous. All the way through the Old Testament God promised material blessings to anyone who would walk perfectly and uprightly before Him. If God had failed to bless Jesus financially, He would have been breaking His own Word.

Jesus never built a worldly empire for Himself. But that doesn't mean He was poor. It means He was the greatest giver who ever walked the face of this earth—and it's about time we started following in His footsteps.

If we'll start giving, if we'll start taking care of the needs in people's pocketbooks, we'll be far more likely to win their hearts.

What do you think will happen to the heart of a starving nation when you bring in a 747 full of food, clothes, and medical supplies to them in the name of Jesus and His love? The hearts of those people are going to soften! They're going to be willing to listen to what we have to say about Jesus.

Don't you ever let anyone tell you it's wrong to want to prosper. It's wrong for you not to want to prosper when that prosperity can mean the difference between heaven and hell for millions of people.

Forget about your own little needs. Raise your vision and set your mind on giving to meet someone else's, on establishing God's covenant in the earth. Then stand fast in faith and get ready to enjoy the greatest prosperity you've ever known.

SCRIPTURE READING: Deuteronomy 8:11-18

When Tough Times Come

"Then had the churches rest throughout all
Judaea and Galilee and Samaria, and were edified;
and walking in the fear of the Lord, and in the comfort
of the Holy Ghost, were multiplied." **(Acts 9:31)**

There are times when life on this earth is hard and uncomfortable... and even downright painful. When those times come, you deeply need the comfort that only the Holy Spirit can bring.

How do you receive that kind of comfort?

By doing just what the believers in Acts did. By "walking in the fear of the Lord."

Now, when I talk about "the fear of the Lord," please understand, I'm not saying you should be afraid of God. He's your Father! You should be as secure and unafraid when you come before Him as a child who knows he is dearly loved. But you must also have so much respect for Him that whenever He reveals something you need to do, you do it immediately—even if it goes against your natural desires. *That's* walking in the fear of the Lord.

Let me show you what I mean. Once, several years ago, I received a very disturbing phone call shortly before I was to preach at one of our meetings. It was painful news about a situation in which one of my children

had been wronged. The news of it wounded my heart.

I cried, and in the natural, I wanted to get angry about it, to strike back in some way. But instead, I began praying in other tongues. As I prayed, I was prompted in my spirit to rejoice and praise the Lord.

I certainly didn't *feel* like praising. I felt like stomping my foot. But, out of respect to the Lord, I put my feelings aside and obeyed. Next, the Holy Spirit impressed me to read a particular prophecy. As I did, I could tell I was being strengthened.

Then suddenly, I realized I was free. By my obedience, I had opened myself to the comforting power of the Holy Spirit. The anger and pain that had filled me just moments before were gone! They had been replaced by the gentle love and reassurance of the Lord.

No matter how tough or painful a situation you may be facing today, trust and obey the directions of your Father. He will make that same supernatural, Holy Spirit-inspired comfort available to you!

SCRIPTURE READING: Matthew 4:1-11

Choose Life

"For to be carnally minded is death; but
to be spiritually minded is life and peace." **(Romans 8:6)**

If you were given the choice between life and death, which would you choose? The answer seems obvious. But, in reality, it's not.

You see, choosing death doesn't necessarily mean jumping from the nearest cliff. It's much more subtle than that.

The Bible says death is being carnally minded, being entangled in this present worldly realm. The Bible also tells us what life is. "My son, attend to my words," says Proverbs 4:20-22, "...for they are life!"

To be worldly minded is death. To be Word minded is life.

In the tenth chapter of Luke, there's a story that illustrates this principle extremely well. It's the story of Mary and Martha. You probably remember it. Mary was sitting at Jesus' feet listening to Him teach while Martha was bustling around in the kitchen cooking dinner for everyone.

Finally Martha couldn't stand it anymore. She came to Jesus and said, "Lord, don't you care that my sister has left me to do all the work myself? Tell her to help me!" Jesus answered, "Martha, Martha, thou art careful and troubled about many things: But one thing is needful: and Mary hath chosen that good part, which shall not be taken away from her" (Luke 10:41,42).

Mary had set everything else aside, so she could hear the Word. But Martha had let the seemingly important business of living take priority over the Word. She'd chosen death, not life.

You see how easy it is to slip into that?

"But Brother Copeland," you say, "if I didn't spend all my time taking care of the business of living, my life would fall apart!"

Oh, really? Martha probably thought that too. She probably thought if she didn't cook dinner for all those folks, they'd go hungry. But they wouldn't have. Jesus had miraculously fed multitudes before and He could have done it again in Martha's home. She could have plopped herself down at Jesus' feet, and they could have had a banquet at God's expense!

Don't make the mistake that Martha did. Don't get so entangled in the business of living that you choose death by default. Decide to put the Word first place. Choose Life!

SCRIPTURE READING: Romans 8:5-13

God Goes Too!

"But the person who is united to the Lord
becomes one spirit with Him." **(1 Corinthians 6:17, AMP)**

I once heard about a great man of God who looked in the mirror every day when he put on his suit and said, "Suit, everywhere you go today, God goes in you." And you know, he's right. If you have united yourself to God by receiving Jesus as Lord, everywhere you go today...God goes too!

As believers, we need to start becoming more conscious of that. We need to train ourselves to be constantly aware of God inside of us, talking to us, teaching us, counseling us, empowering us, and enduing us with Himself.

We need to continually remind ourselves that we are one spirit with Him. That means that every time we face a problem, every time we face an evil spirit that tries to influence and hinder our lives, God is facing it too. When we meet those things, God meets them. And He's already overcome them!

Let me encourage you when you get dressed today to look in the mirror and say, "I am united to the Lord and I have become one spirit with Him. Body, everywhere you go today...God goes. God is in you. The power of God is in you. The wisdom of God is in you. The victory of God is in you."

Say that to yourself every day—many times a day. Keep doing it until you begin to develop the habit of thinking that way. Cultivate a constant awareness of the reality of God living in you!

SCRIPTURE READING: 1 Corinthians 6:17-20

Get Rid of the Frogs

"When shall I intreat for thee, and for
thy servants, and for thy people, to destroy the frogs
from thee and thy houses?" **(Exodus 8:9)**

Have you ever wrestled with one of those problems that stubbornly refuses to go away? It seems to be immune to all solutions. You swat at the thing in every conceivable way, but instead of being eliminated, it expands and multiplies until it's wildly out of control.

An Egyptian pharaoh faced just that kind of problem, the Bible tells us, thousands of years ago. He was in a hot dispute with God over the future of the Israelites, and as a result of that dispute, he woke up one morning to find his country swarming with frogs. Slimy, smelly, hopping-all-over-the-place frogs.

It was a *serious* problem. I'm not talking about a frog or two in the front yard. I mean frogs were everywhere—in their beds, on their tables. Big old frogs in the ovens. Little bitty frogs in the bread dough and the drinking water. Frogs. Frogs in your hair. Frogs in places you wouldn't even want to think about!

Then God made a move. He sent His man Moses in to Pharaoh to ask, "When shall I intreat the Lord to get these frogs out of here?"

Do you know what Pharaoh said? "Tomorrow." Can you imagine that? He could have said, "Right now! Today!" But instead he decided he'd spend one more night among the frogs.

You say, "That's the stupidest thing I ever heard. Why in the world would he do it tomorrow?" I don't know. Probably for the same reason you want to wait until tomorrow to get saved or healed or prosperous.

Here's what I want you to notice. When Moses asked Pharaoh that question and he answered, "Tomorrow," Moses said, "All right. So that you know there's a God in heaven, BE IT DONE UNTO YOU ACCORDING TO YOUR WORDS."

Let me ask you this: How long are you willing to let that persisting problem harass you? When are you going to get rid of the frogs in your life? Do you realize they'll stay around as long as you'll let them? They'll be there until you finally make a quality decision to go with the Word of God and get them out.

Why don't you do it today?

SCRIPTURE READING: Exodus 8:1-13

Take Your Place

"But God, who is rich in mercy, for his great love
wherewith he loved us, Even when we were dead in sins,
hath quickened us together with Christ...And hath raised us up together,
and made us sit together in heavenly places
in Christ Jesus." **(Ephesians 2:4-6)**

God has raised us up to sit together in heavenly places in Christ Jesus! That's what the Word of God says. Very few of us have actually dared to believe this. We've uplifted Jesus. We've exalted Him—and rightly so! But at the same time, we've unwittingly belittled what He did by not allowing Him to bring us alongside Him.

That was God's purpose at Calvary: to bring us alongside Jesus. To make us what He already was.

You see, Jesus didn't need exalting. He was exalted before He ever came to this earth. He was already one with the Father. He didn't need to get authority over the devil—He'd never lost it!

He put on a physical body so that He could come to earth as a man and gain authority over sin and sickness, demons, fear, poverty, and all the other curses that came when the law of death moved into the earth—and He did it.

He succeeded. He mastered everything in the world of the intellect, everything in the physical world.

Before He ascended, He said, "All authority is given unto Me both in heaven and in the earth." Then He turned around and gave that authority to us by giving us His name.

You and I are the reason Jesus came to earth and died and lived again. He didn't do it for Himself. He did it so He could bring us alongside. So we could wear His name and wield His authority on the earth. He did it so that we could stand before God and be everything to Him that Jesus is.

When you were born again, you were made the righteousness of God in Christ! So as a born-again believer, dare to receive this message, to meditate on it and to act on it. Go ahead—dare to take your place!

SCRIPTURE READING: Ephesians 2:1-13

Don't Depend on Guesswork

"Call unto me, and I will answer thee, and shew thee
great and mighty things, which thou knowest not." **(Jeremiah 33:3)**

Who do you turn to when you need help, when you need an important answer to an important question? Do you ask God first?

So many believers fail to do that! They'll stand around wringing their hands and talking to each other all day. They'll inquire of their pastor. They'll inquire of their friends. They'll inquire of their husband or their wife. But do they inquire of God? No.

Don't make that mistake.

Instead, follow the example of King David. In the fourteenth chapter of 1 Chronicles, the Bible tells us he was about to face a battle with the very powerful Philistines who had ALL come out against him. The Philistine nation had been an enemy of Israel for years. David probably could have guessed that God would tell him to go to battle against them. But he didn't

guess! He went to God and inquired, saying, "Shall I go up against the Philistines? And wilt thou deliver them into mine hand? And the Lord said unto him, Go up; for I will deliver them into thine hand."

Don't depend on guesswork. When you encounter a problem, seek the Lord through the Word and in prayer and ask Him what the solution is. No matter how much scripture you learn, no matter how fully you perceive who you are in Christ Jesus, you'll never outgrow your need to do that.

Go to the Lord and find out exactly what He wants you to do. Don't decide your course of action and then ask God to bless your plans. Go to Him and say, "Lord, what are Your plans?" His plans are already blessed. If you follow them, your victory is guaranteed.

SCRIPTURE READING: 1 Chronicles 14:8-17

Enjoy the Victory

"But thanks be to God, Who gives us the victory—making us
conquerors—through our Lord Jesus Christ." **(1 Corinthians 15:57, AMP)**

Victors! More than conquerors! That's what the Bible says we are. I know you've heard that many times before, but today I want you to let the reality of it really sink in. I want you to spend some time meditating about what those terms actually mean.

The dictionary says that *victory* means "final and complete supremacy or superiority in battle or war, success in any contest or struggling involving the defeat of an opponent or the overcoming of obstacles."

To *conquer* means "to get the better of in competition or struggle, to master, suppress, prevail over, overwhelm, surmount, to gain superiority, to subdue, to vanquish, to crush, to defeat."

Once you get those definitions firmly in mind, you'll realize in Jesus you've gotten much more than a ticket to heaven. You've gotten the best of the world you're living in now. Through Him, you've overcome it, mastered it, suppressed it, and prevailed over it.

No wonder 1 Corinthians 15:57 shouts, "Thanks be to God! Because He *gives* us the victory, making us conquerors through our Lord Jesus Christ!"

Why don't you shout too! Shout thanks to God today for making you an overcomer. Praise Him that you are joined up with the One who has conquered the world, the flesh, and the devil. Shout hallelujah and enjoy the victory!

SCRIPTURE READING: Romans 8:29-39

Come, Lord Jesus

"Beloved, now are we the sons of God,
and it doth not yet appear what we shall be:
but we know that, when he shall appear, we shall be like him;
for we shall see him as he is. And every man that hath
this hope in him purifieth himself, even as
he is pure." **(1 John 3:2,3)**

Hopelessness. As this age draws to a close, that's a feeling that's going to be more and more common among the people of this world. But, you know, it's something we as believers never have to feel! Because no matter how much pressure comes on the earth, no matter how dark the natural circumstances around us are, we know that we have hope in the soon return of the Lord Jesus Christ.

Sometimes we forget that. We get our attention focused so intently on the natural things of this life that we lose that hope and get caught up in the hopelessness around us. But we don't have to let that happen.

A friend of mine once met a born-again Arab woman in the Middle East who was living proof of that. The woman was caught in a life most of us would consider almost unbearable. She was living in a war zone that had been torn up by violence. She faced the danger of bombs and bullets every day.

Now that Arab woman had no hope in the natural. Her country was being destroyed around her. She had to go to Israel to work and get money for her family because there were no jobs where she was, no way to make money. Things around her seemed to be going from bad to worse, but she told my friend she had hope because she knew that Jesus was coming back for her. And that hope kept her going.

So, if you're feeling hopeless, get your eyes off this world and get them onto the soon return of Jesus. Not only will that raise your spirits, the Bible says it will purify you. It will cause you to live uprightly, to separate you from the sin and failure of the world around you. It will lift you into the joy and victory of God.

Think about this. When this old world comes to an end, you and I will just be getting started. We'll be stepping into the most glorious life we've ever known. The people of the world may look back wistfully and wish for better days gone by. But for you and me, the best is yet to come. So we can shout hallelujah in the midst of trouble and say with the apostle John, "Even so, come, Lord Jesus." Come, quickly!

SCRIPTURE READING: Revelation 21, 22:1-7

It's Your Decision

"And, behold, there cometh one of the rulers
of the synagogue, Jairus by name; and when he saw [Jesus],
he fell at his feet, And besought him greatly, saying, My little daughter
lieth at the point of death: I pray thee, come and lay thy hands
on her, that she may be healed; and she shall live.
And Jesus went with him." **(Mark 5:22-24)**

I wonder when God is going to *do something* about this problem! Have you ever asked that question? If so, you may be surprised to find out that the answer depends 100 percent on you.

There's an incident in Mark 5 that will show you what I mean. Jesus had just gotten out of a boat and people were pressing all around Him, "thronging Him," it says. They had Him shoved up against the shoreline when suddenly there came a man moving through that crowd to get to Jesus.

Throwing himself at Jesus' feet, Mark records, he prays and beseeches Him greatly, saying, "My little daughter lieth at the point of death: I pray thee, come and lay thy hands on her... and she shall live."

Think about this situation for a moment. Here's a man that's politically on the level of the mayor of the city. But he's so doggedly determined to get to Jesus that he fights his way through the crowd and clears out enough room to fall at Jesus' feet. He's made a decision—and when he gets to Jesus, he says exactly what it is: *Lay your hands on her and she shall live.*

Let me ask you something: Who do you think is directing the ministry of Jesus here? This one man! A man who's made a decision. When he speaks that decision out, Jesus doesn't say anything. He just stops what He's doing, turns around, and follows him.

In a crowd of literally thousands, the faith decision of one man is directing the actions of Jesus.

What does that mean to you? It means that if you're sitting around waiting for Jesus to decide to heal you... for Jesus to decide to help you...for Jesus to decide to prosper you and give you victory...you're in for a long wait. Because that's not Jesus' decision.

It's yours.

SCRIPTURE READING: Mark 5:21-24,35-43

Don't Play Dead

"From the days of John the Baptist until now
the kingdom of heaven suffereth violence, and the violent
take it by force." **(Matthew 11:12)**

The *Amplified Bible* says, "A share in the heavenly kingdom is sought with most ardent zeal and intense exertion."

I want you to get violent today. Yes, violent, determined, zealous. I want you to get so committed to the things of God that you'll withstand any attempt to take them away from you.

Too many believers these days are like the Israelites. They're wandering around in a wilderness of defeat because there's an enemy in the Promised Land. They're being robbed of their rightful inheritance because they're afraid to fight him. They keep hoping that somehow they'll find a way in without using force. But they won't! You have to make demands where Satan and his associates are concerned.

When God sent the Israelites into Canaan, He said, "Send the armed men to go before you." They were to go up armed—ready for the fight. He knew they'd have to fight to take the land. He never promised them that they wouldn't. What He promised them was they'd win every time.

The same is true for you. You can't just lie down and play dead when you're dealing with the devil. He's not going to let go of any area of your life—of your health or your finances or anything else—without a fight. He's not going to give it up unless you force him.

Quit sitting there in the wilderness. Quit sitting there while the devil steals the blessings of God out from under you. You have God's permission and His power and His ability to take the land. Get violent enough to do something about it...today!

SCRIPTURE READING: Deuteronomy 31:1-8

The Power of Love

"But faith...worketh by love." **(Galatians 5:6)**

I used to wonder why we believers didn't see more of the power of God operating among us than we do. With what we know about faith and the Word, it seemed to me signs and wonders and miracles should be happening all the time.

So, one day I asked, "Lord, why isn't the power of God turned up to a higher volume in the Church?"

Do you know what He said? He told me we weren't walking in enough love yet.

God wants us to have power. But first, He has to be sure we'll use that power in love. He wants to know that we won't take it and mix it with judgment and criticism and blast people out of the water.

"Kenneth," He said, "I can't afford to back your words with supernatural power in a church service on Sunday morning and then have you get on the freeway that night and lash out at someone because he pulled over into your lane. You'd blow him off the highway. I can't leave the power of Almighty God at a high volume in the mouth of an unmerciful fool."

Then He reminded me of a time I took my son, John, hunting. He was just a little guy at the time, barely big enough to keep his gun from knocking him on his back every time he'd pull the trigger. I was teaching him how to shoot, and he was coming along pretty well.

That day we were walking along out at Gloria's grandparents' farm and John spotted one of the biggest tarantula spiders I'd ever seen. It was clinging to the wall of the barn. When John saw that spider, he took aim. He was going to blow that bug away.

If I hadn't stopped him, he would have too. And it wouldn't have dawned on him until it was all over that he was going to blow a hole in the barn at the same time. From my grown-up perspective, I could see that would be foolishness. He couldn't. He was looking through the eyes of a child.

Do you want God to put a shotgun of spiritual power in your hand, so you can blow the works of the devil to kingdom come? Then focus on love. Pursue it. Practice it. Study it. Grow up in it. Then you'll see the power of God operating through you.

SCRIPTURE READING: Romans 13:8-14

He Opened the Way

"In the beginning [before all time] was the Word [Christ],
and the Word was with God, and the Word was God Himself....
And the Word [Christ] became flesh (human, incarnate)
and tabernacled — fixed His tent of flesh, lived
awhile — among us...." **(John 1:1,14, AMP)**

The deity of the Lord Jesus Christ is something that can never be brought into question by any born-again believer. Our very salvation rests on the fact that Jesus Christ is divine, the second person of the Godhead, God — the Son.

The beloved disciple and apostle John forever puts to rest any doubt about that in John 1:1,14. Anyone who doubts what those verses say could not possibly have been born in the kingdom of God. For the deity of Jesus forms the very foundation of our faith in Him.

Yet, if you'll search the Gospels, you'll see that Jesus didn't go around proclaiming Himself as God during His 33 years on earth. He acknowledged that He was the Son of God, the Messiah. He referred to God as His Father (which enraged the Pharisees), but He never made the assertion that He *was* the most high God. In fact, He told His disciples that the Father God was greater and mightier than He (John 14:28).

The reason is simple. He hadn't come to earth just as God. He'd come also as man. The Word says He set aside His divine power and took the form of a human being — with all its limitations. Since God was His Father, He was not born with the sin nature that had been passed along to the sons of Adam. But by being born of a woman, in all other respects He became a man and called Himself the Son of Man or, literally, the Son of Adam.

How, then, did He do all those mighty works? The same way He expects us to do them today — by the anointing and the power of the Holy Spirit (Acts 10:38). He said, "It's the Father within Me who does the work."

What does that mean to you? It means that Jesus meant exactly what He said when He said that you, as a believer, would be able to do the works that He did! (John 14:12).

It means that you, as a reborn child of God, filled with the same Holy Spirit as Jesus was, have the opportunity to live as He lived when He was on earth.

In fact, that is exactly what He intends. He went before you, as a man, and opened the way. Don't just admire Him *for* it. Follow Him *in* it today!

SCRIPTURE READING: John 14:1-15

An Experienced Champion

"But they that wait upon the Lord shall renew their strength;
they shall mount up with wings as eagles; they shall run, and not be weary;
and they shall walk, and not faint." **(Isaiah 40:31)**

Did you know that the force of faith has the power to rejuvenate your physical body? It's true. You can see that in the life of Sarah. Most people don't understand the full extent of what God did in her life. All they know is that He enabled her to have a child in her old age.

But if you'll look closer, you'll see that there was more to it than that. When Sarah laid hold of the promise of God by faith, it began to restore her physically to such an extent that when King Abimelech saw her, he wanted her for his wife.

Think about that! At 90 years old, she was so beautiful that a king wanted her in his harem. What's more, after she gave birth to Isaac, the Bible says, she nursed him till he was weaned. Then she kept right on living until that boy was raised!

Now, I'm not telling you you can have a baby at 90 like Sarah did. She had a specific promise from God about that. But I am telling you that if you'll believe God for renewed strength and health in your old age, He'll provide it for you. In fact, Psalm 103 says that's one of His benefits. It says God will fill your mouth with good things so your youth is renewed like the eagle's.

That is God's desire for you in your old age. A powerful, experienced champion of the Word with your strength renewed by faith. Start confessing that today. Fill your mouth with the promises of God. Say, "Praise God, my youth is renewed like the eagle's." You'll still go to heaven when your work on earth is through—but you won't just fade away. You'll fly out of here in a blaze of glory like the conqueror God created you to be.

SCRIPTURE READING: Psalm 92

It Only Takes a Few

"If my people, which are called by my name,
shall humble themselves, and pray, and seek my face,
and turn from their wicked ways; then will I hear from heaven,
and will forgive their sin, and will heal
their land." **(2 Chronicles 7:14)**

You may be thinking, "Can a few people like us actually change the whole nation?"

Let me ask you this: Can one demonic person change a nation for the worse? Definitely. Hitler did it in Germany, didn't he?

Then if the devil's power resting on a man can change a nation for the worse, you can be sure that a group of men and women with God's power resting on them can change a nation for the better.

No nation is so far gone that God can't change it. Israel proved that. Why, even when it didn't exist, the devil couldn't destroy it. God raised it back up before his very eyes.

I want you to notice something in that scripture. It says, "If MY people, which are called by MY name...." God didn't say it would take everybody in the nation to get things turned around. He said, "If MY people...."

Notice also that He didn't say, "If my people will get out there and sign petitions and drum up a majority vote...." He said, "Pray." In other words, we're going to have to quit trying to work this thing out by ourselves. GOD Himself will do the healing in this land. Our job is to pray, to believe, and to seek His face. Seek Him today.

SCRIPTURE READING: 2 Chronicles 7:1-16

Fight the Right Foe

"For though we walk in the flesh, we do not war after the flesh."

(2 Corinthians 10:3)

Do you know why so many believers are losing the battles in their lives?

They're fighting the wrong enemy!

They've been deceived into believing that just because a person said or did something to hurt them, that person is the one they need to fight. But they're wrong.

You see, the Bible says we don't wrestle with flesh and blood. And since people are definitely flesh and blood, they're *never* the source of our problem.

"But, Brother Copeland, you just don't know what So-and-so did to me!"

It doesn't matter. If you waste your time fighting So-and-so, your real enemy will get away scot-free.

Who is that real enemy? Look at Ephesians 6:12, "For we wrestle not against flesh and blood, but against principalities, against powers, against the rulers of the darkness of this world, against spiritual wickedness in high places."

Satan and his demons. They are your lifelong enemies! They are behind every personal affront you encounter.

The people who hurt you and persecute you are only Satan's tools. When he wants to strike out at you, he uses them to get the job done.

Remember this: Persecution is not the manifestation of another person's hate for you. It's a manifestation of Satan's fear of you. When you get into the Word and start swinging it around—using it like the sword of the Spirit it is—he gets scared. So he looks for some person he can send in there to stop you.

Next time someone hurts you, don't let yourself get sidetracked into fighting them. Bind the spirit behind them. Put flesh and blood battles behind and war with the weapons of the Spirit. Zero in on Satan with authority and the Word of God and bring your real enemy down!

SCRIPTURE READING: Ephesians 6:10-18

You're a Winner

"I have written unto you, young men, because
ye are strong, and the word of God abideth in you, and ye have
overcome the wicked one." **(1 John 2:14)**

Man was created to be a winner. The Bible tells us so. We read in Genesis, for example, that man was originally put on this earth as a dominating lord. God gave him dominion over the earth and everything that crept, flew, crawled, and breathed there.

Man didn't even know what losing was until he separated himself from God through disobedience in the Garden of Eden. When that happened, he ran headlong into defeat. He was forced to accept failure as his lot in life, lowering himself to a subordinate position—a position he was never meant to occupy.

It's a sad story. But if you're a born-again child of God, your story has a happy ending. Through faith in Christ Jesus, you've been made a winner once again!

In fact, God has *guaranteed* your success. Let me show you what I mean. Imagine you're about to tackle a really tough job, and before you even get started on it, God speaks to you right out loud and says, "I just want you to know, I'm going to personally see to it that this project you're working on succeeds."

Well, let me tell you something. You *do* have God's promise that you'll succeed. He said in His Word that you're an overcomer! In Him you can overcome any problem the world throws your way (1 John 5:1-5).

It doesn't matter how much you feel like a loser. It doesn't matter how many times you've failed in the past. If you believe that Jesus is the Christ, the Son of the living God, then you've become more than a conqueror (Rom. 8:37) in Him.

Does that mean you won't have any more trouble? No. It simply means you can go through that trouble and emerge triumphant.

If you've been feeling like a failure lately, renew your mind to the Word of God that says you're a success. Every time a challenge comes up, respond by saying, "Well, praise God, I can beat this thing because I'm an overcomer in Jesus!" Let that Word from God abide in your heart. It *will* make a winner out of you.

SCRIPTURE READING: 1 John 5:1-5

Delight Yourself

"Blessed is the man that feareth the Lord,
that delighteth greatly in his commandments. He shall
not be afraid of evil tidings: his heart is fixed,
trusting in the Lord." **(Psalm 112:1,7)**

The man who makes a habit of delighting in God's Word will have a heart that's fixed! He can make it through disastrous situations without losing his balance. His mind's made up before he ever gets to the disaster. He's victorious before he ever gets there. A person like that is hard to whip!

The sad thing is that most believers wait until the disaster hits before they start trying to establish themselves on the Word. They wait until their back is against the wall. Then, suddenly, they get real spiritual and start fasting and praying...and all too often they find they've started too late.

That's like a guy who finds out a burglar is in his house and then starts looking for the barbells, so he can build up enough muscle to throw the burglar out. He ain't gonna make it! If he'd been working out instead of watching TV every night, he'd have been ready. But as it is, he's headed for a painful defeat.

Be ready *before* the devil breaks into your house. Get your heart fixed. Turn off the TV. Turn off the distractions of the world and turn on the Word. The time to start establishing yourself on it is right now!

SCRIPTURE READING: Job 22:21-30

The Hidden Things of God

"Blessed art thou...for flesh and blood hath not revealed it unto thee, but my Father which is in heaven." **(Matthew 16:17)**

Remember when you went to school and learned your ABC's? You learned them by using your five senses and your logical abilities to gather information and sort it out. That kind of knowledge is called natural knowledge and it's the only kind most people know anything about.

But in the kingdom of God, there's another kind of knowing. One that works its way from the inside out instead of from the outside in. It's called revelation knowledge.

Jesus spoke about this kind of knowledge in Matthew 16. He'd just asked the disciples, "Who do you say I am?" Peter had answered Him by declaring, "Thou art the Christ, the Son of the living God."

"Blessed are you, Simon," Jesus responded, "because flesh and blood has not revealed this to you, but My Father which is in heaven."

In other words, Jesus was saying, "Peter, you didn't learn this information through your physical senses. You received it another way. You received it directly from God."

If you've ever had a revelation like that, you know that when it comes, it changes things. It makes you see old things in an entirely new light. It gives you such unshakable confidence that, as Jesus said to Peter, "The gates of hell can't prevail against you."

But revelations like that don't come easily. You have to meditate the Word and search the Spirit of God for them because they are "hidden" in Him. The Bible says God has hidden His wisdom for the saints (1 Cor. 2:7-9). Notice, He's hidden it *for* you, not *from* you. He wants you to have it.

Don't think, however, that God is just going to drop great revelations in your lap while you're watching TV. You have to seek Him.

If you're hungry for revelation knowledge, get yourself in a position to receive it by meditating the Word, praying, and fellowshipping with the Lord. Begin to receive those revelations from Him. It's the most exciting kind of learning there is.

SCRIPTURE READING: 1 Corinthians 2

Brag on God

"Rejoice and exult in hope; be steadfast and patient in suffering and tribulation; be constant in prayer." **(Romans 12:12, AMP)**

We're to live in hope. We're to rejoice. So, when Satan comes to steal your victory and tell you that God is not going to help you this time, you just think on the Word of God and start rejoicing. Rejoice that you're in Him. Rejoice that heaven is your home. Rejoice that greater is He that is in you than he that is in the world. Rejoice. Brag on God today. The devil can't stand it!

"Be steadfast and patient in suffering and tribulation...." *Tribulation* means "being under pressure." When pressure comes, don't cave in. Don't faint. Instead, go to the throne of grace. Go boldly in the name of Jesus and get the help you need.

Remember this: When things get hard isn't when you let go of the Word. That's when you double up on it. That's when you are "constant in prayer" so that you are unmovable.

Rejoice. Be patient under pressure. Be constant in prayer. The devil won't be able to steal one thing from you!

SCRIPTURE READING: Romans 5:1-5

The Inner Witness

"The Spirit itself [Himself] beareth witness with our spirit."
(Romans 8:16)

Do you ever have trouble hearing from God? Do you find yourself caught in confusing circumstances needing guidance, and yet even after praying and reading the Word—you're still not sure what God wants you to do?

I've had that experience. I knew His written Word and acting on it changed my life. But I was uncertain when I had to make decisions about things the Word didn't specifically address. Things like whether to move to one city or another, for example.

What held me back was my ability to *know* that I was doing the right thing. You see, God's written Word and the inward witness are two different things. They never contradict each other, but they're both a vital part of our walk with God.

God expected Israel, for example, to obey His written Word. But He also said to them, "Obey my *voice*" (Jer. 7:23) because He wanted them to know His will in specific situations. That's what happened when Israel invaded Jericho. They heard God's voice. Where else do you think they would have gotten that strange battle plan? It wasn't written in the law of Moses. And certainly, no human being would suggest a seven-day march around a city as the most effective form of invasion!

But exactly how, you may wonder, does God speak to us? Does He just shout down at us from heaven?

Not usually! Romans 8 says the Holy Spirit bears witness with our spirit. That means that God's directions come from *inside*, not outside, of you.

At times when you hear His guidance, you may even wonder, "Was that me, Lord, or was that You?" That's because God doesn't normally inject thoughts directly to your mind from the outside. Instead, He speaks to your spirit, and your spirit translates it into a thought.

Tune in today to that inward witness, to that quiet knowing, that urging, prompting, and leading arising within you.

If when you hear it, it sounds like you, don't be surprised. It is you! It is your spirit being influenced by the Spirit of God! After you're born again, your spirit is a safe guide because you are born of God's Spirit. You have His nature. And the Holy Spirit lives in your spirit to teach you and to give you direction.

SCRIPTURE READING: Joshua 6:1-20

A Powerhouse of Protection

"No weapon that is formed against thee shall prosper;
and every tongue that shall rise against thee in judgment thou shalt
condemn. This is the heritage of the servants of the Lord, and their
righteousness is of me, saith the Lord." **(Isaiah 54:17)**

No weapon formed against you shall prosper. Isn't that great news! Isn't it good to know that no sickness, no circumstance, no problem that rises against you can successfully bring you down?

Some years ago, one of our friends was facing a lawsuit. He and I prayed together according to this scripture and agreed it was the final word in the situation, not the allegations against him. We stood in faith, believing that lawsuit had to fail.

Sure enough, when my friend went to court, they just couldn't beat him. He didn't win that case because of his keen and witty lawyers. He won because he was innocent and because he had believed that powerful promise of God.

Follow his example. When the devil attacks you in some area of your life, don't sit around crying and begging God to save you. Open up your Bible to Isaiah 54:17 instead. Remind yourself of what God has promised you. Use that promise to strengthen you against sin and every other evil work the devil would like to use to keep you bound.

Then establish yourself on it through prayer. Say, "Lord, I refuse to be afraid of this weapon the devil has brought against me because I know that according to Your Word, it cannot prosper. I trust You to protect me, and I thank You for it now. In Jesus' name. Amen."

Don't let the powerhouse of God's protection go to waste. Put it to work in your life. It *is* your rightful heritage as a servant of the Lord.

SCRIPTURE READING: Isaiah 54:10-17

Open the Flow

"Wherefore seeing we also are
compassed about with so great a cloud of witnesses,
let us lay aside every weight, and the sin which doth so easily
beset us, and let us run with patience the race that is set
before us, looking unto Jesus the author and finisher
of our faith." **(Hebrews 12:1,2)**

Disciplining the flesh. For many believers that phrase stirs memories of frustration and failure. They know it's important—the Word of God clearly teaches that. But they're not sure exactly how to go about it.

Some have given up, shrugging off such discipline as impossible. Others are still fighting stubbornly to get their flesh under control—and losing one battle after another.

But it doesn't have to be that way. In fact, we can't afford to let it be that way. It will cost us too much.

You and I are blessed to be part of the generation that will see the signs and wonders which the prophets of old wished they could have lived long enough to see. We will witness the Spirit of God poured out upon all flesh. But sin hinders the Spirit's flow. And only as we rid ourselves of it will the power and glory of God be manifested through us. Only then will we experience the wonderful things that are prophesied to take place in our generation.

So put your past failure behind you. Make up your mind that you're not going to let the sins of the flesh rob you of the glory of God. It *is* possible to step out of the sin you've struggled with so long and live under the Spirit's control. Look to Jesus...He will show you how.

SCRIPTURE READING: 2 Timothy 2:19-23

Stake Your Claim

"Praise ye the Lord. Blessed is the man
that feareth the Lord, that delighteth greatly in his commandments.
Wealth and riches shall be in his house: and his righteousness
endureth for ever." **(Psalm 112:1,3)**

I 'll never forget the time Gloria discovered that scripture. We didn't have any money at the time, and the walls in our house were as bare as they could be. But she was ready to decorate. So she took that promise, "Wealth and riches shall be in his house" and laid claim to it by faith.

Suddenly, everywhere we went, somebody was giving us a painting or some other little treasure for our house.

Unfortunately, most believers aren't as quick to believe God for that kind of thing as Gloria was. Some even claim God doesn't promise us New Testament believers physical prosperity, just spiritual. But the truth is, you can't separate the two. That's why Jesus says, "If you'll seek first the kingdom of God and His righteousness, then all these [material] things will be added to you." He knows the spiritual realm and the material realm are connected.

The physical world cannot operate independently from the spiritual world. What happens in one is simply a reflection of what happens in the other.

Obviously, your spiritual standing profoundly affects your financial standing. That's why, when you get hold of the gospel and begin to prosper spiritually, you can begin to prosper physically and materially as well.

Don't let anyone talk you out of God's promises of prosperity. You don't have to choose between financial and spiritual prosperity. Both belong to you. Lay claim to them by faith. As a born-again child of God, dare to reach out and receive the riches that belong to you!

SCRIPTURE READING: Deuteronomy 7:8-13

When the Pressure is On

"Then they that feared the Lord spake often
one to another: and the Lord hearkened, and heard it,
and a book of remembrance was written before him for them
that feared the Lord, and that thought upon
his name." **(Malachi 3:16)**

Have you ever noticed that those who have the most exciting, faith-inspiring testimonies are those who've been under pressure at some time in their lives? They're the people who stayed faithful when the pressure was on. People who believed God's promises of prosperity in the midst of desperate financial situations or people who trusted God for healing in the face of a terminal disease.

My friend, when you get into a hard spot, that's not the time to back out on God and begin to say, "Well, God, why did You let this happen to me?" It's not the time to step back and reevaluate His faithfulness.

What I'm saying to you is this: When tough times keep dragging on and the situations around you seem to refuse to get in line with the promises of God, don't reevaluate God! He is not missing it, and He's not failing.

If you're going to reevaluate anything, reevaluate yourself! Look and see where you may have failed. If you still can't find out what the problem is, just say, "God, I don't know what's wrong here, and I'm asking You to show me. But one thing I know, the problem's not with You, and I continue to be moved by Your Word and not by circumstances." Then, when He reveals something to you, be quick to make changes.

I want to encourage you to stand firm and to keep honoring God with your words. The Lord is listening to you when the pressure is on. What is He going to hear?

SCRIPTURE READING: Psalm 62

Put Love to Work

"And now abideth faith, hope, charity, these three;
but the greatest of these is charity." **(1 Corinthians 13:13)**

What do you do when you're facing a particularly stubborn problem? A problem that resists your every effort to solve it?

Put the power of love to work on it! The power of love is the greatest power in the universe. It's beyond defeat. It *never* fails (1 Cor. 13:8).

The Bible says God *is* love. So when you release love into a situation, you have released God into it. Think about that! When you start releasing love into a situation, Jesus becomes responsible for its success.

What is this love I'm talking about?

First Corinthians 13 tells us it's patient and kind. It's not jealous or haughty or conceited or rude. It doesn't insist on its own way. It's not touchy or resentful and it pays no attention to a suffered wrong.

Love rejoices when right and truth prevail and it bears up under anything and everything that comes. It's ever ready to believe the best of every person. Its hopes are fadeless under all circumstances and it endures everything without weakening (AMP).

The person who refuses to love is missing out on the very best God has to offer.

Don't *you* miss out on any of it. Release love every moment into every situation, every prayer, and every thought until it totally consumes your life. It will strengthen you and cast out every fear that has robbed you of God's greater blessings. It will drive the devil out of your affairs and set you free from every torment of darkness.

Put love to work on the stubborn problems in your life. It's the one solution they'll never be able to resist.

SCRIPTURE READING: 1 Corinthians 13

Pick Up Your Sword

"But thou, O man of God...fight the good fight of faith."

(1 Timothy 6:11,12)

When you're up against the wall, don't start begging God to break through it for you. That's not the way He works. He'll give you the plan. He'll give you the power. And He'll guarantee the victory. But your hand, not His own, is the instrument He's going to use to get the job done. You're going to have to stretch forth your hand by speaking and acting on the Word, even when circumstances are against you.

God gave me a striking revelation of that over 20 years ago through a vision He gave me in Beaumont, Texas. I was preparing to minister in a service there, spending some time in prayer, when suddenly I saw myself standing in the pulpit of the church. Looking up, I saw a dragon—a horrible, ugly thing—poke his head through the front door of the church.

As he came into the church, his body expanded like a balloon, filling the whole room. He was snorting fire and smoke. When, in the vision, he turned it on me, he almost burned my clothes!

As I fell back onto the floor, I saw Jesus standing nearby with a sword in His hand. "Why doesn't He do something about this?" I thought. "Can't He see I'm hurting?"

But He didn't move. He just stood by with a frown on His face. I could tell He was really put out with me. The Bible says God was not pleased with those who were overthrown in the wilderness (1 Cor. 10:5). And He wasn't pleased with me either as I lay there on my back in defeat.

Then Jesus held out the sword to me and pointed at the dragon. The look on His face said, "Get up!"

I reached up to catch hold of the sword, and an instant before I touched it, Jesus turned it loose.

The sword stayed in midair of its own accord. I grabbed it and began to pull myself up. Not only did it hold firm, but it began to lift me!

I stood and touched the dragon's chin with my sword and it split him from one end to the other. It laid him open right before my eyes. In amazement, I looked down at the sword. "Why haven't I used this before?" I thought.

Don't wait for God to slay the dragon in your life. You have the sword of the Spirit, the all-powerful Word of the living God, at your fingertips. Pick it up and use it today!

SCRIPTURE READING: Joshua 11:5-23

The Power to Create

"Therefore be imitators of God — copy Him and follow
His example — as well-beloved children [imitate their father]."
(Ephesians 5:1, AMP)

Creating new things, changing old things. Because you and I are made in the image of God that's something we're always trying to do. But if we're to be successful at it, we need to learn a lesson about it from the Creator Himself, our very own heavenly Father.

You know, He didn't just come upon creation by accident and say, "Well, what do you know! There's light!" No, before He began to make His universe, He first had a desired result (an inner idea, or image, of what He wanted to create) and then said, "Light be!" and light was.

If we're going to imitate Him, we're going to have to put the principle of the inner image to work too.

"But, Brother Copeland," you say, "that was God. Surely you don't expect me to try to act like God." I most certainly do. Ephesians 5:1 says to!

Let me warn you about something though. Don't waste your time sitting around trying to dream up a positive inner image all on your own. That's nothing more than positive thinking, and while it's better than negative thinking (or not thinking at all), it will eventually fall flat.

If you're a born-again child of Almighty God, God has given you the principle and the power to make permanent changes in your life and in your circumstances.

Think again about creation. God wanted light. So He said, "Let there be light." The words He spoke were directly related to His inner image. He used His Words to get that image from the inside to the outside.

What you need to use as the basis for your inner image and for the words you speak is the Word of God. The Word has supernatural power. And if you fill that Word with faith and speak it out, it will work for you to change your life and circumstances as surely as it did for your Father.

Find out what real creativity is all about. Dig into the Word of God and start rebuilding your world today.

SCRIPTURE READING: 2 Corinthians 4:6-13

Do You Know What to Ask For?

"And Jesus answered and said unto him,
What wilt thou that I should do unto thee? The blind man
said unto him, Lord, that I might receive
my sight." **(Mark 10:51)**

All of us know what it's like to go round in circles. To pray our way through one financial disaster only to be met by another. To receive healing for one illness just in time to be knocked off our feet by the next.

Oh, we try. We pray. We exercise our faith. But we keep getting caught in the same old problems over and over again. Why? Because all too often, we don't actually know what it is we need to be praying *for*.

I can almost hear your reaction. "Believe me, Brother Copeland, that's not *my* problem. I know what I need. It's getting that need met that's got me running in circles."

That's what most other folks think too. So they spend all their time working on *getting*. They waste their energy praying for things they don't really need and asking for things they don't really want. Then they wind up going nowhere fast.

Look with me to the tenth chapter of Mark, and I think you'll see what I mean. Blind Bartimaeus sat by the roadside begging when Jesus passed by. "And when he heard that it was Jesus of Nazareth, he began to cry out, and say, Jesus, thou son of David, have mercy on me.... And he, casting away his garment, rose, and came to Jesus. And Jesus answered and said unto him, What wilt thou that I should do unto thee? The blind man said unto him, Lord, that I might receive my sight. And Jesus said unto him, Go thy way; thy faith hath made thee whole. And immediately he received his sight, and followed Jesus in the way" (verses 47,50-52).

Now I want you to think about something for a moment. In the light of what the Scriptures tell us, how many needs did Bartimaeus have? Did he have just one? No! He wasn't simply a blind man, he was a beggar. He probably had more problems than you could shake a stick at, and all those problems would have seemed like legitimate needs to Bartimaeus. But it was sight he *needed*. If he could obtain his sight, all the rest would fall into line.

He *knew* that. So, when Jesus said, "Bartimaeus, what do you want Me to do for you?" he knew exactly what to ask for and he got it.

Jesus is just as available to you today as He was to Bartimaeus. He's just as willing to meet your need. The question is, do you really know what to ask for?

Think about that. Pray about it. Let the Lord Jesus open your eyes and show you what you really need. If you do that, your prayers will take on a whole new power. Instead of hitting around at the edges of your problems, they'll go straight to the heart— and solve them. And you won't have to waste your life running in circles anymore.

SCRIPTURE READING: Mark 10:46-52

From Milk to Meat

"For when for the time ye ought to be teachers,
ye have need that one teach you again which be the first principles
of the oracles of God; and are become such as have need of milk,
and not of strong meat." **(Hebrews 5:12)**

Do you want to know why the Body of Christ has been in such a mess over the past few years? Do you want to know why the devil has been able to make a public display of our weaknesses? Do you want to know why instead of being unified and strong, we've often been torn apart by division and criticisms that come not from without but within?

It is because, as the Lord said in Hebrews, the people of God have need of milk and not of strong meat. They're babies! The people of God for the most part don't know His ways.

That's why He's commissioned you and me to train believers who are unskilled in the Word of righteousness and help bring them to maturity.

"Sure," you say, "you're a preacher, but what about me? What can I do?" Well, I'll tell you. I believe God has called us both to do something. You'll find it in Hebrews 3:13. "Exhort one another daily, while it is called To day."

That's no longer just a Bible verse to me. It's a direct command from the Lord. Gloria and I received that command a few years ago when we were preaching in Australia. It prompted us to step out in faith on daily television. But it's not a command that was just meant for us. It's one we all must obey in our own way.

"Exhort one another daily." Pray over that scripture today, won't you? Fellowship with your Father over it. Ask Him how He wants you to fulfill that command. He may tell you to help support ministries like Gloria's and mine who teach the uncompromised Word of God daily. He may tell you to fill yourself so full of His Word that it spills out on everyone you meet and encourages them to go on— and grow on—in Jesus.

Whatever He says, do it! There's a Church full of spiritual babies out there and more are being born all the time. You *can* help bring them from milk to meat. Begin to exhort them. Today.

SCRIPTURE READING: Hebrews 3:7-19

Recall God's Mercies

"This I recall to my mind, therefore have I hope.
It is of the Lord's mercies that we are not consumed, because
his compassions fail not. They are new every morning:
great is thy faithfulness." **(Lamentations 3:21-23)**

God is faithful. He's full of compassion. His mercies are new every morning. As a believer, you know all that. But simply knowing it is not enough.

For it to do you any good, you have to recall it. You have to remember it again and again in order to rekindle your hope and stir your faith.

So, make it a point to remind yourself of God's faithfulness every morning. Remind yourself of the benefits that are yours in Jesus.

What are those benefits? Psalm 103 spells them out:

1. He forgives all your sins.

2. He heals all your diseases.

3. He redeems your life from destruction.

4. He crowns you with loving kindness and tender mercies.

5. He satisfies your mouth with good things so that your youth is renewed like the eagle's.

6. He executes righteousness and judgment for you against oppression. He sets you free.

7. He makes known His ways to you.

8. He gives you His grace and mercy in times of need.

Make it a point every morning this year to say those things out loud to the Lord. Stand before Him in prayer and recall His mercies to you. Keep it up and by the end of this year you'll be stronger in faith and more confident of God's love than you've ever been before.

Don't just settle for *knowing* God's blessings. Remember them every day and watch them come alive in you.

SCRIPTURE READING: Psalm 103:1-17

Give God the Glory

"Herein is my Father glorified, that ye bear
much fruit; so shall ye be my disciples." **(John 15:8)**

There's an old Full Gospel tradition that says God gets glory from the wonderful way His children bear pain and agony and that the world is impressed by that. What a lie! That's simply a tool of the devil to keep God's children in bondage.

People of the world already have all the pain and agony they want. They aren't looking for a way into it. They are looking for a way out. They don't care what you preach. It's the religious people who get worried about that. The world, the sinners, are smarter than that. All they care about are the results.

That's why they'll come to your church when they hear people are getting healed, delivered, and set free from suffering. That's what they're looking for, and that's what God wants them to receive.

The Bible says that God gets glory when they see the lame walk and the blind see (Matt. 15:31). Jesus said, "Herein is My Father glorified, when you bear much fruit" (John 15:8). What is that fruit? Lives being restored and healed by the power of God.

There was a man who came to one of our healing meetings who was so far gone with cancer he had almost no energy or life about him. He didn't even know the Lord, but he came expecting a miracle. During the miracle service, the Lord told Ken someone was being healed of cancer, in the glands, in the throat, and in the chest. When the man came up and received his healing, he said, "I left the hospital this morning with cancer, and I'm healed." He went back to the hospital that afternoon and the doctors checked and dismissed him. As a result, the man received Jesus as his Lord, and later that day he was restored to his wife whom he'd been separated from. He got born again, healed, and his marriage put back together in one day!

Now that's fruit! That brings God glory. When we minister healing and deliverance like Jesus on the earth, that brings God glory. Let's do away with religious tradition and go with what the Word says. Let's impress the world with Jesus and give God the glory today!

SCRIPTURE READING: John 15:1-16

Become Sensitive Again

"Let all bitterness, and wrath, and anger,
and clamour, and evil speaking, be put away from you,
with all malice: And be ye kind one to another, tenderhearted,
forgiving one another, even as God for Christ's sake
hath forgiven you." **(Ephesians 4:31,32)**

A few years ago I was in Detroit, and I met a woman who was raised in a communist-bloc country. While I was visiting with her, a news broadcast came on. And as we sat there listening to it, suddenly tears came to her eyes.

"What's the matter?" I asked.

Although I hadn't noticed it, the news commentator had said something derogatory about the president. "I don't like to hear anybody talk about this country like that," she said. "I don't care whether it's true or not. I don't want to hear it."

The newscaster's comment had slipped right by me. But it had brought tears to her eyes. Why? Because she had a sensitive heart where this country is concerned.

We need to be more like that dear lady when it comes to our pastors, our teachers, our evangelists, and even our fellow believers.

We need to realize that our own insensitivity has driven the anointing of the Holy Spirit from many of our lives and our churches. We need to realize that the license we've given ourselves to criticize other members of the Body of Christ has weakened us all.

What will strengthen us again?

The power and the anointing of the Holy Spirit that falls on every sensitive and seeking heart.

I urge you to regain the tender heart you once had. Remove the callouses within you by repentance, by a commitment to live the law of love, by a renewed devotion to the Word, and by fellowship with your Father.

Don't allow the condition of your heart to hold back the Spirit of God. Become sensitive again!

SCRIPTURE READING: Ephesians 4:1-13

Obey Him in the Little Things

"He who is faithful in a very little [thing], is faithful also in much."

(Luke 16:10, AMP)

Have you ever wanted to take on some really big project in the kingdom of God, but the Lord just wouldn't seem to let you? If so, there's probably a good reason why.

You can see what I'm talking about if you'll read about what God did with the children of Israel after He brought them out of Egypt. He wanted to take them on into the Promised Land. But before He could do it, God had to know if they would obey Him. He had to know if they would listen to His voice. Because if they didn't, the enemies they were about to face would wipe them out.

So, do you know what He did? He tested them in a small matter.

Exodus 16:4 tells us about this simple test. "Then said the Lord unto Moses, Behold, I will rain bread from heaven for you; and the people shall go out and gather a certain rate every day, that I may prove them, whether they will walk in my law, or no."

God took a little, insignificant matter, the food they ate—and used it to see if they would listen to Him or not. He told them how much of it to gather, when to gather and when not to, and what to do with it after they brought it in.

And the Israelites went right out and violated those instructions. They showed God by their actions that His voice was not important to them. They were not willing to obey even His simplest commands.

God works the same way today. Before He sends you on a major mission, He gives you the opportunity to prove you can be trusted with small instructions.

But most of us miss that opportunity. We pray, "What do You want me to do, Lord? Where do You want me to go? I'll do anything You say." But then when the Lord says, "I want you to get up and pray in the Spirit one hour every morning," we fail to obey Him. We say, "Oh yeah, that would be good. I ought to do that." But somehow we never quite get around to it.

Don't make that mistake. Start today obeying God in the little things. Let Him see that He can trust you out there in a place of much authority. Let Him know you'll be faithful to His words and to the voice of His Spirit. Once He knows you won't let disobedience wipe you out, He'll start sending bigger assignments your way.

SCRIPTURE READING: Exodus 16:1-28

Let Your Life Shine

"Be thou an example of the believers, in word, in conversation, in charity, in spirit, in faith, in purity." **(1 Timothy 4:12)**

One thing the world needs to see is good examples. They need to see believers walk in love and purity and faith in their homes, in their schools, and in their businesses.

The apostle Paul exhorts us in Romans 12:17 to live above reproach in the sight of all men. Other scriptures teach us to avoid all appearance of evil. So, when you go after God, don't walk out on the edge, trying to see how much you can get by with. Go all out in God's direction. Conduct yourself in a way that will put to rest any question about whether or not you're a Christian. Let the people around you see your love and faith and purity in every situation.

Your example will go a lot further than your words. When our son, John, was a little boy, we were spending time with my grandparents. John was sleeping with my granddaddy and he woke him up in the night and said, "Pop, I have an earache. Would you pray for it?" Well, my grandparents

were raised in a church that didn't believe in healing. I don't know what Pop did, but it didn't work. So, John just got up and said, "I'm going to go get in bed with my mother. When she prays, it stops hurting." About 18 years later, Pop told me the story.

You see, I had set an example of faith and love and John remembered it. While your children are growing up, they might forget some of the sermons you've preached or act like they're not interested in the things of God. But they'll never forget your example.

Even at the place where you work or go to school or just in your neighborhood, people might reject or argue with the words you say. But they'll never refute or forget your acts of love.

Don't let petty sins and spiritual compromises cast a shadow over your example. Live above reproach and let the light of Jesus shine brightly through you.

SCRIPTURE READING: Romans 12:9-21

Stir Up the Power

"Greatly desiring to see you, being mindful of your tears....
I remind you to stir up the gift of God which is in you.... For God has not
given us a spirit of fear but of power and of love
and of a sound mind." **(2 Timothy 1:4,6,7)**

There are times when you know what God has called you to do, but you just don't feel you have the inner resources you need to do it. Somehow you've simply run dry. You know the Word says that "out of your belly shall flow rivers of living water" (John 7:38). But, during those times, you can't even find the creek bank, much less the river.

The Word of God tells us how to handle those situations through a clear command: "Stir up the gift inside you."

YOU stir YOURSELF up! Everything you need is already in you. Jesus put it there. Everything you'll ever need to accomplish what God has called you to do has been placed inside you by God Almighty.

Faith is in there. Power is in there. Love is in there. Believe that. Speak it out. Say it to yourself now, right out loud:

"In the name of Jesus, I stir up the gift that's within me by faith. I'm stirring up my faith. I'm not going to wait until I *feel* stirred up. I'm stepping out by faith and expecting my feelings to follow!

"I'm stirring up the love of God that's in me. I'm stirring up the power. I'm stirring up myself and running the devil out of my affairs. I'm stirring myself up in the Spirit of the living God! I AM stirred up!"

SCRIPTURE READING: 2 Timothy 1:1-8

What's Your Name?

"And whatsoever ye do in word or deed,
do all in the name of the Lord Jesus, giving thanks to God
and the Father by him." **(Colossians 3:17)**

Did you know your name has been changed? It's no longer the same as it was before you were born again. You gave your old name away when you made covenant with Jesus.

To fully appreciate what that means, you have to think about it in the light of what we know about blood covenant. When someone enters a covenant of blood, he is giving himself completely away. He is no longer his own. His assets and his debts, his strengths and his weaknesses belong forever to his covenant brother.

When you're in blood covenant with someone, that person's name becomes your name forever. You cannot escape it—good or bad—it's yours.

When you received Jesus as your Lord and Savior, *He took your name!* Your name was sin. Your name was weakness. Your name was fear and poverty and every other evil thing you inherited from Adam.

Jesus took those names from you and gave you His own in exchange. That's right! Ephesians 3:15 says that the whole Body of Christ has been named after Him both in heaven and earth. That means you have been given Jesus' name. Its authority is now yours!

Just think about who you're named after:

"Jesus, Mighty God, Wisdom, Deliverer, Lion of the Tribe of Judah, Word of Life, Advocate, Provider, The Great I Am, Helper, Savior, Prince of Peace, Wonderful Counselor, Lamb of God, Lord of Hosts, Root of David, Author and Finisher of our Faith, The Way, Healer, Son of God, The Truth, Chief Cornerstone, King of Kings, Light of the World, Chief Shepherd, My Strength and Song, Righteous Judge, Son of Righteousness, Resurrection and Life, The Alpha and Omega."

Praise God, those names cover any need you'll ever have. What's more, the power of God is in His name to bring that name to pass in your life (Acts 3:16).

You can't call yourself discouraged anymore. That's not your name. You can't answer when the devil yells, "Hey, poor boy." That's not your name. Jesus has taken those old names of yours. They're gone. So meditate on the names of the Lord. They're all wrapped up in the name of Jesus, the name above all names, and that name with all its power and authority has been given to you!

SCRIPTURE READING: Ephesians 3:16-21

Occupy Till Jesus Comes

"Wherefore take unto you the whole armour of God,
that ye may be able to withstand in the evil day, and having done all,
to stand. Stand therefore, having your loins girt about with truth,
and having on the breastplate of righteousness; And your feet shod with
the preparation of the gospel of peace; Above all, taking the shield of faith,
wherewith ye shall be able to quench all the fiery darts of the wicked.
And take the helmet of salvation, and the sword of the Spirit,
which is the word of God." **(Ephesians 6:13-17)**

The Bible teaches that as believers, you and I are to occupy until Jesus comes. "Occupy" is a military term meaning to hold possession, or control, of conquered troops and territory. If we're to do that effectively, most of us are going to have to change our attitudes. We're going to have to recognize that Jesus has already won the victory.

That's right. Satan is already defeated. He was whipped at Calvary. We're not on the defensive, he is!

What's more, Jesus has given you His very own armor and sword to use to keep that defeated devil in line. You may be a 90-pound weakling on your own, but if you'll put on God's armor, the devil will never know it. He'll run from you just like you were Jesus.

Think about it. What would you do if you were the devil and you came face-to-face with some fellow wearing God's armor and God's helmet with God's weapons in each hand? As long as that fellow only spoke God's words, you would think that must be God inside there!

Don't neglect any of the armor you've been given. Wear it all. Keep the devil on the defensive—and occupy till Jesus comes!

SCRIPTURE READING: Luke 12:35-44

Imitate the Faithful

"Remember your leaders and superiors in authority,
[for it was they] who brought to you the Word of God. Observe
attentively and consider their manner of living...and
imitate their faith." (Hebrews 13:7, AMP)

Apart from the Word of God itself and prayer, nothing can do more for you than watching and imitating a real man of faith. I found that out in a big way many years ago when I was a student at Oral Roberts University. As co-pilot on the airplane that transported him and his staff to his healing meetings, I had the opportunity to study Oral Roberts up close. I followed him around. I heard him preach. I watched him lay hands on the sick.

I'll never forget the day I had the opportunity to put some of what I'd learned from him into action. I'd just been to a few of his meetings. Spiritually, I was still as green as a gourd. But I'd been assigned to help the people in the "invalid room" get ready for Brother Roberts to lay hands on them. I was standing there for the first time surrounded by every kind of sickness and disease you can imagine. And when Brother Roberts came in, instead of laying hands on the people himself, he caught me by the coat sleeve and said, "You're going to do the praying. You're going to lay hands on them."

I know all the blood must have drained out of my face because I'd never prayed for anything like that in my life. I might have considered praying for a headache or maybe a serious hangnail, but that's it!

The first lady we came to had cancer of the stomach. She weighed less than 80 pounds. She was just the picture of death. I walked over toward her and before I could open my mouth, I heard a voice from behind me say, "In the name of Jesus, take up your bed and walk." She instantly spit that cancer out on the floor. Then she jumped off that bed and screamed, "I'm healed," and started running around the room.

Let me tell you, that moment changed me. When I stepped up to the next person and raised my hands, I could see the healing coming. I'd seen Jesus heal through Brother Roberts, so in my mind's eye, I could see Him healing through me.

You can do the same thing. Find someone who's operating in more faith and power than you are and learn from him. Watch Jesus in them and then copy Him. Sooner or later, others will start seeing Jesus in you.

SCRIPTURE READING: 2 Kings 2:1-15

Don't Buy a Lie

"And all these blessings shall come on thee, and overtake thee, if thou shalt hearken unto the voice of the Lord thy God." **(Deuteronomy 28:2)**

Well, brother, in the end I'm sure you'll see these financial problems are actually a blessing in disguise. Have you ever heard anybody say that to someone who's hurting financially? Chances are, you have. It's a popular idea. The problem is, it's a lie used by the devil to keep believers down.

As a result, many believers today are suffering one financial defeat after another. So let's go to the Word of God today and get the issue of prosperity and poverty straight. Let's find out, once and for all, which is the blessing, which the curse.

You can find the answer to that question in Deuteronomy 28. What God describes in verses 1 through 14 is the blessing—prosperity. In verses 15 through 31, God describes poverty—and He has called it a curse.

The curse is meant to destroy. Not to teach people a lesson. Not to make them more spiritual. But to destroy them.

Regardless of how intense the lack is, the nature of poverty remains the same. It is, and will always be, a curse.

Satan has gone to great lengths to convince God's people that poverty is a blessing in disguise. But poverty is something the devil contrived!

Don't buy into his lies. Get your thinking in line with the Word of God. If you're a born-again child of God, you no longer have to live under the curse of poverty or any other curse for that matter. You've been redeemed!

SCRIPTURE READING: Deuteronomy 28:1-31

Abide in the Word

"If ye abide in me, and my words abide in you, ye shall ask what ye will, and it shall be done unto you." **(John 15:7)**

That word "abide" is so important. When Jesus told us to obey His commandments and keep His Word, He wasn't just telling us to follow a bunch of religious rules and regulations.

He was telling us to allow His Word— which is a living thing!—to make its home within us. He was telling us to spend time with it, to meditate on it, to fill our minds and our mouths with it, and to let it guide our every action.

The apostle Paul put it this way, "Let the word of Christ dwell in you richly..." (Col. 3:16). Most believers don't have any idea what that means. That's one of the reasons they're so short on power.

Oral Roberts once said that when the Word is really abiding in you, when it's alive and producing like it should, you can *hear* it. You know what it's like when you get a song on your mind and you just keep hearing it over and over inside you? Well, when you start abiding in the Word, you're probably going to hear it in much that same way.

Many times, I've been in desperate situations, wondering what I was going to do when suddenly I'd hear a scripture down on the inside of me. Suddenly, I'd know exactly what the answer to my situation was. I'd be delivered by the Word of God that was dwelling in me.

So, invite the Holy Spirit to go to work on your behalf. Just keep telling Him, "Whatever You bring to my remembrance from the Word is exactly what I'm going to act on. I'm going to be obedient to every command of Jesus that You bring to mind."

Make a quality decision to abide in the Word. You'll soon discover that the Word is abiding in you.

SCRIPTURE READING: Colossians 3:1-16

Moving Forward or Slipping Back?

"Therefore we ought to give the more earnest heed to the things which we have heard, lest at any time we should let them slip." **(Hebrews 2:1)**

It's happened to all of us. We get a little of the Word of God under our spiritual belts. We have a few victories. Our lives are going great for the first time in years. Then suddenly we slip and it all falls apart. We find ourselves having to start all over again.

That's what happened to the people the Book of Hebrews was written to. They made such great spiritual progress that they got to the place where they should have been teachers. Then they slipped back so much, they needed baby food again. (See Hebrews 5:12.)

What caused them to fall so far? They let other things get in the way of their faith. They let the promises of God slip, so they slipped.

That's happened to a multitude of believers in the last several years. "Well, Brother Copeland," they said, "we're tired of that faith stuff." Or, "We just don't have time to spend that much time in the Word."

They've turned their attention away from the promises of God. It's not that they didn't believe them any more. It's just that they directed their attention to other things. They let their Word level drop and since low Word level equals low faith level, they soon began suffering defeat in areas they once had victory in.

Don't let that happen to you. When things are going well, don't just ride the tide of God's blessing. Dig deeper into what God has for you. Give more earnest heed to the promises of God. Concentrate on moving ahead, on becoming so strong in the Spirit you can not only get your own needs met, you can meet others' needs as well!

Remember: Low Word Level = Low Faith Level = Slip.

Don't get so busy enjoying today's victory that tomorrow ends up in defeat. Look into the things you've learned. Give the Word more of your attention—not less. Keep moving from faith to faith. Instead of trying to trip you up, Satan and his bunch will be crying, "Oh no, that faith man is coming after us again!"

SCRIPTURE READING: Hebrews 5:11-14, Hebrews 6:1-12

Free Your Faith

"And when ye stand praying, forgive,
if ye have ought against any." **(Mark 11:25)**

Few people realize just how closely connected faith and forgiveness are. Jesus taught about that connection in His sermon on mountain-moving faith that's recorded in Mark 11:22-26.

He said, "What things soever ye desire, when ye pray, believe that ye receive them, and ye shall have them. And when ye stand praying, forgive."

Jesus backed those two sentences up together on purpose. He wanted us to know that releasing those who have wronged us is fundamental to receiving from God. He wanted to impress on our hearts the fact that we cannot have our prayers answered and hold grudges in our hearts at the same time.

Unforgiveness clogs the faith channel and keeps you powerless against the mountains in your life!

If you've been praying for something and you just can't seem to get an answer, check your heart for unforgiveness. Ask the Holy Spirit to bring any grudge that's hidden there to light. Unclog the channel of faith and you will soon see things you've been praying for come to pass.

SCRIPTURE READING: Matthew 18:21-35

Talk Like God!

"Whosoever shall say unto this mountain,
Be thou removed, and be thou cast into the sea;
and shall not doubt in his heart, but shall believe that those things
which he saith shall come to pass; he shall have
whatsoever he saith." **(Mark 11:23)**

Jesus didn't say, "Whosoever shall speak to God about this mountain." He said we should speak directly to the mountain the desired end result.

From a worldly point of view, that sounds foolish. But 1 Corinthians 1:27 explains that God has chosen the foolish things of the world to confound the wise. It's always going to sound foolish to the world when a Christian talks as if what God has promised is reality, especially when those promises seem to contradict the natural evidence around us. But if you want to keep the enemy defeated, that's the kind of talking you'd better be doing.

The Bible says God Himself talks that way! In Romans 4:17, it says, "[He] calleth those things which be not as though they were." God doesn't wait for circumstances to line up before He speaks. He *causes* them to line up *because* He speaks. You can do the same thing if you'll make your words agree with His and speak them out of your mouth by faith.

"But what if nothing happens right away?" you may ask. "What if the circumstances don't immediately change?" When Jesus spoke to the fig tree in Mark 11:14, He didn't go back and check to see if anything had happened to it. No, once He had spoken it, He considered it done.

Follow His example. Let your faith speak. Agree with God's Word!

SCRIPTURE READING: Mark 11:12-23

Honor God and He'll Honor You

"Honour the Lord with thy substance,
and with the firstfruits of all thine increase: So shall
thy barns be filled with plenty, and thy presses shall burst
out with new wine." **(Proverbs 3:9,10)**

The Book of Proverbs gives us a very basic principle of success. It is this: If you want God to honor you and bless you in any area of your life, you're going to have to honor Him in that particular area.

If you want God to bless you financially, you're going to have to honor Him with your money, or as this verse puts it, with the firstfruits of all your increase. In other words, you're going to have to tithe.

Ken and I know that from experience. When we started our life with the Lord, we were in terrible shape financially. And we stayed that way for several years because we failed to tithe consistently. Oh, we tried to tithe, but we'd never last long at it.

Then, one day, we made a quality decision that we were going to tithe no matter what. That's when we started coming out of trouble financially. When we began honoring God with our money by tithing, He began to help us in that area in miraculous ways.

You may say, "Well, Gloria, I just can't afford to tithe right now."

But let me tell you, you can't afford not to! If you don't start honoring God with your money, you'll be in the same financial position next year that you're in today.

So do it—even if it looks like you can't afford to. God is faithful! If you'll honor Him by giving Him the ten percent that belongs to Him, He'll help you with the rest.

Give God His first. Do it in faith expecting. As you tithe, worship Him and be grateful for what He has already done in your life. You'll be amazed when you see what He can do.

SCRIPTURE READING: Malachi 3:8-12

What Riches Were Meant to Do

"Let him that stole steal no more: but rather let him labour, working with his hands the thing which is good, that he may have to give to him that needeth." **(Ephesians 4:28)**

It always amazes me when I preach about prosperity and someone comes up to me and says, "I don't need much prosperity. I'm a simple person with a simple life. So I just ask God for enough to meet my needs."

They think that's humility, but it's not. It's selfishness! They don't realize it, but they're actually saying, "All I care about is meeting my own needs. I have no ambition to help meet anyone else's."

They could ask God for a million dollars, take out just enough to meet their needs, and give the rest away. But that doesn't even occur to them because when it comes to money, they've been brainwashed by a world that says if you have it, you've got to keep it.

That philosophy has hindered the ministry of Jesus Christ on the earth today. It has caused preachers to set aside their calling and get secular jobs just to survive. It's handicapped churches and stunted the growth of ministries that could have reached thousands more for the Lord.

It takes money to preach the gospel. Jesus Himself knew that, and contrary to what some people think, His ministry was not a poor one. He had so much money coming in and going out through His ministry that He had to appoint a treasurer. His name was Judas.

But Jesus didn't store up that money for Himself. He gave it to meet the needs of those around Him. He had such a reputation for giving that on the night of that last Passover when Judas left so abruptly, the disciples assumed that Jesus had sent him out to give to the poor.

Can you imagine how much and how often Jesus must have given to the poor for the disciples to make that assumption?

Jesus never built a worldly empire for Himself. But that doesn't mean He was poor. It means He was the greatest giver who ever walked the face of this earth, and it's time we started following in His footsteps.

Don't turn down the wealth God wants to give you just because you don't "need" it. Dare to accept it, then pass it along to those who do. Stop working for a living and start working for a "giving." Discover for yourself what riches were really meant to do.

SCRIPTURE READING: Luke 12:15-31

Your Children Released From Captivity

"Thus saith the Lord; Refrain thy voice
from weeping, and thine eyes from tears: for thy work
shall be rewarded, saith the Lord; and they [your children]
shall come again from the land of the enemy. And
there is hope in thine end, saith the Lord, that
thy children shall come again to their
own border." **(Jeremiah 31:16,17)**

Jesus *has* redeemed us from the curse. Many of us have been well taught about that redemption where sin, sickness, and poverty in our own lives are concerned. But we often fail to realize that that redemption has power over the destruction the devil tries to bring on our children's lives as well.

Deuteronomy 28 states the curse of the law in verses 16-68. Notice what that curse says about children. "Thy sons and thy daughters shall be given unto another people, and thine eyes shall look, and fail with longing for them all the day long: and there shall be no might in thine hand" (verse 32).

"Thou shall beget sons and daughters, but thou shalt not enjoy them; for they shall go into captivity" (verse 41).

Many Christian parents are still suffering needlessly under that curse. Their children are being taken captive by drugs, alcohol, and perversions.

But it doesn't have to be that way! Since Jesus broke the curse of the law, these parents have the authority in the name of Jesus to order Satan out of their children's lives.

Don't let the devil run roughshod over your children! When you see the first warning signs of rebellion in them, confess the promises of God over them and refuse to give the devil any room to operate.

Remember, the children don't understand the unseen forces that are coming against them. So it's your responsibility to stand against those forces on their behalf. Exercise that responsibility. Then take every opportunity to minister love to them.

God knows how to deliver your children. Do your part and trust Him to do His. He *will* bring them back from the land of the enemy!

SCRIPTURE READING: Isaiah 60:1-5

Press In

"Let the word of Christ dwell in you richly...." (Colossians 3:16)

Things in this old world aren't getting any better, and in recent times, the Holy Spirit has been speaking an urgent message to my heart. He's been saying, "Press in. Draw in to a more intimate relationship with your heavenly Father. If you don't, you won't make it. If you do, you will see more glorious outpourings of God than you can imagine."

That message isn't just for me. It's also for you—and for every other believer on the earth today. We are in the last of the last days of this age. Jesus is coming soon. It's an exciting time, but it's also a dangerous time. Those who don't do what the Spirit says, who don't press in to the Lord, are going to go from disaster to disaster. But those who do will defeat the disasters and turn them into glory, in Jesus' name!

Your first step in drawing closer to God is to realize that you know God first in His Word. Time spent meditating in the New Testament is time spent with Jesus.

Most people don't realize that. So, instead of getting to know the Lord through His Word, they try to know Him through their feelings and that just won't work.

Letting the Word dominate your thinking is to allow the Holy Spirit to have control over your mind. As you do that, your feelings will eventually fall in line.

Remember this: The first chapter of John tells us that Jesus *is* the Word. That means, when you spend time in it, you're spending time with Jesus. When His Word is dwelling in you richly, then Jesus is dwelling in you richly too!

Don't go from disaster to disaster. Take those disasters and turn them into glory, in Jesus' name. Press in to Jesus. Press in to the Word and you'll make it through these dangerous days just fine!

SCRIPTURE READING: John 1:1-14

Get the Two Together

"As ye have therefore received Christ Jesus the Lord,
so walk ye in him: Rooted and built up in him, and stablished
in the faith, as ye have been taught, abounding therein
with thanksgiving." **(Colossians 2:6,7)**

Established in the faith and abounding with thanksgiving. These days it seems that's a rare combination.

A lot of people have been taught faith over the last several years, and a lot of people have been taught to abound with thanksgiving. But it's been hard to set the two together. Faith folks want to confess the Word all the time, but they don't praise God very much. And those who like to praise God just want to jump and shout and dance and have a good time in the Lord. You can't get them to get very serious about the Word.

Success comes from combining the two.

So, do it! Put them together in your life. When you run into a challenge, don't just stand around grim-faced and white-knuckled holding onto your faith. Raise your hands high and praise. Start thanking God in the midst of what's happening around you. Keep thanking Him for the answer until it comes.

Instead of just standing on the Word, let the joy of the Lord enable you to dance around on it a little. It will get you where you're going a whole lot faster...and you and God both will have a much better time on the way.

SCRIPTURE READING: Colossians 2:1-10

Love: The Secret of Success

"Love never fails." **(1 Corinthians 13:8, AMP)**

Fear of failure. It's haunted all of us at some time in our lives. Popular psychology tells us to adjust to it. But the Word of God tells us that there is a failure-proof way to live without it. It is the way of LOVE.

If you want to know real success, you must learn to be moved and motivated by love. That's how Jesus was when He was on the earth.

Even when John the Baptist was senselessly, brutally murdered and Jesus went away to be alone, He didn't deviate from the way of love. For Matthew 14:6-14 says that even then in that emotionally taxing time when the people followed Him and would give Him no solitude, He was moved with compassion and healed their sick.

I used to wonder how Jesus could just turn away from that terrible crime and not retaliate. What I didn't realize was that He *did* retaliate. He overcame the works of Satan with compassion. He defeated hatred with love. He attacked Satan in the spirit realm by destroying his works of sickness and disease.

Compassion doesn't strike at the surface of things. It goes to the root of the problem. That's why it always succeeds.

"But wait!" you may say. "I can't operate like that. I'm not Jesus."

Yes you can, because the Word of God says that His love has been shed abroad in your heart! (Rom. 5:5). And 1 John 2:5 says His love is perfected in you as you keep His Word.

Commit to living the life of love today. Watch God turn failure into success at home, at work...in any situation. LOVE NEVER FAILS!

SCRIPTURE READING: Matthew 14:1-14

Seek God First

"Seek ye first the kingdom of God, and his righteousness;
and all these things shall be added unto you." **(Matthew 6:33)**

Whenever Ken and I talk about living by faith, I know there are some people who think, "Oh, that's easy for *you*. You're preachers. You have it made!" And, in some ways, we do. We have it made because our calling demands that we give God our attention, and giving God your attention always brings success.

But we haven't always lived that way. In fact, the first time I ever saw Kenneth Copeland, he was about as far from a preacher as I figured you could get. He flew planes and sang in nightclubs. As for me, I was a college girl who said she would never marry a preacher and who had never even heard about the new birth.

Right after we got married, Ken went into a business enterprise that we thought was going to make us rich. So I quit my job and went to work for this new company. Two weeks later it folded.

We ended up sleeping on a rented roll-away bed that sagged in the middle. We had a wrought-iron coffee table Ken made in high school and a black and white TV. Nothing else. No refrigerator. No stove. I cooked in my coffeepot and an electric skillet and used a cardboard box on the porch to keep our food cold.

We were flat broke. Unemployed. Deeply in debt. I had nowhere to go. No furniture. No nothing.

Then one day I picked up the Bible Ken's mother had given him for his birthday. In the front she'd written this verse, "Seek ye first the kingdom of God, and his righteousness; and all these things shall be added unto you." I turned and read Matthew, chapter 6. It said God cared for the birds. For the first time in my life it got into my heart that God cared where I was and what I was doing. I figured if He cared for birds, He cared for me! I knelt in that bare room and told Jesus that if He could do anything with my life, He could certainly have it. That's all I remember saying.

I had no idea I'd just gotten born again. Two weeks later Ken found a new job. We moved to a new furnished apartment and bought a better car. In the midst of it all, something else happened—Ken got born again.

Don't worry if you don't "have it made." We certainly didn't when all this started. Just stick with God and let Him make you. He is a good God who is good to all (Ps. 145:9).

Make a decision in your heart to seek *HIM* first. Then *all* the other things will be added.

SCRIPTURE READING: Psalm 128

Spread Peace This Christmas

"And suddenly there was with the angel a multitude
of the heavenly host praising God, and saying, Glory to God in the highest,
and on earth peace, good will toward men." **(Luke 2:13,14)**

Christmas is a very important time of year. It's a time of year when the whole world is hearing the message of the birth of Jesus. It's a time when people are tenderhearted... the perfect time to plant seeds of love in the lives of those you meet.

Sometimes those seeds may just take the form of a kind word in the middle of rush hour shopping. Other times, you may get the opportunity to pray and minister to someone. But whatever the situation, keep a sharp eye out for even the smallest chance to assist people.

I've had some outstanding experiences giving a few dollars to someone in need. As they are taking the money, I tell them, "This money is from the Lord Jesus Christ. I serve Him. He is the One who instructed me to help you."

It's amazing how many people are ready to hear what you have to say when you say it in love. They're starved for someone to really care. Be that someone this Christmas season. Spread the Word about the peace that's available in Jesus. Tell about His goodwill toward men.

Who knows how many of those small seeds may one day take root and bring one more precious person into the glorious kingdom of God?

SCRIPTURE READING: Luke 2:1-20

Tune In

"He that speaketh in an unknown tongue
speaketh not unto men, but unto God: for no man
understandeth him; howbeit in the spirit he
speaketh mysteries." **(1 Corinthians 14:2)**

Have you ever looked around at your own life or the life of the Church and wondered why it's taking the Lord so long to get things in order?

If so, let me tell you something I learned a few years ago. He's not the One who's slow. We are!

It's not God's fault that the Church still has spots and wrinkles. It's not His fault that we're not living in total victory. He's always ready. He's the great "I AM." We're the ones who fall short.

Compare it to turning on a radio. If you don't have it tuned to exactly the right frequency, you won't be able to hear the station. It's not the station's fault. It's sending out signals perfectly. The problem is, you haven't tuned in to it.

That's what's happening with you and me. We haven't fine tuned our spirits enough to pick up the voice of the Spirit. Oh, we pick up a few things now and then, but mostly, we just fade in and out. We don't stay on God's wavelength all the time.

How do you adjust your spiritual tuner?

By praying in the Spirit. Praying in other tongues is the fastest, most effective method I know of to tune in to God—because instead of praying your own thoughts and plans, you're praying His!

The Bible says that when you pray in tongues, you're speaking mysteries to God. In the Spirit, you're calling forth parts of God's plan you don't even understand with your natural mind. By the unction of the Holy Spirit, you're praying the perfect will of God.

You see, God knows how to deliver His people. He knows how to turn us into the glorious Church without spot or wrinkle. He has a plan that will do it. And if we'll tap into that plan and start releasing it into the earth by praying in the Spirit, praying according to His will and not our own, this age will draw to a close quickly. If we'll all get our minds and hearts in tune with what God's doing, there will be an explosion of the power of God that will turn this world around!

Start adjusting your spiritual tuner today. Spend an hour praying in other tongues. Set your spirit on God's wavelength and just see how quickly the spots and wrinkles begin to disappear from you.

SCRIPTURE READING: 1 Corinthians 14:1-19

Don't Panic

"Roll your works upon the Lord — commit and trust them
wholly to Him; [He will cause your thoughts to become agreeable
to His will, and] so shall your plans be established
and succeed." **(Proverbs 16:3, AMP)**

Right now you may be on the edge of a major decision...about to make a change in your job or your church or your personal life. You know you need divine guidance. And you're hoping desperately to hear from the Lord.

If that's your situation, don't panic. Being led by the Lord isn't some complicated process that only the spiritual "pros" can master.

I found that out years ago when I was a new believer. I wanted to live in a way that was pleasing to God, but I didn't know how to make decisions that were in line with His will.

Then one day as I was studying my *Amplified Bible,* I came across Proverbs 16:3. Immediately, I latched onto this verse and began to use it in my life — and I can tell you now from experience, it works!

It will work for you too if you'll do what it says. Roll your works over on God, commit your ways to Him, trust them wholly to Him. He'll start adjusting your thoughts to be like His until, at some point, you'll just know the right thing to do. Of course, faith is involved. One of the requirements is trust, and you won't be able to do that without feeding on God's Word. Then as you practice rolling your works upon the Lord and trusting Him, you become more confident in your ability to hear. Start now with whatever problem is bothering you. Pray and trust God with it. In other words, believe you receive when you pray. Stop worrying and begin believing.

Learn to live this way and it doesn't matter whether you've been a Christian 30 minutes or 30 years, your plans shall be established and succeed!

SCRIPTURE READING: Psalm 37:1-7

No Deposit—No Return

"Blessed is the man that feareth the Lord,
that delighteth greatly in his commandments. He shall not
be afraid of evil tidings: his heart is fixed,
trusting in the Lord." **(Psalm 112:1,7)**

Are you ready to face a crisis? Don't wait until one hits to find out. Prepare yourself now.

That's what a couple of my Partners did. They faced a situation that would have made many people panic. But when the crisis hit, their hearts were so deeply established on the Word of God that their first response was not one of fear but of faith.

What affected me most when I heard their testimony was one particular phrase they kept using:

No Deposit—No Return

What they meant by that was that if you don't take the time to deposit the Word in your heart now, it won't be there later when you really need it. You'll end up in a crisis with only doubt and unbelief instead of the faith and power you need to see you through. In a situation like the one this couple faced that could be deadly.

You see, their two-year-old son had suffered a fall that had cracked his skull and critically injured his neck. He had no feeling in his arms and legs and was unable to move. Yet as they rushed him to the emergency room, a great sense of peace rested on them. Rather than crying with fear, they prayed in faith and declared, "By Jesus' stripes, our son is healed!"

Sure enough, within hours, their boy was totally restored. Even the X rays verified the fact that a miracle had taken place.

What's important to understand about that story is this: The victory was not won when the damage to that little boy's body disappeared. It was won all during the days and weeks and months before when his parents were listening to tapes and studying the Word and praying in the Spirit. It was won because these people had spent time building a foundation on the Word so that when this storm came, they were able to stand.

Now is the time for you to build a rock-solid foundation! Don't wait around until you're faced with a crisis. Get the Word in your heart in abundance now, so when you really need it, it will flow out in power.

Remember: No deposit—no return.

Start making those precious deposits today!

SCRIPTURE READING: Psalm 112

A Carefree Christmas

"Be careful for nothing; but in every thing
by prayer and supplication with thanksgiving let your requests
be made known unto God." **(Philippians 4:6)**

Can you really have a merry Christmas even when you have a thousand and one pressures bearing down on you? Yes, you can—and you don't have to leave the country to do it. No matter how intense or how trivial the problems are that you're facing right now, you can have the most wonderful, most carefree Christmas season you've ever had in your life; and you can start having it today.

As a believer, you're probably familiar with that scripture that says to be anxious for nothing. But, have you ever taken it seriously enough to put it into action? There's a good chance you haven't because you haven't understood just how dangerous those anxieties are. You probably haven't realized that they're a deadly part of the devil's strategy against you.

That's right. Worry is one of the chief weapons of his warfare. If he can get you to worry about them, he can use the financial pressures and family pressures and scheduling problems that are just a "normal" part of everyday life to weigh you down and drag you into more trouble than you think possible.

Medical science tells us that a high percentage of the people hospitalized in the U.S.A. are there with ailments caused by worry and tension. Yet, a great many believers worry without even thinking about it. They'll worry about being too short or too skinny. They'll stew over this and that and not even realize they've been sinning.

"Sinning, Brother Copeland?"

Yes! For the born-again, Spirit-filled believer who owns a Bible—worrying is a sin. So, even if the Christmas cards are late and 45 people are coming to your house for Christmas dinner, don't worry.

Instead, do what the Bible says to do. Pray, making your request known to God...and praise Him for the answer. Then you'll have peace.

Now, go ahead and have a truly merry Christmas, you carefree thing you!

SCRIPTURE READING: Matthew 6:24-34

Run Him Out of Town

"Stand therefore...having shod your feet in preparation
[to face the enemy with the firm-footed stability, the promptness
and the readiness produced by the good news] of
the Gospel of peace." **(Ephesians 6:14,15, AMP)**

reparation. When it comes to fighting spiritual battles, that's a word you'd do well to remember. Most believers don't pay much attention to it. They don't prepare themselves in advance. They fiddle around until the devil makes his move, then they jump up and try to fight him with the Word... and they usually lose.

I used to do the same thing until the Lord taught me differently. I used to wait until my meetings began to pray for their success. As Satan would come against them from one direction, I'd fight him there. Then he'd move around and attack them in another area, and I'd fight him there.

One day the Lord showed me that by waiting until the last minute to take my stand, I was giving Satan time to build up his forces against me. And consequently, I was losing many of my battles. Then the Lord said something to me I'll never forget. He said, "If they had kicked Al Capone out of Chicago when he was just a small-time operator, he wouldn't have been so hard to handle; but they waited until he became a first-class criminal with his forces built up around him. Then it took an army to bring him down."

When I heard that, I made up my mind never to be caught unprepared again. I started praying about those meetings weeks in advance, getting the stage set spiritually before they ever began. Instead of letting Satan get his forces entrenched, I started throwing him out before he got a single foothold. When I did, I saw more victories than I ever had before.

Don't let the devil catch you off guard. Be prepared! Start praying and speaking the Word of faith now over your family, your business, your church. Get your feet shod with the preparation of the gospel of peace. Then if Satan causes trouble, you'll be well-equipped to run him out of town.

SCRIPTURE READING: 1 Samuel 17:12-51

Dare to Take Your Place

"But after that the kindness and love of God our Saviour
toward man appeared...Which he shed on us abundantly through
Jesus Christ our Saviour; That being justified by his grace,
we should be made heirs." **(Titus 3:4,6,7)**

A covenant of grace. That's what you and I have with Almighty God. If you could truly grasp the significance of that, you'd never be the same again.

What exactly *is* a covenant of grace? It's a relationship of favor that gives you access to someone else's power.

An illustration of a covenant of grace is the covenant the old Sicilian "family" members have with the "godfather" of the "family."

In that group, a weak person might come in and ask the Don for a favor. The Don would say, "I will grant this favor and I will ask a favor of you, and when that time comes, I will collect it."

Once that was said, the weak person would become excited. Suddenly he knew he would no longer have this problem because anyone who tried to rough him up would now have to face the godfather, the one with all the power. Suddenly, that little guy's attitude would change. He would leave the presence of the head of the family in the full assurance that he didn't have a thing to worry about. He was no longer small and powerless in his own mind. He had gained favor (grace) with the powerful.

He'd walk out thinking, "Everything is handled. All I have to do now is whatever the Don asks me to do—and the Don knows I don't have anything, so whatever he asks me to do, he'll provide the wherewithal to do it."

That's grace. God's willingness to enter into blood covenant with you and give you everything He has in exchange for everything you have.

He took your sin to give you His righteousness. He took your sickness to give you His health. He took your poverty in order to meet all your needs according to His riches in glory. Whenever He asks you to do something, He provides everything you need to carry it out.

The great Jehovah, God of heaven and earth, is your Father God. Can you understand that? If you're under the blood of Jesus, you've been made a covenant child of the most powerful being in the universe.

Dare to take your place in the family!
SCRIPTURE READING: Luke 4:14-21

Extremely Blessed

"A gift is as a precious stone in the eyes of him that hath it: whithersoever it turneth, it prospereth." **(Proverbs 17:8)**

I f I could give you a gift this Christmas, the Word is what I'd give you. I'd rather give it to you than a check for a million dollars. Because you can run through a million dollars real quick, but the truth of God's Word never quits—and it will get you out of situations a million dollars can't get you out of.

Ken and I are just ordinary people. But when we latched onto God's Word, we latched onto something out of the ordinary, something that changed our lives. Every area of our lives.

Nothing that's happened to us has happened because of us. It's happened because of God's Word. In fact, I don't even have to know you to promise you this: If you'll give God's Word your full attention—and not be afraid of His will for your life—you're going to be happier and more prosperous than anything you could ever dream up.

Of course, if you do that, people may call you extreme. They say that about us all the time. But we don't mind. We *are* extreme. And if you'll set your faith on the Word of God, you can be extreme too. Extremely well. Extremely prosperous. And extremely blessed. Merry Christmas.

SCRIPTURE READING: Psalm 119:56-65

Don't Settle for Second Best

"My brethren, count it all joy when ye fall into divers temptations;
Knowing this, that the trying of your faith worketh patience." **(James 1:2,3)**

I admit, it's tough to be enthusiastic about going through tests and trials. But can you get excited about being totally supplied in every way, in want of nothing? Well, according to the Word of God, if you'll use your trials to develop patience, that's precisely the position you're going to be in!

You see, patience doesn't mean what you thought it meant. It does not mean settling sweetly for second best. It does not mean standing meekly by while the devil romps all over you.

No, patience is a powerful word. The New Testament meaning of it as translated literally from the Greek is "to be consistently constant or to be the same way all the time, regardless of what happens."

To understand how much power is involved in that, you have to realize that it's one of the most outstanding attributes of God Himself. The Bible says He's the same yesterday, today, and forever.

Think about that for a minute. The guy who absolutely cannot be changed by anyone or anything is an extremely powerful fellow, wouldn't you say? Obviously, God has that much power.

But you know what? You do too!

By the power of the Holy Ghost working within you, you can be the same every day no matter what happens. If you'll put your trust in the Word of God and let patience go to work, it won't matter what happens. You won't ever have to accept anything less than victory again.

Now *that's* something to get excited about.

SCRIPTURE READING: 2 Timothy 3:10-17

A Little Bit of Heaven on Earth

"Put on therefore, as the elect of God,
holy and beloved, bowels of mercies, kindness,
humbleness of mind, meekness, longsuffering; Forbearing
one another, and forgiving one another...even as
Christ forgave you." **(Colossians 3:12,13)**

Living in a home filled with the love and the peace of God Himself is almost like living in heaven right here on earth. We all know that's true. And we long to live in such a home. Yet, time and time again, we short-change our families. We spend our kindest words and our most winning smiles on those beyond our front door.

Have you ever wondered why?

The answer is simpler than you might suspect. Spiritually speaking, your family is under attack. You see, it is not only one of your most precious gifts, when it's operating in harmony, it's one of your most powerful resources. Satan knows that even if you don't—and he's out to destroy it.

His battle plan is simple. He will do everything he can to create strife in your home. He'll stir up feelings of self-pity and jealousy. He'll encourage you to nurse resentments and harbor bitterness. And through it all, his purpose remains the same, to divide and destroy your home.

When God's people get in harmony with each other, miracles start to happen. Their agreement creates an atmosphere in which God's supernatural, miracle-working power is free to flow! So Satan is constantly tempting us to spoil that atmosphere, to foul things up by being at odds with each other. All too often we fall prey to his tactics simply because we don't realize just how dangerous strife really is. One close look at the Word of God will solve that problem, however. James 3:16 says, "Where envying and strife is, there is confusion and every evil work."

Don't open the door of your home to Satan by allowing your family the "luxury" of a few quarrels.

Stop the destruction before it starts. Anchor yourself to God's Word. Find out what He has to say about the power of agreement. Stop looking at your family from your own limited perspective and start seeing it as God sees it—as a powerhouse! That way you won't drift helplessly into an argument every time a gust of emotion blows through your home.

Determine right now not to let the devil have your family. Instead, pray for them, support them, and love them. Bring them together, so you can all enjoy a little bit of heaven on earth.

SCRIPTURE READING: Colossians 3:12-25

Stick to Your Calling

"Wherefore I put thee in remembrance
that thou stir up the gift of God.... Who hath saved us,
and called us with an holy calling, not according to our works,
but according to his own purpose and grace, which
was given us in Christ Jesus before the
world began." **(2 Timothy 1:6,9)**

A re you doing what God called you to do?

If you haven't ever thought about it before, that may sound like an odd question to you. You may be tempted to shrug it off and say, "Oh, I'm not really called to do anything. I'm not a pastor or a teacher or a minister of any kind...I guess I'm just what you might call a little finger on the Body of Christ."

Let me tell you something: No matter who you are, God has put a holy calling in you. He's designed you and called you to meet a need in the Body of Christ that nobody else can meet quite like you can.

You may be called to be so successful in business you can finance the gospel worldwide. You may be called to a ministry of prayer and intercession. You may be called to a ministry of healing right there in your own neighborhood. But no matter what that calling is, it's important and you need to follow it!

If you're like many believers I know, you may have let your life become so overgrown with other things that you just don't have time to pursue your calling. You may be so overwhelmed with the cares of life that you can't imagine how you can fit anything else in.

Over the years, a pastor friend of mine got involved in so many different areas of ministry that he was about to fold up physically under the strain of it. The overload was actually about to kill him. Finally, the Lord spoke to him one night and said, "John, it's not your calling that's nearly killed you. It's everything else you've added to it."

I've had to deal with that in my own life. I've had to quit doing things just because they need doing. I've had to discipline myself to sticking to what *I'm* called to do.

Make up your mind to prayerfully trim away the extra things you've added to your life. Stir up the gift God has placed inside you. Get back to what He has called you to do.

After all, that calling is vital. It's holy...and it's yours. Don't ever let it slip away from you.

SCRIPTURE READING: Acts 9:1-20

Don't Just Sit There...Arise!

"Now four men who were lepers were at the entrance of
the city's gate; and they said to one another, Why do we sit here
until we die.... So they arose." **(2 Kings 7:3,5, AMP)**

No matter how bad the problem is you may be facing today, no matter how far under the circumstances you may be, in 24 hours you can be back on top!

"Oh, Brother Copeland, that would be impossible!"

That's what the Samaritans thought in 2 Kings, chapter 7. Their land was being ravaged by famine. Enemy troops had surrounded them and cut off all source of supply. Mothers were eating their own children just to survive.

But right in the middle of that, the Lord told the prophet Elisha that in 24 hours the whole situation would change. Flour and barley would sell for just a few pennies and there would be abundance for all.

What did God use to turn that situation around?

Four lepers! Four lepers who, instead of sitting around feeling sorry for themselves and waiting to die, decided to arise and take their chances in the enemy camp. When they got there, they found it abandoned. All the warriors had been frightened away by the angels of God, and they'd left enough food behind to feed all of Samaria!

Sometimes you and I are like the officials in that story. We get problem-centered instead of Word of God centered. We let ourselves be so surrounded with the loud voice of the world that the vision of our victory is pushed out of sight.

When that happens, faith and power begin to subside and life caves in on us from every side.

If that's happened to you, stop crying about it. Stop looking at your problem and feeling sorry for yourself. That won't change anything!

Just like He did for Elisha, God's given you a word. He's promised you victory. He's promised to make you an overcomer.

So don't just sit there till you die. Don't accept defeat. Rise up in faith. Stand up on God's Word and fight for your life. Get mad at Satan. Cast him out. Get mad at that sickness. Get angry with poverty and start giving.

Rise up and receive the deliverance of the Lord!

SCRIPTURE READING: 2 Kings 6:24-33, 2 Kings 7:1-20

Go When You're Ready

"With long life will I satisfy [you], and shew [you] my salvation." **(Psalm 91:16)**

Did you know that it's not God's will for you or anyone to die young? His will for you is to live the full number of your days. You ought to live 70 or 80 years, and if you are not satisfied, live a while longer! The Bible says that when Abraham died, he died at a good old age, *full* of years. That's the way it ought to be with all of us.

Some believers don't realize that and they've gotten themselves in a mess. When they get sick instead of just believing for healing, they start wondering if it's God's will for them to die. "Maybe He's ready to call me home," they think.

Don't ever entertain thoughts like that. If God has His way, He won't call you home until you're good and ready to come. The apostle Paul understood that. In 2 Timothy 4:6,7, he said, "For I am now *ready* to be offered, and the time of my departure is at hand. I have fought a good fight, I have finished my course, I have kept the faith." Paul didn't die until he and Jesus were ready for him to go.

Regardless of your age, if the devil is telling you God isn't going to heal you because it's time for you to go home, he is lying to you. God promises in Psalm 91:16 that if you are living under the shadow of the most High, He will satisfy you with long life. (That means that you are abiding in Him as Jesus taught in John 15.)

If you're not satisfied that you have finished your course yet on this earth, it's not time for you to die. So ignore the devil and keep right on living. Resist sickness and disease in the name of Jesus. Stand on God's promise!

Then, when you're ready to go on to heaven, go! But go satisfied, healed, and ready! Go in victory shouting the words of that old joy-filled song— "Heaven is near and I can't stay here. Good-bye world, good-bye."

SCRIPTURE READING: Deuteronomy 34

Good Success

"This book of the law shall not depart out of thy mouth;
but thou shalt meditate therein day and night, that thou mayest
observe to do according to all that is written therein: for then
thou shalt...have good success." **(Joshua 1:8)**

Good success is a way of life that comes from being established in the Word of God. It comes from spending so much of your time and your thought life on the Word that it becomes what you and I could call "second nature." It comes from hearing and obeying the Word so consistently that it begins to guide your actions even when you're not consciously thinking about it.

When I started flying airplanes, I learned to train myself by getting the handbook for a certain airplane and reading it over and over again. In my mind's eye, I'd visualize everything that could occur in that airplane. I trained myself by meditating on what I needed to do.

And that's exactly what I started doing with the Word of God. I thought about it day and night. Before long, I started getting excited about what I was reading.

I'd sit at home and think about how I'd apply the Word in different situations. I'd see myself praying for the sick and having them recover. The Word became "second nature" to me.

Practice meditating on the Word that way. Let it become part of you. See yourself obeying it in every possible circumstance. It will guarantee you "good success."

SCRIPTURE READING: Psalm 1

A Time to Forget

"Lord, how oft shall my brother sin against me,
and I forgive him? till seven times? Jesus saith unto him...
Until seventy times seven." **(Matthew 18:21,22)**

Remember when...? That's a question we hear a lot this time of year. Reminiscing with family and friends, we browse through Christmases gone by, enjoying the memories until inevitably, we stumble across the memories we would rather forget.

Suddenly, the pain comes rushing back. The sting of a parent's criticism, the broken promise of a friend, the rejections, the disappointments, the heartaches...

What should we do with memories like that? Do we have to drag them along, like so much baggage, from year to year?

No. We can leave them behind. In fact, we *must* leave them behind. And there's only one way to do it—through forgiveness.

Forgiving someone sounds like a simple thing to do. Yet few of us actually do it. We treat forgiveness as if it were one of life's additional options, something we can take or leave alone. But it's not. It's a basic requirement for every believer. In fact, as far as God is concerned, unforgiveness is wickedness. And in Matthew 18, Jesus tells a parable that illustrates the terrible consequences of it. The parable involves a servant who owed his lord a debt equivalent to millions of dollars. When the debt came due, he pleaded with his master, "Lord, have patience with me and I will pay thee all." His master was so moved that he canceled the entire debt!

Soon after, that same servant sought out a man who owed him $15. Finding him unable to pay, he ignored the man's pleas for mercy and had him cast into prison.

When his lord heard about it, he was incensed. He called him a wicked servant and delivered him to the tormentors until he paid all that was due.

Look again at the size of that unforgiven debt. *Fifteen dollars.* The little debts are the ones that most often trip us up. The petty resentments between husband and wife, between brother and sister. Tiny bits of unforgiveness that seem too insignificant to bother with. Beware. Those are the kinds of debts Satan uses to torment you.

After all, Jesus paid off a mountain of debts for you. You can afford to be generous about the nickel and dime debts of others.

Spend time with the Holy Spirit, allowing Him to reveal the unforgiveness in you. Then repent and release it. Make this Christmas more than just a time for remembering. Make it a time to forget.

SCRIPTURE READING: Matthew 18:21-35

Know Him as Daddy

"For [the Spirit which] you have now received [is] not
a spirit of slavery to put you once more in bondage to fear,
but you have received the Spirit of adoption — the Spirit
producing sonship — in [the bliss of] which we cry,
Abba! [That is,] Father!" **(Romans 8:15, AMP)**

One night after a worship service a friend of mine and I stepped outside and were suddenly awed by the beauty around us. It was one of those crisp, clear winter nights when the brilliance of the moon and stars nearly takes your breath away. I said to my friend, "Tommy, will you look at that!" Then he looked up with one of those Holy Ghost whole face smiles and with a voice full of tenderness said, "My Daddy made that!"

"My Daddy...." I'll never forget the way he said that.

Some people might think he shouldn't have been talking in such familiar terms about God, but they'd be wrong. It's scriptural to talk that way about Him. In the New Testament there's a Greek word for father— "Abba." The most accurate translation for that word in English is "Daddy."

It's a word that signifies closeness. It speaks of a relationship that's been developed through time spent together.

"Father" is one thing. "Daddy" is another.

Growing up, my father was sometimes my "Father" and sometimes my "Daddy." When we were out duck hunting, he was "Daddy." When he gave commands he meant to be obeyed instantly, he was "Father."

God is like that too. He's your Father and He's your Daddy. There are times you'll be very serious and down to business with one another. Other times you'll be more lighthearted. But either way, once you fellowship with Him enough to get to know Him, I guarantee, you'll want to be close to Him *all* the time.

SCRIPTURE READING: Romans 8:14-18

Don't Answer

"And be not conformed to this world: but be ye transformed by the renewing of your mind, that ye may prove what is that good, and acceptable, and perfect, will of God." **(Romans 12:2)**

Be not conformed to this world. If you live like the world, you'll be overcome by the world. It's as simple as that. So don't let the world squeeze you into its own mold.

Instead..."be transformed" by the entire renewal of your mind. Overcome the world by having your mind transformed to think like God thinks. In other words, when you see something in the Word, say, "I agree with that. From now on I'm acting on that instead of what I used to think."

For example, when sin calls your name, don't answer. Agree with the Word instead and say, "I'm dead to that, Devil. You can't pull me into it anymore!"

As you do that, you'll find yourself changing. You will find yourself living like a world overcomer!

SCRIPTURE READING: Romans 6:1-11

Major on Mercy

"I beseech thee, shew me thy glory." **(Exodus 33:18)**

What would you say is the single, most outstanding thing about God? What's His most important characteristic? Some people would say it's His power. Others, His holiness. But God Himself would give a different answer.

You can find that answer in Exodus 33. There Moses is asking God to show him His glory.

Now the word "glory" could literally be translated "heavy weight." It refers to the heaviest, biggest, grandest thing about someone. It's the sum total of their worth.

So what Moses was actually saying was, "Lord, I want to see the weightiest thing about You. I want to know Your grandest attributes." What did God say to him in response?

Chapter 34:6,7 tells us, "The Lord passed by before him, and proclaimed, The Lord, The Lord God, merciful and gracious, longsuffering, and abundant in goodness and truth, Keeping mercy for thousands, forgiving iniquity and transgression and sin, and that will by no means clear the guilty; visiting the iniquity of the fathers upon the children...unto the third generation and to the fourth generation."

Just think about that! When Moses asked God to show him the most important thing about Himself, God showed him His mercy.

That means if you and I are to imitate God (Eph. 5:1) we must major in mercy too. Mercy, goodness, forgiveness, and compassion must mark our behavior above all else.

Major on mercy and others will see the glory of God in you.

SCRIPTURE READING: Exodus 33:7-23, Exodus 34:5-10

Remember Noah

"And the Lord said, I will destroy man
whom I have created from the face of the earth;
both man, and beast, and the creeping thing, and the fowls
of the air; for it repenteth me that I have made them.
But Noah found grace in the eyes
of the Lord." **(Genesis 6:7,8)**

One of the dirtiest, most damaging lies that the devil ever told you was when he said, "You aren't important." Don't you ever believe that.

You *are* important! Every born-again member in the Church of Jesus Christ has a part to play in God's plan. God has something for you to do that no one else can do just like you can. If you don't take your place and do your part, things won't be quite right.

I can just hear you thinking, "Oh, Gloria, I'm just one person. What could I possibly do that could be so significant?"

Look in Genesis, chapter 6, and you'll see the answer to that question. There you'll see that the people on the earth had gotten so wicked that God had regretted that He'd made them. He was ready to wipe the whole population out—but He didn't. Why? Because of one man: Noah! One obedient man saved the human race.

Think about that. What if Noah had said, "Well, this is just too much pressure for me. I can't live upright before God in the middle of this ungodly generation. I mean, everybody around me is living the other way. Every man around me imagines only evil in his heart. I can't make any difference in this dark world anyway. I'm just one man."

Praise God, Noah didn't say that. He didn't picture himself as an insignificant man whose life didn't matter. Really, he saw himself as a man to whom God had spoken and by faith he obeyed God according to the Book of Hebrews. And because of that he ended up being the only thing that stood between mankind and total destruction.

Next time you're tempted to shrug off the instructions of God and be disobedient, next time you catch yourself thinking, "It doesn't matter what I do"—remember Noah. Consider the fact that, whether you understand it or not, God is counting on you to carry out your part of His plan. Live like you're someone important in the kingdom of God. And sooner or later you'll realize, you are.

SCRIPTURE READING: Genesis 6

Born to Victory

"I have told you these things so that in Me
you may have perfect peace and confidence. In the world
you have tribulation and trials and distress and frustration;
but be of good cheer...I have overcome
the world." **(John 16:33, AMP)**

Jesus said as long as you live in the world, you're going to have trouble. (I can vouch for that!) But you're not just in the world. You're in JESUS in the world, and that makes all the difference. You're in Him and He's overcome every kind of trouble there is.

As God's child, you're not the defeated trying to get victory. You're the overcomer, and Satan's trying to rob you of the victory that already belongs to you.

When you made Jesus the Lord of your life, you were born into victory... because the Victor came to live in you. Think about it. The victorious Jesus. The Anointed One. The glorified and resurrected Lord. The Ruler of the Universe.

Cheer up, my friend. Have "perfect peace and confidence." That's *Jesus* who lives in you!

SCRIPTURE READING: John 16:15-33

Don't Speak – *Shout* Your Victory!

"From the rising of the sun unto the going down of the same the Lord's name is to be praised." **(Psalm 113:3)**

Praise God. Praise Him in the morning. Praise Him at noon. Praise Him at night. If you've never praised God in your life, then get started right now. Praise Him for freedom. Praise Him for healing and Calvary. Praise Him for the name of Jesus.

You ought to be shouting your way to work and shouting your way back home! If there's anything the devil can't stand, it's praise.

If you've taken territory from the devil and he's coming against you to get it back, this is not the time to sit down and whine about how things aren't working out. It's not time to decide that God has taken His hand off your life.

It IS time to get into the Word and get yourself reanchored in God's promises. It's time to keep that promise constantly before your eyes and in your heart. It's time to pray the prayer of faith and take your stand on the basis of His provision. It is time to continue to do the things you know to do.

When Satan starts shaking your mountain, don't retreat and run for cover. Speak to the mountain with the authority you wield in the name of Jesus Christ. Then, when you're done with that, start to praise and shout the victory.

You don't have to be afraid of Satan. He'll be afraid of you!

SCRIPTURE READING: Psalm 50:1-23

"For the earth shall be full of the knowledge of the Lord, as the waters cover the sea" (Isaiah 11:9b).

JANUARY

1	Gen. 1, 2, 3	Matt. 1
2	Gen. 4, 5, 6	Matt. 2
3	Gen. 7, 8, 9	Matt. 3
4	Gen. 10, 11, 12	Matt. 4
5	Gen. 13, 14, 15	Matt. 5:1-26
6	Gen. 16, 17	Matt. 5:27-48
7	Gen. 18, 19	Matt. 6:1-18
8	Gen. 20, 21, 22	Matt. 6:19-34
9	Job 1, 2	Matt. 7
10	Job 3, 4	Matt. 8:1-17
11	Job 5, 6, 7,	Matt. 8:18-34
12	Job 8, 9, 10	Matt. 9:1-17
13	Job 11, 12, 13	Matt. 9:18-38
14	Job 14, 15, 16	Matt. 10:1-20
15	Job 17, 18, 19	Matt. 10:21-42
16	Job 20, 21	Matt. 11
17	Job 22, 23, 24	Matt. 12:1-23
18	Job 25, 26, 27	Matt. 12:24-50
19	Job 28, 29	Matt. 13:1-30
20	Job 30, 31	Matt. 13:31-58
21	Job 32, 33	Matt. 14:1-21
22	Job 34, 35	Matt. 14:22-36
23	Job 36, 37	Matt. 15:1-20
24	Job 38, 39, 40	Matt. 15:21-39
25	Job 41, 42	Matt. 16
26	Gen. 23, 24	Matt. 17
27	Gen. 25, 26	Matt. 18:1-20
28	Gen. 27, 28	Matt. 18:21-35
29	Gen. 29, 30	Matt. 19
30	Gen. 31, 32	Matt. 20:1-16
31	Gen. 33, 34, 35	Matt. 20:17-34

FEBRUARY

1	Gen. 36, 37, 38	Matt. 21:1-22
2	Gen. 39, 40	Matt. 21:23-46
3	Gen. 41, 42	Matt. 22:1-22
4	Gen. 43, 44, 45	Matt. 22:23-46
5	Gen. 46, 47, 48	Matt. 23:1-22
6	Gen. 49, 50	Matt. 23:23-29
7	Exod. 1, 2, 3	Matt. 24:1-28
8	Exod. 4, 5, 6	Matt. 24:29-51
9	Exod. 7, 8	Matt. 25:1-30
10	Exod. 9, 10, 11	Matt. 25:31-46
11	Exod. 12, 13	Matt. 26:1-35
12	Exod. 14, 15	Matt. 26:36-75
13	Exod. 16, 17, 18	Matt. 27:1-26
14	Exod. 19, 20	Matt. 27:27-50
15	Exod. 21, 22	Matt. 27:51-66
16	Exod. 23, 24	Matt. 28
17	Exod. 25, 26	Mark 1:1-22
18	Exod. 27, 28	Mark 1:23-45
19	Exod. 29, 30	Mark 2
20	Exod. 31, 32, 33	Mark 3:1-19
21	Exod. 34, 35	Mark 3:20-35
22	Exod. 36, 37, 38	Mark 4:1-20
23	Exod. 39, 40	Mark 4:21-41
24	Ps. 90; Lev. 1, 2	Mark 5:1-20
25	Lev. 3, 4, 5	Mark 5:21-43
26	Lev. 6, 7	Mark 6:1-29
27	Lev. 8, 9, 10	Mark 6:30-56
28	Lev. 11, 12	Mark 7:1-13

MARCH

1	Lev. 13	Mark 7:14-37
2	Lev. 14	Mark 8:1-21
3	Lev. 15, 16	Mark 8:22-38
4	Lev. 17, 18	Mark 9:1-29
5	Lev. 19, 20	Mark 9:30-50
6	Lev. 21, 22	Mark 10:1-31
7	Lev. 23, 24	Mark 10:32-52
8	Lev. 25	Mark 11:1-18
9	Lev. 26, 27	Mark 11:19-33
10	Num. 1, 2	Mark 12:1-27
11	Num. 3, 4	Mark 12:28-44
12	Num. 5, 6	Mark 13:1-20
13	Num. 7, 8	Mark 13:21-37
14	Num. 9, 10, 11	Mark 14:1-26
15	Num. 12, 13, 14	Mark 14:27-53
16	Num. 15, 16	Mark 14:54-72
17	Num. 17, 18, 19	Mark 15:1-25
18	Num. 20, 21, 22	Mark 15:26-47
19	Num. 23, 24, 25	Mark 16
20	Num. 26, 27	Luke 1:1-20
21	Num. 28, 29, 30	Luke 1:21-38
22	Num. 31, 32, 33	Luke 1:39-56
23	Num. 34, 35, 36	Luke 1:57-80
24	Deut. 1, 2	Luke 2:1-24
25	Deut. 3, 4	Luke 2:25-52
26	Deut. 5, 6, 7	Luke 3
27	Deut. 8, 9, 10	Luke 4:1-30
28	Deut. 11, 12, 13	Luke 4:31-44
29	Deut. 14, 15, 16	Luke 5:1-16
30	Deut. 17, 18, 19	Luke 5:17-39
31	Deut. 20, 21, 22	Luke 6:1-26

APRIL

1	Deut. 23, 24, 25	Luke 6:27-49
2	Deut. 26, 27	Luke 7:1-30
3	Deut. 28, 29	Luke 7:31-50
4	Deut. 30, 31	Luke 8:1-25
5	Deut. 32, 33, 34	Luke 8:26-56
6	Josh. 1, 2, 3	Luke 9:1-17
7	Josh. 4, 5, 6	Luke 9:18-36
8	Josh. 7, 8, 9	Luke 9:37-62
9	Josh. 10, 11, 12	Luke 10:1-24
10	Josh. 13, 14, 15	Luke 10:25-42
11	Josh. 16, 17, 18	Luke 11:1-28
12	Josh. 19, 20, 21	Luke 11:29-54
13	Josh. 22, 23, 24	Luke 12:1-31
14	Judg. 1, 2, 3	Luke 12:32-59
15	Judg. 4, 5, 6	Luke 13:1-22
16	Judg. 7, 8	Luke 13:23-35
17	Judg. 9, 10	Luke 14:1-24
18	Judg. 11, 12	Luke 14:25-35
19	Judg. 13, 14, 15	Luke 15:1-10
20	Judg. 16, 17, 18	Luke 15:11-32
21	Judg. 19, 20, 21	Luke 16
22	Ruth 1, 2, 3, 4	Luke 17:1-19
23	1 Sam. 1, 2, 3	Luke 17:20-37
24	1 Sam. 4, 5, 6	Luke 18:1-23
25	1 Sam. 7, 8, 9	Luke 18:24-43
26	1 Sam. 10, 11, 12	Luke 19:1-27
27	1 Sam. 13, 14	Luke 19:28-48
28	1 Sam. 15, 16	Luke 20:1-26
29	1 Sam. 17, 18	Luke 20:27-47
30	1 Sam. 19, Pss. 23, 59	Luke 21:1-19

MAY

1	1 Sam. 20, 21; Ps. 34	Luke 21:20-38
2	1 Sam. 22; Ps. 56	Luke 22:1-23
3	Pss. 52, 57, 142	Luke 22:24-46
4	1 Sam. 23; Pss. 54, 63	Luke 22:47-71
5	1 Sam. 24, 25, 26, 27	Luke 23:1-25
6	1 Sam. 28, 29	Luke 23:26-56
7	1 Sam. 30, 31	Luke 24:1-35
8	2 Sam. 1, 2	Luke 24:36-53
9	2 Sam. 3, 4, 5	John 1:1-28
10	2 Sam. 6, 7; Ps. 30	John 1:29-51
11	2 Sam. 8, 9; Ps. 60	John 2
12	2 Sam. 10, 11, 12	John 3:1-15
13	Pss. 32, 51	John 3:16-36
14	2 Sam. 13, 14	John 4:1-26
15	2 Sam. 15; Pss. 3, 69	John 4:27-54
16	2 Sam. 16, 17, 18	John 5:1-24
17	2 Sam. 19, 20	John 5:25-47
18	Pss. 64, 70	John 6:1-21
19	2 Sam. 21, 22; Ps. 18	John 6:22-40
20	2 Sam. 23, 24	John 6:41-71
21	Pss. 4, 5, 6	John 7:1-27
22	Pss. 7, 8	John 7:28-53
23	Pss. 9, 11	John 8:1-27
24	Pss. 12, 13, 14	John 8:28-59
25	Pss. 15, 16	John 9:1-23
26	Pss. 17, 19	John 9:24-41
27	Pss. 20, 21, 22	John 10:1-21
28	Pss. 24, 25, 26	John 10:22-42
29	Pss. 27, 28, 29	John 11:1-29
30	Pss. 31, 35	John 11:30-57
31	Pss. 36, 37, 38	John 12:1-26

JUNE

1	Pss. 39, 40, 41	John 12:27-50
2	Pss. 53, 55, 58	John 13:1-20
3	Pss. 61, 62, 65	John 13:21-38
4	Pss. 68, 72, 86	John 14
5	Pss. 101, 103, 108	John 15
6	Pss. 109, 110, 138	John 16
7	Pss. 139, 140, 141	John 17
8	Pss. 143, 144, 145	John 18:1-18
9	1 Kings 1, 2	John 18:19-40
10	1 Kings 3, 4; Prov. 1	John 19:1-22
11	Prov. 2, 3, 4	John 19:23-42
12	Prov. 5, 6, 7	John 20
13	Prov. 8, 9	John 21
14	Prov. 10, 11, 12	Acts 1
15	Prov. 13, 14, 15	Acts 2:1-21
16	Prov. 16, 17, 18	Acts 2:22-47
17	Prov. 19, 20, 21	Acts 3
18	Prov. 22, 23, 24	Acts 4:1-22
19	Prov. 25, 26	Acts 4:23-37
20	Prov. 27, 28, 29	Acts 5:1-21
21	Prov. 30, 31	Acts 5:22-42
22	S. of Sol. 1, 2, 3	Acts 6
23	S. of Sol. 4, 5	Acts 7:1-21
24	S. of Sol. 6, 7, 8	Acts 7:22-43
25	1 Kings 5, 6, 7	Acts 7:44-60
26	1 Kings 8, 9	Acts 8:1-25
27	1 Kings 10, 11	Acts 8:26-40
28	Eccl. 1, 2, 3	Acts 9:1-22
29	Eccl. 4, 5, 6	Acts 9:23-43
30	Eccl. 7, 8, 9	Acts 10:1-23

JULY

1	Eccl. 10, 11, 12	Acts 10:24-48
2	1 Kings 12, 13	Acts 11
3	1 Kings 14, 15	Acts 12
4	1 Kings 16, 17, 18	Acts 13:1-25
5	1 Kings 19, 20	Acts 13:26-52
6	1 Kings 21, 22	Acts 14
7	2 Kings 1, 2, 3	James 1
8	2 Kings 4, 5, 6	James 2
9	2 Kings 7, 8, 9	James 3
10	2 Kings 10, 11, 12	James 4
11	2 Kings 13, 14	James 5
12	Jonah 1, 2, 3, 4	Acts 15:1-21
13	Amos 1, 2, 3	Acts 15:22-41
14	Amos 4, 5, 6	Gal. 1
15	Amos 7, 8, 9	Gal. 2
16	2 Kings 15, 16	Gal. 3
17	2 Kings 17, 18	Gal. 4
18	2 Kings 19, 20, 21	Gal. 5
19	2 Kings 22, 23	Gal. 6
20	2 Kings 24, 25	Acts 16:1-21
21	Pss. 1, 2, 10	Acts 16:22-40
22	Pss. 33, 43, 66	Phil. 1
23	Pss. 67, 71	Phil. 2
24	Pss. 89, 92	Phil. 3
25	Pss. 93, 94, 95	Phil. 4
26	Pss. 96, 97, 98	Acts 17:1-15
27	Pss. 99, 100, 102	Acts 17:16-34
28	Pss. 104, 105	1 Thess. 1
29	Pss. 106, 111, 112	1 Thess. 2
30	Pss. 113, 114, 115	1 Thess. 3
31	Pss. 116, 117, 118	1 Thess. 4

AUGUST

1	Ps. 119:1-88	1 Thess. 5
2	Ps. 119:89-176	2 Thess. 1
3	Pss. 120, 121, 122	2 Thess. 2
4	Pss. 123, 124, 125	2 Thess. 3
5	Pss. 127, 128, 129	Acts 18
6	Pss. 130, 131, 132	1 Cor. 1
7	Pss. 133, 134, 135	1 Cor. 2
8	Pss. 136, 146	1 Cor. 3
9	Pss. 147, 148	1 Cor. 4
10	Pss. 149, 150	1 Cor. 5
11	1 Chron. 1, 2, 3	1 Cor. 6
12	1 Chron. 4, 5, 6	1 Cor. 7:1-19
13	1 Chron. 7, 8, 9	1 Cor. 7:20-40
14	1 Chron. 10, 11, 12	1 Cor. 8
15	1 Chron. 13, 14, 15	1 Cor. 9
16	1 Chron. 16; Pss. 42, 44	1 Cor. 10:1-18
17	Pss. 45, 46, 47	1 Cor. 10:19-33
18	Pss. 48, 49, 50	1 Cor. 11:1-16
19	Pss. 73, 85	1 Cor. 11:17-34
20	Pss. 87, 88	1 Cor. 12
21	1 Chron. 17, 18, 19	1 Cor. 13
22	1 Chron. 20, 21, 22	1 Cor. 14:1-20
23	1 Chron. 23, 24, 25	1 Cor. 14:21-40
24	1 Chron. 26, 27	1 Cor. 15:1-28
25	1 Chron. 28, 29	1 Cor. 15:29-58
26	2 Chron. 1, 2, 3	1 Cor. 16
27	2 Chron. 4, 5, 6	2 Cor. 1
28	2 Chron. 7, 8, 9	2 Cor. 2
29	2 Chron. 10, 11, 12	2 Cor. 3
30	2 Chron. 13, 14	2 Cor. 4
31	2 Chron. 15, 16	2 Cor. 5

SEPTEMBER

1	2 Chron. 17, 18	2 Cor. 6
2	2 Chron. 19, 20	2 Cor. 7
3	2 Chron. 21; Obad.	2 Cor. 8
4	2 Chron. 22; Joel 1	2 Cor. 9
5	2 Chron. 23; Joel 2, 3	2 Cor. 10
6	2 Chron. 24, 25, 26	2 Cor. 11:1-15
7	Is. 1, 2	2 Cor. 11:16-33
8	Is. 3, 4	2 Cor. 12
9	Is. 5, 6	2 Cor. 13
10	2 Chron. 27, 28	Acts 19:1-20
11	2 Chron. 29, 30	Acts 19:21-41
12	2 Chron. 31, 32	Acts 20:1-16
13	Is. 7, 8	Acts 20:17-38
14	Is. 9, 10	Eph. 1
15	Is. 11, 12, 13	Eph. 2
16	Is. 14, 15, 16	Eph. 3
17	Is. 17, 18, 19	Eph. 4
18	Is. 20, 21, 22	Eph. 5:1-16
19	Is. 23, 24, 25	Eph. 5:17-23
20	Is. 26, 27	Eph. 6
21	Is. 28, 29	Rom. 1
22	Is. 30, 31	Rom. 2
23	Is. 32, 33	Rom. 3
24	Is. 34, 35, 36	Rom. 4
25	Is. 37, 38	Rom. 5
26	Is. 39, 40	Rom. 6
27	Is. 41, 42	Rom. 7
28	Is. 43, 44	Rom. 8:1-21
29	Is. 45, 46	Rom. 8:22-39
30	Is. 47, 48, 49	Rom. 9:1-15

OCTOBER

1	Is. 50, 51, 52	Rom. 9:16-33
2	Is. 53, 54, 55	Rom. 10
3	Is. 56, 57, 58	Rom. 11:1-18
4	Is. 59, 60, 61	Rom. 11:19-36
5	Is. 62, 63, 64	Rom. 12
6	Is. 65, 66	Rom. 13
7	Hos. 1, 2, 3, 4	Rom. 14
8	Hos. 5, 6, 7, 8	Rom. 15:1-13
9	Hos. 9, 10, 11	Rom. 15:14-33
10	Hos. 12, 13, 14	Rom. 16
11	Mic. 1, 2, 3	Acts 21:1-17
12	Mic. 4, 5	Acts 21:18-40
13	Mic. 6, 7	Acts 22
14	Nah. 1, 2, 3	Acts 23:1-15
15	2 Chron. 33, 34	Acts 23:16-35
16	Zeph. 1, 2, 3	Acts 24
17	2 Chron. 35; Hab. 1, 2, 3	Acts 25
18	Jer. 1, 2	Acts 26
19	Jer. 3, 4, 5	Acts 27:1-26
20	Jer. 6, 11, 12	Acts 27:27-44
21	Jer. 7, 8, 26	Acts 28
22	Jer. 9, 10, 14	Col. 1
23	Jer. 15, 16, 17	Col. 2
24	Jer. 18, 19	Col. 3
25	Jer. 20, 35, 36	Col. 4
26	Jer. 25, 45, 46	Heb. 1
27	Jer. 47, 48	Heb. 2
28	Jer. 49, 13, 22	Heb. 3
29	Jer. 23, 24	Heb. 4
30	Jer. 27, 28, 29	Heb. 5
31	Jer. 50	Heb. 6

NOVEMBER

1	Jer. 51, 30	Heb. 7
2	Jer. 31, 32	Heb. 8
3	Jer. 33, 21	Heb. 9
4	Jer. 34, 37, 38	Heb. 10:1-18
5	Jer. 39, 52, 40	Heb. 10:19-39
6	Jer. 41, 42	Heb. 11:1-19
7	Jer. 43, 44	Heb. 11:20-40
8	Lam. 1, 2	Heb. 12
9	Lam. 3, 4, 5	Heb. 13
10	2 Chron. 36; Dan. 1, 2	Titus 1
11	Dan. 3, 4	Titus 2
12	Dan. 5, 6, 7	Titus 3
13	Dan. 8, 9, 10	Philemon
14	Dan. 11, 12	1 Tim. 1
15	Ps. 137; Ezek. 1, 2	1 Tim. 2
16	Ezek. 3, 4	1 Tim. 3
17	Ezek. 5, 6, 7	1 Tim. 4
18	Ezek. 8, 9, 10	1 Tim. 5
19	Ezek. 11, 12, 13	1 Tim. 6
20	Ezek. 14, 15	2 Tim. 1
21	Ezek. 16, 17	2 Tim. 2
22	Ezek. 18, 19	2 Tim. 3
23	Ezek. 20, 21	2 Tim. 4
24	Ezek. 22, 23	1 Pet. 1
25	Ezek. 24, 25, 26	1 Pet. 2
26	Ezek. 27, 28, 29	1 Pet. 3
27	Ezek. 30, 31, 32	1 Pet. 4
28	Ezek. 33, 34	1 Pet. 5
29	Ezek. 35, 36	2 Pet. 1
30	Ezek. 37, 38, 39	2 Pet. 2

DECEMBER

1	Ezek. 40, 41	2 Pet. 3
2	Ezek. 42, 43, 44	1 John 1
3	Ezek. 45, 46	1 John 2
4	Ezek. 47, 48	1 John 3
5	Ezra 1, 2	1 John 4
6	Ezra 3, 4	1 John 5
7	Hag. 1, 2	2 John
8	Zech. 1, 2, 3, 4	3 John
9	Zech. 5, 6, 7, 8	Jude
10	Zech. 9, 10	Rev. 1
11	Zech. 11, 12	Rev. 2
12	Zech. 13, 14	Rev. 3, 4
13	Pss. 74, 75, 76	Rev. 5
14	Pss. 77, 78	Rev. 6
15	Pss. 79, 80	Rev. 7
16	Pss. 81, 82, 83	Rev. 8
17	Pss. 84, 90	Rev. 9
18	Pss. 107, 126	Rev. 10
19	Ezra 5, 6, 7	Rev. 11
20	Esth. 1, 2	Matt. 1; Luke 3
21	Esth. 3, 4, 5	Rev. 12
22	Esth. 6, 7, 8	Rev. 13
23	Esth. 9, 10	Rev. 14
24	Ezra 8, 9, 10	Rev. 15
25	Neh. 1, 2, 3	Rev. 16
26	Neh. 4, 5, 6	Rev. 17
27	Neh. 7, 8, 9	Rev. 18
28	Neh. 10, 11	Rev. 19
29	Neh. 12, 13	Rev. 20
30	Mal. 1, 2	Rev. 21
31	Mal. 3, 4	Rev. 22

For more information about this ministry and a free catalog, please write:

Kenneth Copeland Ministries
Fort Worth, Texas 76192

World Offices of Kenneth Copeland Ministries

CANADA
P.O. Box 58248
Vancouver, BC V6P 6K1

AUSTRALIA
Locked Bag 8
Australia Square
Sydney, N.S.W. 2000

ENGLAND
P.O. Box 15
Bath, BA1 1GD

SOUTH AFRICA
P.O. Box 830
Randburg 2125